W9-AFM-207

In his latest book, *Everyone's Guide to Demons and Spiritual Warfare*, Ron Phillips skillfully lays a solid foundation addressing the important issues of spiritual warfare like a wise master builder. All the while he places top priority on the atoning work of Christ on the cross by providing the biblical and commonsense tools of how to fight our enemy by the authority and lordship of Christ. This book provides the spiritual keys necessary for every believer desiring to live an overcoming life beyond the norm and mundane. It's a must-read for every Christian seeking God's best for their lives.

—MARCUS D. LAMB
PRESIDENT/FOUNDER, DAYSTAR TELEVISION NETWORK

Pastor Ron Phillips has put a lot of study and prayer into the writing of this book. It is factual, informative, and will be a blessing to you. As you read it, God will help you to know more about Him and His wonderful plan for His children.

—DODIE OSTEEN
COFOUNDER, LAKEWOOD CHURCH
HOUSTON, TX

For too many people today, "spiritual warfare" is a wacky mix of new age teaching and bad theology. Ron Phillips has done a great service by anchoring this book in solid biblical doctrine. This will change the way the church looks at spiritual warfare, and it's long overdue.

—PHIL COOKE
FILMMAKER AND AUTHOR OF *JOLT! THE POWER OF INTENTIONAL CHANGE IN A WORLD THAT'S CONSTANTLY CHANGING*

* page 22

EVERYONE'S GUIDE *to*

DEMONS & SPIRITUAL WARFARE

RON PHILLIPS

Charisma
HOUSE
A STRANG COMPANY

Most Strang Communications Book Group products are available at special quantity discounts for bulk purchase for sales promotions, premiums, fund-raising, and educational needs. For details, write Strang Communications Book Group, 600 Rinehart Road, Lake Mary, Florida 32746, or telephone (407) 333-0600.

Everyone's Guide to Demons and Spiritual Warfare by Ron Phillips
Published by Charisma House
A Strang Company
600 Rinehart Road
Lake Mary, Florida 32746
www.strangbookgroup.com

This book or parts thereof may not be reproduced in any form, stored in a retrieval system, or transmitted in any form by any means—electronic, mechanical, photocopy, recording, or otherwise—without prior written permission of the publisher, except as provided by United States of America copyright law.

Unless otherwise noted, all Scripture quotations are from the New King James Version of the Bible. Copyright © 1979, 1980, 1982 by Thomas Nelson, Inc., publishers. Used by permission.

Scripture quotations marked KJV are from the King James Version of the Bible.

Scripture quotations marked NIV are from the Holy Bible, New International Version. Copyright © 1973, 1978, 1984, International Bible Society. Used by permission.

Cover design by Justin Evans
Design Director: Bill Johnson

Copyright © 2010 by Ron Phillips
All rights reserved

Library of Congress Cataloging-in-Publication Data:
Phillips, Ron M.
  Everyone's guide to demons and spiritual warfare / Ron Phillips.
      p. cm.
  Includes bibliographical references (p.   ).
  ISBN 978-1-61638-127-1
  1. Spiritual warfare. I. Title.
  BV4509.5.P485 2010
  235'.4--dc22

                                        2010020327

First Edition

10 11 12 13 14 — 9 8 7 6 5 4 3 2 1
Printed in the United States of America

contents

SECTION V: ENFORCING THE VICTORY OVER YOUR ENEMY

SECTION VI: MAINTAINING THE VICTORY OVER YOUR ENEMY

Introduction

A MONG THE MOST popular television programs in recent years is the reality show *Survivor*. A group of people are left in a desolate location and must survive on what is at hand. As a part of the intrigue, only one can win the large cash prize at the end of the contest. As the show progresses, the contestants never know who are their friends or who are their enemies!

Major Nidal Hasan was a psychiatrist in the United States Army. His education was paid for by the taxpayers. At thirty-nine years of age, the major had never served in a combat zone. In November of 2009 he shouted "Allahu Akbar" at a troop enlistment center in Fort Hood, Texas, and began to fire two weapons, killing thirteen and wounding more than thirty-five individuals, both civilian and military.[1] As his background was investigated, it was discovered that he had connections with Islamic terrorists.[2] Pretending to be a friend of the American soldiers, he was a plant of the enemy. The U.S. Army did not know an enemy was among them.

We live in a beautiful world, yet to survive we must know our real enemies. Our strong enemies are not people but invisible forces of darkness. These forces from the dark side carry out the order of a former ally who turned against our God. Satan, along with the forces of evil demons, is very near and ready to take out God's soldiers. Yet God has given us the resources to survive and thrive. But to do so we must know our enemy and be fully aware of the resources and weapons at our disposal.

This thought is captured beautifully by the psalmist in Psalm 126. This passage is a song of freedom, celebrating the return of captive Israelis from Babylon to Zion. Their emotion and confession picture for us freedom from Satan's snares and chains! Keeping us captive to wrong living, wrong thinking, wrong decisions, and wrong relationships is Satan's strategy to hold us down. His plan is to keep us from ever discovering our true selves and our way home.

In this psalm we observe the five legacies of liberty. These facets of freedom will be clearly seen in the life of the individual or in the life of the liberated church.

1. Freedom in Christ Is Like a Dream Come True

When the Lord brought back the captivity of Zion, we were like those who dream.

—Psalm 126:1

The Christian life experienced to its fullest is also a dream come true. Most believers are living far beneath their privileges. Jesus promised, "I have come that they may have life, and that they may have it more abundantly" (John 10:10). Are you living with an abundance of power, resources, and joy? The supernatural power of God is our heritage. The fruit of the Spirit is our promise.

Having led hundreds of people to freedom in Christ, I can say honestly that for many of them life becomes new, fresh, and exhilarating. One young lady was suffering from anorexia nervosa—self-destructive starvation. Although she had seen some counselors, her problem was not physical but spiritual. After extended counseling she rejected the enemy and his deception. The truth set her free. She is now active for Christ and especially enjoys singing in the choir.

People who have been set free from the enemy's strongholds invariably experience an amazing awakening to the spiritual life. Suddenly their eyes are open to all that they have in Christ.

In the early 1950s, before cruises became the vogue, a poor man booked a passage from London to the United States in order to see his family. On board he stuck to himself and never entered the dining room. Toward the end of the journey, passengers asked him why he did not eat in the dining room. "Oh, I could afford only a ticket for the trip. But I brought along cheese and crackers to sustain me," he assured them.

"Sir, the food is included in the price of the ticket!" his fellow passenger said.

It is possible to live the Christian life this way. We must realize that our commitment to Christ has brought us all that we need for this life and the life to come.

2. CHRISTIAN FREEDOM IS A SOURCE OF JOY

Then our mouth was filled with laughter, and our tongue with singing.

—PSALM 126:2

Never have I seen more joyless people than in the average church or religious gathering. People seem restrained and bound by tradition, denomination, or religious pride. Where are the exuberance, the whole-hearted singing, the joyful shout, and the sounds of laughter?

No wonder so many believers and churches are insipid and weak. Nehemiah 8:10 says, "The joy of the LORD is your strength." Shortly before the cross, Jesus prayed these words: "These things I speak in the world, that they may have My joy fulfilled in themselves" (John 17:13). You may protest and say that Jesus was talking about our future joy in heaven. Yet Jesus went on to say, "I do not pray that You should take them out of the world, but that You should keep them from the evil one" (v. 15). It is "the evil one" who hinders our joy in the Christian life. Joy is the birthright and privilege of every Christian.

Once I was preaching the truths of spiritual freedom in an east Tennessee church. I was focusing on freedom from the spirit of heaviness or depression. (See chapter 17.) After teaching, I led the people through a prayer, repudiating the spirit of heaviness and releasing the fruit of the Spirit, which includes joy. I began reading Isaiah 61:3: "[I will] give them…the garment of praise for the spirit of heaviness." I then turned to Romans 14:17: "For the kingdom of God is not eating and drinking, but righteousness and peace and joy in the Holy Spirit." Suddenly a young woman, normally extremely shy, began to laugh, weep, and shout, "Praise the Lord! I am free! I'm free!" The truth of her freedom exploded in joy and poured out of her. Joy is the birthright of every Christian.

3. FREEDOM IN CHRIST IS EVIDENT TO THE UNCHURCHED

Then they said among the nations, "The LORD has done great things for them." The LORD has done great things for us, and we are glad.

—PSALM 126:2–3

The joy of ended captivity is convincing evidence to the unreached around us. Seeing people delivered who have been in bondage is persuasive proof for witnessing. Christians who cannot handle the vicissitudes of life faithfully and joyfully have no effective witness for Christ. Yet when the unreached see the believer coping with anger, bitterness, pride, depression, and other problems in a victorious manner, then the message of Christ gets through. You see, friend, being a witness means that your lifestyle is a part of the evidence.

A young married woman began to experience real freedom in Christ from the assaults of depression by Satan. Though her problems and pressures were unchanged, her perspective changed as she began to see herself in Christ. Soon her children and husband came to Christ. Since that time, others in her family have come to the Lord.

When our lives are lived in Christ, it is evident to the unchurched.

4. FREEDOM IN CHRIST RELEASES THE FLOW OF REVIVAL

Bring back our captivity, O LORD, as the streams in the South.

—PSALM 126:4

Not long ago I was in Israel, and we were scheduled to travel into normally dry southern Israel. Our Masada trip was postponed a day because of rains in Jerusalem. Southern Israel by the Dead Sea is the lowest point on the earth, so rains in upper Israel fill the streambeds in the South. These flowing streams give life to the land.

What a beautiful picture of revival! When believers are set free from the bondage of captivity, it releases the flow of the life of God into the church. The dry places are where demons live, according to Luke 11:24. When revival comes, God's enemies are scattered (Ps. 68:1). Real revival cannot come until the church knows her identity in Christ and begins to walk in the heritage of freedom.

Spiritual warfare is not destruction to revival; it is an impetus to revival. When believers experience the liberating power of the truth of the good news of Christ, then the power of God is released through them. Only when the church is released from carnal captivity will the spirit of God be released in heaven-sent revival.

5. FREEDOM IN CHRIST INSPIRES WITNESS

Those who sow in tears shall reap in joy. He who continually goes forth weeping, bearing seed for sowing, shall doubtless come again with rejoicing, bringing his sheaves with him.

—PSALM 126:5–6

These familiar verses are usually preached alone, calling the church to passionate soul winning. Yet the sowing and reaping can only take place if the people have come home from spiritual bondage to the promised land of the Spirit-filled life.

How futile to call on people to sow and reap in the rocky and infertile soil of a spiritual wasteland. It is in the fertile land of the will of God that believers find the Bible to be a rich bag of precious, life-giving seeds. Only when one is free can he or she effectively sow in tears and reap in joy.

God promises revival and a harvest to those who come home from bondage. Believers can experience freedom that leads to a new effectiveness in their witness.

What you hold in your hand is the result of this decade of frontline combat against the forces of darkness. I have done hand-to-hand combat with demonic forces and rejoiced as they fled, terrified and defeated, their victims.

Author Jack Taylor reminds us that Satan and the demons are decisive forces but defeated foes. The victory has been won at the cross and empty tomb, yet the battle rages on Earth. You do not have to live in bondage and defeat. You can know the joy of victory and release.

While by no means all encompassing, this manual can assist the church and individual believers in moving to the next level of spiritual warfare. Unless we restore unity and move together in the body of Christ, we shall live in defeat. Revival awaits us if we will move into battle against Satan together.

I summon all who are following Christ to train themselves for war. We will not see a moral revolution, nor can we stop the erosion of our own Western culture, without a spiritual fight. An increasingly militant Islam will not stop its advance unless the church takes the truth, empowered by the Spirit, into battle.

The victory is ours, but we must enforce it.

SECTION I

FACING THE REALITY OF YOUR ENEMY

chapter 1

A RUDE AWAKENING

I N THE CLASSIC movie *Shenandoah*, Jimmy Stewart portrays a widowed patriarch over a large farm in the Shenandoah Valley of Virginia. As the Civil War erupts, he longs to keep his family intact and mind his own business. Soon the war comes to his house with a son and daughter murdered and another son missing. But in the climatic scene while the family is worshiping, the young lost son finds his way home.

This pictures human life. Despite all of your efforts, Satan will soon make your life a battleground. I had both a great awakening and a rude awakening that brought me to the battlefront.

A GREAT AWAKENING

Some of the most miserable people I know are active, professing Christians. As I sped westward toward Albuquerque, I knew I had become one of that tribe! For whatever accumulated reasons, after ten years of a busy, successful ministry I wanted to quit.

This was not normal ministerial wanderlust—a disease that affects the clergy and whose symptoms include a mad belief that another place of service can fill the void of a lost spiritual relationship. No, this awful agony was a desire to leave the ministry.

While I was flying at six hundred miles an hour toward a speaking engagement, I was writing out my resignation from the ministry. Was this burnout? I had no idea that the living God had different plans. I was about to begin a journey to fullness.

I arrived the night before my scheduled morning speaking time and was immediately frustrated by my room assignment. It was the only one on the hall—far away from the action. I checked the program to see who the other speakers would be. I knew the preacher scheduled to speak, but I had never heard the woman on the program.

But it would be her message on prayer and knowing God that would utterly crush my proud heart.

The next day I sat in the back of the auditorium and listened to her story unfolding. As the wife of a seminary professor who became a state denominational executive, she was thrust into crisis by her husband's sudden death. He had been her spiritual resource and rock. In the back of an ambulance, she faced the reality that all of their shared life was abruptly ending. Now she needed Jesus as never before, and He proved Himself faithful.

This message hammered at my self-pity and self-sufficiency. I believed right. I worked hard. I had read all the deeper-life books, yet I had lost the reality of God's presence. Joyless and burned out, God's Word hammered at my desire to go AWOL.

Struggling inside, I made my way back to my room and collapsed on the bed, weeping. That night, out of a deep sleep I heard my name being called. Awakened, I went to the door and found no one. Soon I was sleeping again and was startled awake by hearing my name called a second time. The same thing had happened again. Like Samuel, I knew God awakened me.

This proved to be a great awakening for me. I was led to pick up my Bible and turn to Psalm 91–95. Graciously God spoke to me out of that ancient account. You see, God had not moved; I had! He was still in the secret place awaiting my fellowship. Further, He had "fresh oil" with which to anoint my stale spiritual life. That little room became a sanctuary, and the presence of Jesus swept over me.

In Psalm 91:1–2 we read, "He who dwells in the secret place of the Most High shall abide under the shadow of the Almighty. I will say of the LORD, 'He is my refuge and my fortress; my God, in Him I will trust.'" I rediscovered the importance of a devotional life. I became aware that we are in spiritual warfare, facing infernal and invisible forces of wickedness. Prayer came alive in me again. "He shall call upon Me, and I will answer him; I will be with him in trouble; I will deliver him and honor him" (v. 15).

Prayers poured forth from my aching heart—prayers of repentance, worship, and intercession. Through the night God visited me with a fresh filling of His Holy Spirit.

These scriptures came alive! God spoke to me through His precious Word. Here was the message I received that evening.

Psalm 92:10–15 challenged my heart to understand the fullness of the Holy Spirit. Verse 10 says, "I have been anointed with fresh oil." As I read the verses in that psalm, I could see what had been available to me all the time through the anointing of the Holy Spirit.

My eyes and ears would be open and perceptive to the things of God (Ps. 92:11). My life could again flourish and grow (v. 12). The house of God would again be a place I would enjoy (v. 13). The aging process would have no effect on my spiritual life (v. 14). My mouth would be open to praise the Lord for His goodness (v. 15).

After speaking later that day, I flew home thinking everything was going to be better! Little did I know that I had begun a hard journey with Jesus— a journey that contained dark valleys between the mountaintops. I had no idea how desperately I would need the resources I had rediscovered.

The year ahead would be, in the words of Charles Dickens, "the best of times...the worst of times." The Spirit-filled life is not only a life of spiritual worship. The enemy saw what God was beginning, and he unleashed a relentless attack on everything precious in my life.

A RUDE AWAKENING

I heard of a boxer who was taking blow after blow. His manager kept hollering, "Stay with it, Joe. You are winning." After several rounds of this, Joe turned to his manager and said, "If I am winning, I wish somebody would tell *him*."

This is the way I felt as my life became a veritable battleground on all fronts for a two-year period. Depression lived at our house. When I returned from that life-changing encounter with the Lord, I found myself immediately in a struggle at home.

DIFFICULTIES AT HOME

In the fall of 1990, both my daughter and my wife totaled their cars on successive days. Heather, my daughter, was not seriously injured, and miraculously her car did not go into the flooded creek nearby. She did, however, suffer a blow to the head that has created recurring difficulties, including minor seizures.

My wife, Paulette, was nearly killed. I remember that September morning and the man on the telephone telling me Paulette had been in an accident not far from the house. I drove over the hill on Highway 153 and saw a terrifying scene before me.

Paulette was trapped for forty-five minutes in her little Sunbird. All the bones on the left side of her upper body were broken or crushed. Even some of her teeth were cracked from the blow. She went into shock and nearly died, but the rescue team saved her life. For three months she had to have constant care.

In March of 1991, my dad died suddenly. After struggling all his life with alcohol addiction, he was saved and ordained a deacon at the age of fifty-nine. We had become very close. On Sunday night before his death, he and I talked by phone for an hour. He was my great encourager. Now, at age sixty-nine, Dad was gone.

TROUBLE AT CHURCH

On the church front a woman committed suicide. Then her best friend was hospitalized in a mental unit. She threatened suicide unless I came immediately to see her. I and my associates went up to visit. When we sat down in the room, other voices poured forth from the woman. One of my associates who is gifted in the area of prayer and spiritual warfare began to identify and dismiss these cursing infernal enemies.

In less than an hour thirteen demonic entities identified themselves as suicide, lust, death, cancer, depression, fear, rebellion, rejection, and others. All of them had English names, but as they were asked their real names, in the authority of Jesus, they would reveal their real natures only after a struggle. This dear lady is still recovering and needs counseling because of past wounds of the enemy, but she is better and, I believe, will be totally well in the future.

This experience opened my eyes to another world, another realm. Suddenly I realized that what had been theory was real warfare! Had I been, as a pastor, some kind of spiritual Don Quixote, fighting with windmills while my people were living in bondage?

I fell to my knees, and God's Spirit spoke gently to my spirit. He said, "This is what you asked Me for." Yes, I wanted the reality of God, and I was discovering from my own pain and from the bondage of others a new direction and passion for ministry.

Immediately the Lord led me to invite a gifted minister friend to come and lead a spiritual warfare conference. He was a longtime friend in whom God had brought renewal. He and I, along with others, prayed together for months for God to move in life-changing power.

Bishop J. Tod Zeiger came and began to preach on "Strongholds in the Believer's Life." From the very first service God began to set people free. Revival came to the church, and the meeting had to be extended. Literally hundreds of people had their lives changed during the meeting. Since that day we have seen hundreds more set free through prayer and spiritual warfare. Some of their stories will be found later in this book.

Some were not happy. Years before, through the ministry of Jack Taylor, God had revealed to me the truth of praise and worship. Later, in a worship seminar with Dr. Jack Hayford, God convicted me of my own lack of worship and taught me to worship and love Jesus publicly. As old forms, ideas, and traditions fall, some people grow uncomfortable. Surprisingly, a staff member came and accused me of frightening the people and of not being a true Baptist. Already the enemy had rallied a small group to try to kill the revival and renewal that had come.

At this point one of our members lost her husband to a sudden heart attack. She was left with a teenage son and daughter. She was diagnosed with a bad heart and faced the possibility of life-threatening surgery. When I got the news, my wife and I went immediately to pray for her before she went into the hospital. The Holy Spirit spoke clearly to me and told me, "This sickness is not from Me and will not stand." I prayed over my friend, rebuking a spirit of infirmity and death. Miraculously, when they examined her the next day, all the symptoms were gone!

Subsequently the staff and members who opposed the renewal and delivering ministry left. For three years the church went through ups and downs of turmoil. Eventually all of the opposition was exposed, and some were found to be guilty of criminal acts. The church survived the difficulty and a multimillion-dollar lawsuit.

PERSONAL STRUGGLES

In the middle of these struggles I was attacked with a life-threatening situation. One Thursday evening, Kelli, my grown daughter, came over to spend the night because she had dreamed that I was sick. That night around 1:00 a.m. I awoke sick and dizzy. I went to the bathroom and collapsed there, losing consciousness. My daughter heard the fall in the other room and came in to see what it was.

In my unconscious state I was at peace. I caught a fleeting glimpse of the brightness and glory of another world, and for a moment I smelled the sweet atmosphere of the other world. Then, as if far away, I could hear Kelli's voice calling, "Dad, Dad...," and I came back. I was hospitalized for a week with stress-related heart problems and still take a pill every day to keep the heartbeat steady.

It was this experience that taught me the key truth of spiritual warfare: the battle is not ours but His. My heart doctor walked in to see me and said, "Pastor, you must practice what you preach if you are going to live." Out of this time God taught me what I will be sharing with you in the rest of this book. God can equip you to do His work and His will.

SEASON OF WAR AND PEACE

I have discovered that spiritual warfare's intensity is seasonal. God cycles include seasons of rest, and yet it is His will that we "fight the good fight of faith" (1 Tim. 6:12).

We must be alert to our enemy at all times. "Be sober, be vigilant; because your adversary the devil walks about like a roaring lion, seeking whom he may devour" (1 Pet. 5:8). It is our task to resist his schemes. "Therefore submit to God. Resist the devil and he will flee from you." (James 4:7).

The material that follows is designed to equip you to do battle over the spiritual darkness that comes against you. The Christian walks through a war zone. Yet the victory is ours. God rarely removes difficulty, but He walks us through these valleys. God is determined to teach us that we cannot live without Him. We need to be fully furnished with the spiritual armor and resources that are already ours.

chapter 2

GAINING A VICTORY
PERSPECTIVE

WARFARE BATTLES ARE often won or lost before the first engagement. In the war rooms strategies are developed and decisions made that ultimately reveal the victor! So it is for all of us in the kingdom. Our war manual, the Holy Scriptures, reveals the record of a victory already determined and decided. In the incarnation, life, death, and resurrection of Jesus the Messiah, God struck the decisive blow and declared victory over Satan and his forces.

Our present age seems to defy this conclusion. The rise of radical Islam, with its terror-driven threats to control the earth, is the new player on the war front. With more subtle attacks against Christianity and its values, the "cultural war" is going on in education, government, and the media.

The New Testament, however, clearly proclaims that believers are already transferred from the kingdom of darkness into the kingdom of Jesus Christ (Col. 1:13). Though invisible and not yet fully manifest, the kingdom of God has come in Jesus Christ of Nazareth. Furthermore, in spite of its faults, the church lives in this present world more than one billion strong. Conversion to Christianity far exceeds conversion to Islam! It is true as Jesus promised: "The gates of hell shall not prevail against it [the church]" (Matt. 16:18, KJV).

In the invisible realm, Jesus Christ has disarmed the powers of darkness and publicly triumphed over them. "Once and for all the decisive battle with the power of evil had been fought and won; yet the long campaign continued and the first Victory Day had not come in sight."[1]

Evil cannot be explained by nature, education, psychology, or evolution. There is lurking behind the terrible acts of human history malignant forces of evil! The Scriptures declare a hidden history of covert evil affecting all of history and all of humanity.

Listen to the late Professor James S. Stewart from his book *A Faith to Proclaim*:

> Were Paul to come back today and look upon the tragic conflict of our world, he would still say that "our wrestling is not against flesh and blood," not against any group of men or nations, Caesarism or Communism, as though the interests of democracy were synonymous with the righteousness of God; it is nothing so simple and naïve as that—God pity the facile imagination which assumes our own policies are blameless and our own hands clean. No, the real warfare cuts across all such alignments, and lies deeper down in the invisible realm where sinister forces stand flaming and fanatic against the rule of Christ. And the only way to meet that demonic mystic passion is with the Súvaµis and passion of the Lord. Was it not Christ's declared intention to kindle that flame in human hearts? "I am come to send fire on the earth." For only Spirit can conquer spirit. The children of darkness are wiser in this than the children of light. The devil knows better than to stifle emotion. And it is no use, in a day when spirit forces of passionate evil have been unleashed upon the earth and when fierce emotions are tearing the world apart, it is no use having a milk-and-water passionless theology: no good setting a tepid Christianity against a scorching paganism. The thrust of the demonic has to be met with the fire of the divine. As indeed it can: since Christ has overcome the world.[2]

The church must rediscover spiritual warfare. We must open our biblical and spiritual armory and outfit the people of God to take the faith to the enemy. Though the victory is already ours, we remain in this present world, and it is our obligation to enforce the victory of Christ. Christ's coming was a paradigm shift in the ancient battle, a turning point in human history!

So I must begin this book at the end, not at the beginning. The apostle John fought the enemy and was such a threat to government and culture that he was exiled to the island of Patmos. The rulers of that age breathed a sigh of relief, believing that at last they were done with this upstart faith of Christianity. From that lonely exile we have the breathtaking panorama of God's future for us all unfolding!

As a great drama comes to a conclusion with a final act, so God has written the last act in this present age. In the Book of Revelation, the wall between the eternal world and the present world is broken down. History and prophecy merge as God ties up the loose ends of the ancient war.

Revelation chapter 5 is the centerpiece of the human struggle. As it is enacted around the throne of God, we see the history, mystery, and victory of humanity.

> And I saw in the right hand of Him who sat on the throne a scroll written inside and on the back, sealed with seven seals. Then I saw a strong angel proclaiming with a loud voice, "Who is worthy to open the scroll and to loose its seals?" And no one in heaven or on the earth or under the earth was able to open the scroll, or to look at it. So I wept much, because no one was found worthy to open and read the scroll, or to look at it.
>
> —REVELATION 5:1–4

UNLOCKING THE SECRET OF THE SCROLL

In this dramatic scene, in the extended right hand of the enthroned Yahweh is a scroll. The scroll is in the possession of the One in authority, as demonstrated by the throne and the right hand. The right hand represents authority and government. The scroll is written on the inside and outside and sealed with seven seals. What is on the inside is hidden from view. Seven seals represent complete sealing. Thus the decrees on the inside of that scroll cannot be undone by any human power.

In order to understand the scroll's mystery, we must find out what it means. There are over four hundred direct quotes or allusions to the thirty-one books of the Old Testament in Revelation. It would make sense to see if Jewish history can give us a hint about the scroll. That hint is found in the laws of redemption and in the celebration of Jubilee. In the ancient world of Israel a family could never *completely* forfeit land, freedom, or the rights to an heir. Under Jewish law one could forfeit land if they borrowed against it and failed to pay the mortgage. One could also forfeit his or her freedom by becoming an indentured servant in order to pay debt. Also a childless widow had rights in a family to obtain a male heir by levirate marriage.

Let me explain further. If through failure you lost land, freedom, or family rights, they could be redeemed! Redemption meant that all debts had been satisfied.

If someone fell into one of these circumstances, the loss was recorded on a scroll, the scroll was sealed, and the price of redemption was written on the outside. Either the person who forfeited his property or a near relative (a kinsman) could buy back the inheritance.

This is clearly pictured in the Book of Ruth. Elimelech and Naomi mortgaged their property in Bethlehem and journeyed to live in Moab (Jordan). There Elimelech died, and so did his sons Mahlon and Chilion. This left Naomi as a widow with two daughter-in-laws, Orpah and Ruth. Ruth returns with Naomi to Bethlehem in dire poverty. Naomi is a penniless widow; Ruth is a Gentile. Naomi has a relative (a near kinsman) named Boaz. He is rich and willing to redeem Naomi. However, he must also be willing to redeem Ruth by marrying her and raising up seed for the family of the dead Elimelech.

In the process there is a nearer relative who cannot redeem. He indicates his inability by taking off his shoe. Boaz redeems the land of Naomi, marries Ruth, and redeems the whole family.

The scroll in the hand of God represents man's failure from Adam until now. It is the record of Satan's war against humanity and the purposes of God. The scroll represents every sin, every war, every grave, every tear, every defeat, and every misery of the human race. In fact, the scroll is the record and reason for all evil and evil acts on the earth. Just as Naomi's scroll would have recorded all of her losses, so there is a scroll of human misery.

Now the ancient story comes to life as in this scripture the drama of the ages unfolds. In God's right hand is the record! The tragedy in the Garden of Eden turned the earth into a vast graveyard. Our world continues to be ravaged by wars, devastated by disasters, stalked by disease, pursued by terror, limited by mortality, and tinged with terror.

The river of sin and wrong choices flows through the pages of history. The tyranny of Satan and the limitations of mortality have crashed the hope out of humanity. That is what is written in that scroll.

The Tears of Humanity

The apostle John, who had the courage to stand by the cross and survive torture and exile, could not be brought to tears by the enemy, yet now he weeps at this scene. The tears of John are your tears and my tears. They represent the heartache of every person who ever felt crushed by failures.

The unopened scroll speaks of human inadequacy. No one could open the scroll of human bondage! Only the tearing away of those seals could open the gates of hell and let humanity go free. All human power, wisdom, education, and progress are inadequate. So tears of despair wet the earth across the ages. This is the record of Satan as the demons wreak havoc upon humanity and upon the planet.

Behold a Deliverer

The price of redemption is written on the outside of the scroll.

- A near kinsman, Jesus Christ, became a human that He might redeem us.

- The kinsman must be able to redeem: Jesus Christ alone had the price of our freedom, His precious blood.

- The kinsman bust be willing: Jesus Christ willingly suffered to bring us back to freedom.

The angel cries out, "Who is worthy to open the scroll and to loose its seals?" (Rev. 5:2). The answer is that a Second Adam has come onto the battleground. He is the Lion of Judah; the Jewish Messiah has come to set the entire world free.

Greater than David, a new King has come to reclaim what is rightfully His. When John looks at the Lion, he sees a Lamb! This victory has been won by the Lamb. In the Book of Revelation, the Lamb of God is worthy of worship (Rev. 5:12), the executer of wrath (Rev. 6:16), and the overcomer of Satan (Rev. 12:11). Revelation 5:5 declares that Jesus the Lamb of God has "prevailed." When you see the Lamb, He is standing, not lying in a grave. He is crowned with all authority. He bears the marks of battle, yet He is standing in eternal triumph.

The word *prevailed* is the Greek word *nikao*. It is translated "overcome," "conquest," "victory," and "triumph." Here it is in the aorist tense, which means "once and for all." Jesus Christ has prevailed once and for all over all the power of Satan.

THE OVERCOMING CHURCH

The history of the church can be traced in the seven churches of Revelation. Though literal churches, these seven churches seem to represent the timeline of church history. Each of the churches is called upon to overcome. This is the same as the word *prevail* used to describe Jesus's victory. Those in the church can overcome the enemy.

> To him who overcomes I will grant to sit with Me on My throne, as
> I also overcame and sat down with My Father on His throne.
> —REVELATION 3:21

We can overcome just as Christ overcame. We can live an enthroned, victorious life with Him. Our overcoming is possible only through His blood.

> And they overcame him by the blood of the Lamb and by the word
> of their testimony, and they did not love their lives to the death.
> —REVELATION 12:11

Our future inheritance is tied to spiritual warfare. If we overcome, we are sons and daughters of God and have a rich inheritance to claim now and in the future.

> He who overcomes shall inherit all things, and I will be his God
> and he shall be My son.
> —REVELATION 21:7

THE BOOK OF WAR

Therefore we will look at the opened scroll of human struggle. In doing so, we will unfold the enemy's hysteria, tirade, and strategy. Furthermore, we will learn how to take the battle to him. Finally, we will learn how to overcome instead of being overwhelmed. We will embrace the lifestyle of victory not victims.

chapter 3

END TIME MISCONCEPTIONS ABOUT SPIRITUAL WARFARE

ON JANUARY 3, 1980, the world heard the shocking news that Joy Adamson had been killed in the Shaba Game reserve in northern Kenya, where she had been observing leopard behavior. Even more shocking was the original explanation for Adamson's death—that she had been attacked by a lion. Her body had been found on a road near her camp in Mawson, and it quickly became apparent to George Adamson and the authorities that human forces were responsible. Her injuries were caused by stabs by a sword-like weapon, not by a lion's fangs and claws. Plus, her tent had been opened, and the contents of a trunk had been scattered about. Although the authorities eventually convicted someone for the murder of Joy Adamson, the true story behind her death remains a mystery.[1]

Do not make the mistake of thinking you can tame the tormentor. You cannot have peaceful coexistence with the enemy. Sooner or later the enemy will destroy the careless and foolish. There are some dangerous misconceptions that are hindering spiritual victory and freedom.

> Now the Spirit expressly says that in latter times some will depart from the faith, giving heed to deceiving spirits and doctrines of demons.
>
> —1 TIMOTHY 4:1

The last days shall be characterized by a departure from the faith. Included in this apostasy will be those deceived by seducing spirits and doctrines of demons. First Corinthians 10:20 warns about religion without Christ and calls it a "sacrifice to demons." Second Corinthians 11:13–15 warns us of counterfeit ministries: "For such are false apostles, deceitful workers, transforming themselves into apostles of Christ. And no wonder! For Satan himself transforms himself into an angel of light. Therefore it is no great thing if his ministers also transform themselves into ministers of righteousness, whose end will be according to their works."

Ephesians 6:11 challenges us all to "put on the whole armor of God." Today many Christians are deceived to the point they do not believe in the power of Satan and the awful influence of the demonic.

First Timothy 1:18 calls us to "war a good warfare" (KJV).

First Timothy 6:12 calls us to "fight the good fight of faith."

Christians have ignored the enemy and allowed him free rein in their lives. Let me clear up some dangerous misconceptions.

Demons were only active in the time of Christ or today in pagan cultures.

There is nothing in the Bible that restricts demonic operation to a certain time or culture. On the contrary, all Scripture speaks of the constant battle that is ours. Second Corinthians 2:11 warns us, "Lest Satan should take advantage of us: for we are not ignorant of his devices." One of his devices is to lead people to deny his existence and operation.

Demons cannot bother believers.

There is much debate over the term *demon possession*. In the New Testament there is no such phrase; rather the term *demonization* is used. No Christian can be totally taken over by demons, but every Christian can be oppressed, harassed, and dominated by the enemy's activity.

In Acts 5:3 Satan filled Ananias's heart "to lie to the Holy Spirit." Unrepentant believers are turned over to Satan for the destruction of the flesh (1 Cor. 5). Ephesians 6:10–17 speaks of our wrestling against the powers of darkness, quenching the enemy's fiery darts, and standing firm against his assaults. The enemy can attack the mind and body of a Christian. Christians need to embrace deliverance as a part of their salvation.

In the Lord's Prayer in Matthew 6:13 we are told to pray daily, "Deliver us from the evil one."

Only occult involvement leads to demonic difficulties.

Occult involvement leads to demonization. However, occult involvement is not the only avenue to oppression by the enemy. Every believer is subject to temptation, deception, oppression, and strongholds.

Demonic operation incites only extreme behavior such as violence and gross sin.

It is true as seen in Mark 5 that total demonization can lead to extreme behaviors. However, look at Mark 1:23–24. We have a man in the synagogue who cries out in his oppression. There is no violence here at all.

Also in Luke 13:10–16 we find a woman called "a daughter of Abraham" bound by "a spirit of infirmity." The word *infirmity* is *astheneia* in Greek. It means "feeble," "lack of strength," "weak," "disability." Jesus says to her, "You are loosed" (v. 12). That word *loosed* is *apoluo*, which means "to free fully and set at liberty." Demonic oppression had kept this woman was sick and helpless for eighteen years. She was a churchgoing believer but was bound by Satan for eighteen years. Jesus set her free on the day of worship!

Christians are in danger when dealing with demons.

I often hear people say in fear, "I do not want to stir up anything by getting involved in warfare." My friend, Jesus laid hands on this poor woman, and she was delivered. Demons are under the authority of believers and can only affect us if we give them place.

What kind of surgeon would not operate because of the fear of inflicting pain? What kind of doctor would not treat a disease for fear of exposing himself? The doctor would put on protection and do his job. Likewise we can suit up in God's armor and help others to freedom. (See chapter 31, "Arming for Victory," for more on this topic.)

Christians should fear touching or being around others demonically afflicted.

Fear invites the attack of the enemy. However, the demonically afflicted are not transmitters. A person right with God has nothing to fear from the enemy.

Christians can plead the blood of Jesus without understanding and faith.

The blood of Jesus cannot be "pleaded" like some good luck charm! We honor the blood of Jesus and trust its cleansing, protection, and delivering power. The blood pleads itself when applied to the life of the believer. Revelation 12:11 speaks of the blood's overcoming power against Satan: "And they overcame him by the blood of the Lamb and by the word of their testimony, and they did not love their lives to the death." The blood speaks of forgiveness and cancels the enemy's right to attack. The blood does not "plead to Satan" for anything. The blood's plea is to the Father. The blood rebukes Satan!

Spiritual warfare instruction is unnecessary.

Recently a pastor and a former long-standing member of this church informed me that the church had gotten along without this teaching for years. I replied, "Look at your church and mine. Half your membership does not attend. Sin is rampant. Depression and oppression dominate many of your people's lives." Ignoring the truth leads to disaster. Second Corinthians 2:11 warns us to be "not ignorant of Satan's devices."

Christians can make light of Satan and the truth of spiritual warfare.

I had an evangelist tell me that Satan is a toothless tiger! That cliché sounds good, but is it true? Look at 1 Peter 5:8–9: "Be sober, be vigilant; because your adversary the devil walks about like a roaring lion seeking whom he may devour. Resist him, stand fast in the faith." The word *devour* means "to gulp down." We are to realize our enemy is defeated but still dangerous.

Resisting the devil is enough over a period of time.

Resisting the devil is necessary and important. Yet this is defensive. There is an offensive side to spiritual warfare whereby ground gained by the enemy must be retaken. Ephesians 4:27 warns us about "giving place" to the devil. In Matthew 12:43 demons seek "places." It is the same word found in Ephesians 4:27!

We must come to the rescue of those captured by the enemy. Colossians 1:13 speaks of salvation as being "delivered from the power of darkness." In Matthew 16 Jesus said of the church, "The gates of hell shall not prevail against it" (KJV). This text speaks of the church attacking the very gates of hell's strongholds.

In John 12:31 Jesus spoke of the cross as a place where the enemy would be "cast out." Every lost person lives under the domain of "the prince of the power of the air, the spirit who now works in the sons [children] of disobedience" (Eph. 2:2).

When Paul stood before King Agrippa, he stated his mission: "To open their eyes, in order to turn them from darkness to light, and from the power of Satan to God that they might receive forgiveness of sins and an inheritance..." (Acts 26:18). Salvation is a rebirth of those in darkness, those who are under the rule of Satan.

Freedom from multiple attacks is instantaneous.

Sometimes it takes intensive warfare to get rid of all the invaders in your life. Years after his entry in the ministry, Timothy battled a stronghold of fear. God will do a complete work if we let him. "For God has not given us a spirit of fear, but of power and of love and of a sound mind" (2 Tim. 1:7).

Freedom gained is the end of spiritual warfare.

No, it is only the beginning of a life of discipleship. Ground retaken in one's life must be defended. Sin must be purged and a life of commitment continued. We must wear our armor until that day we exchange it for a robe of white!

chapter 4

TRAINING FOR REIGNING

THE CHRISTIAN LIFE is a victory won but also a battle to be fought. As I set my pen again to the subject of spiritual warfare, I do so with the battle scars of a veteran. I have learned much on the battlefront that I must share. The spiritual warrior must be prepared to take the battle to the next level.

From the smoke and fire of the battlefield, I have learned much additional help for the body of Christ. The church must become a "spiritual armory," taking the basic training of its people more seriously.

David's life is an example of warfare as preparation for greater anointing and authority. Beginning with a study of David's growth and wilderness experience, let us allow the Lord to train us to reign.

A MISFIT OF THE MASTER

David rose to prominence as a soldier from the obscurity of a shepherd. David was no ordinary boy from the beginning. In a dark-skinned, dark-haired, dark-eyed culture, David was ruddy and fair. He was called "bright eyes." The Bible indicates that David had a glorious crown of bright red hair. His skin was fair, and his eyes were blue.

David was so different that he was given the assignment of shepherd and sent away from the family home. When Samuel came looking for the next king, David was not included in the list of candidates by his father, Jesse.

WORSHIPING WARRIOR

Alone with the sheep, David cultivated a spirit of praise. The Holy Spirit sang poems we call "psalms" through him. This young worshiper also defended his sheep. He killed both a bear and a lion to protect his father's flock.

You see, a shepherd (or a pastor) needs to develop the heart of a worshiper. It is from that commitment that the heart of a warrior is born. David's habits were considered strange and different from others. But poets make powerful soldiers!

ANOINTED BUT UNTRAINED

David was discovered by Samuel, who anointed him king over Israel. He was appointed to be Saul's successor. However, Saul was still very much alive! When David killed the giant Goliath, he instantly became a national hero. Saul then took David into his household and made him like a son. All seemed to be well for a season.

David soon fell into disfavor with Saul and was forced into wilderness exile. Amid much difficulty, God trained David to rule and win in every situation.

IN THE SHADOW OF THE SHEPHERD

You may feel you are not living your destiny or dream. Could it be that you are in your basic training period so that you will know how to lead and win in your place of gifting? David's anointing would take him to the throne, but not before a training experience in the wilderness. In the fields with the sheep, David got to know the Chief Shepherd. He summons His flock in that great passage of Psalm 23:

> The LORD is my shepherd;
> I shall not want.
> He makes me to lie down in green pastures;
> He leads me beside the still waters.
> He restores my soul;
> He leads me in the paths of righteousness

For His name's sake.
Yea, though I walk through the valley of the shadow of death,
I will fear no evil;
For You are with me;
Your rod and Your staff, they comfort me.
You prepare a table before me in the presence of my enemies;
You anoint my head with oil;
My cup runs over.
Surely goodness and mercy shall follow me
All the days of my life;
And I will dwell in the house of the LORD
Forever.

In this psalm David confessed his faith in Yahweh, the "I AM," as the God of the covenant. David calls Him *Rohi*—the shepherd. David cried out in faith, "I shall not want—He is *Jireh* the provider." The Lord brings rest, for He is *Shalom*—our peace. David learned to follow the Lord because he knew He was *Nissi*—the banner. Looking at his life as a sinner in need of righteousness, David talked of those "paths of righteousness" because he trusted in *Jehovah Tsidkenu*. David learned that he was never alone because *Jehovah Shammah* was always present!

David's relationship with God prepared him for a relationship with God's people. Yet there had to be a period of proving. David had to learn not to trust in the flesh. He had anointing, but Saul's armor did not fit. Saul's household wasn't for him. In fact, David was willing to be different in order to fit into God's plan for his life. So after being a misfit in the house of Jesse, David found himself to be unwelcome in the house of Saul. God had plans to raise up David's own house as one of distinction.

YOUR PLACE IN THE ARMY OF GOD

Here in this new millennium, those who have a heart after God may not seem to fit anywhere. Jesse's house represents tradition—the comfort zone for most people. David was not comfortable in that traditional setting, nor were his brothers comfortable with him. The faithful shepherd is not ashamed of singing, laughing, dancing, and celebrating in the majesty of God. His only concern is to lead, feed, reproduce, and protect his flock. This shepherd is willing to trek into the unknown in order to feed his sheep. He is not afraid of Lucifer the roaring lion or of the bear of oppression.

Saul's house represents those who cling only to the latest religious fad. The Saul crowd liked the fighting spirit of David, someone who would face the fearsome Goliath. Saul liked David's ability to quiet the disturbed soul. Yet in the end, the Saul crowd hated the anointing, and David could not fit in that inconsistent house of religion.

David stood with a destiny and a sure anointing to lead; he obviously was not a good fit for the structure of the past. He knew a war was coming for the people and their land, but he needed an army with a heart to fight.

Like David, you are called and anointed, but where will you land? Who will help you move from the place of a misfit to the seat of a monarch in your spiritual life? God has a plan for you, but it may look strange at first. God is getting you ready to move from a cave to coronation and conquest!

Jeremiah Denton was a POW in Vietnam for seven years. Later he was elected to the Alabama Senate. When asked what sustained him during his difficult imprisonment, he said that it was the Bible verses he had memorized.[1] Although a POW physically, his soul was free and victorious!

THE CAVE BEFORE THE CROWN

It wasn't easy to be anointed for kingship while the current king still reigned. David found himself hunted and hated for being the chosen one of God.

The Old Testament tells the story of how David fled from an insane and murderous King Saul into the wilderness toward Philistia. In order to steer him off course, the enemy tempted David to come over to his side. David fled to the city of Gath, where Goliath, the giant he slew, had been born. But David was recognized, and he feared that Achish, the king of Gath, would have him killed. David feigned mental illness and escaped death, but he also found no home in enemy territory.

This story is a picture of the church moving from her wilderness season to her warfare season! David's training of his "cave church" parallels our need in the contemporary church.

THE CAVE CHURCH

David escaped Saul and Gath and found refuge in the cave of Adullam. Soon, word filtered back to Bethlehem that the would-be king was living in a cave. About four hundred brave supporters sought out David in the wilderness.

This crowd did not look like much! God's Word describes them in this way: "And everyone who was in distress, everyone who was in debt, and everyone who was discontented gathered to him. So he became captain over them. And there were about four hundred men with him" (1 Sam. 22:2).

Here was the beginning of David's army—the distressed, the destitute, and the discontent. What an unlikely beginning for an army that would take David to the throne of Israel! The cave would be the beginning of the Davidic church.

Some people would say you can't build something great in a cave! They think you can't have church on the backside of nowhere. Some believe you can't build a church on discontented people who have no money! Yet this ragtag band of David would become a mighty army for God! (See 1 Chronicles 12:22.)

SPIRITUAL BASIC TRAINING

When young people enlist in the military, they must first go through weeks of rigorous instruction. They must be conditioned physically, emotionally, and mentally to fight the enemy. One Web site for military strategy states this of U.S. Marine recruits: "After successfully completing recruit training, including the Crucible, a final endurance test of teamwork, the recruit is transformed both physically and mentally into a vital part of a highly effective team. Then, and only then, is the recruit awarded the title of Marine."[2]

Interestingly enough, we know David had training procedures, for he stated in the Book of Psalms, "He teaches my hands to make war, so that my arms can bend a bow of bronze" (Ps. 18:34).

In the preface to this psalm, we are told that it was written on the occasion of David's escape from Saul and his enemies. This psalm, I believe, represents David's training manual for his people. God desires for the believer to know how to fight spiritually!

SIX ESSENTIALS FOR THE WARRIOR

Today most armed services have a six- to thirteen-week period of what they term basic training. During that time, the recruits have a leader called a drill instructor. After this basic training, the young soldier or sailor begins to look and act differently.

As you continue through this book, I pray that you will get in shape for more intense spiritual warfare. A timid, untrained army is no match for hell's terrorists! No, we must get into spiritual shape, pick up our armor, and go to the battlefront. The destiny of humanity hangs in the balance.

David trained his four hundred soldiers with the truth we find in Psalm 18, which contains six basic charges every warrior needs to hear.

1. Get under authority—submission

> For You will save the humble people, but will bring down haughty looks.
>
> —PSALM 18:27

The soldier must begin the day knowing how to obey orders. From the moment of arrival in boot camp, nothing belongs to the recruit anymore! His hair is cut, his clothing is selected for him, and his schedule is determined by his leaders. For a season, freedom is lost and submission is taught.

It is essential to understand that putting the devil to flight requires submission to God. James 4:7 tells us, "Therefore submit to God. Resist the devil and he will flee from you."

One of my high school buddies was always a rebel at heart. His dress was unconventional, as well as his attitude. Finally he quit school to live free. His choice? He joined the Marines. I laughed when I saw him after boot camp! His long hair was now a crew cut, and he wore a crisp U.S. Marine uniform instead of jeans. He had learned to live under orders! Hebrews 12:1–2 gives the Christian his or her marching orders:

> Therefore we also, since we are surrounded by so great a cloud of witnesses, let us lay aside every weight, and the sin which so easily ensnares us, and let us run with endurance the race that is set before us, looking unto Jesus, the author and finisher of our faith, who for

the joy that was set before Him endured the cross, despising the shame, and has sat down at the right hand of the throne of God.

2. Get on fire for the cause—passion

For You will light my lamp.

—PSALM 18:28

The second goal of boot camp is to inspire the recruit to have a passion for the cause of the nation. All things being equal, the one with the most passion for the fight will win. In our struggle against the enemy, we must be on fire to win the souls of men for God's kingdom.

One admirable thing about Islamic fundamentalists is their unbridled passion for their cause. They are willing to die in order to further their purposes. While their teaching is in error and their methods are horrific, they are on fire for what they believe. All the weapons of a militia cannot stop such passion; it must be met by Christians who have a passion for Jesus Christ.

3. Be prepared for warfare—discipline

The LORD my God will enlighten my darkness.

—PSALM 18:28

God will "enlighten" His soldiers. We have been given the right armor and the right instructions. Every church must become a spiritual armory, preparing its people for the struggle against the darkness.

4. Believe you can win—vision

For by You I can run against a troop, by my God I can leap over a wall.

—PSALM 18:29

Here the recruit confesses his faith. By the power of God he can overcome a troop. With the strength of God he can leap over a wall. The enemy's army and obstacles fall before the spiritual soldier who has faith.

5. Know your weapons—power

> As for God, His way is perfect; the word of the LORD is proven; He is a shield to all who trust in Him. For who is God, except the LORD? And who is a rock, except our God? It is God who arms me with strength, and makes my way perfect....He teaches my hands to make war, so that my arms can bend a bow of bronze.
>
> —PSALM 18:30–32, 34

Notice first that God has a perfect battle plan. The word *perfect* means "absolutely complete." We must fight according to His plan.

Secondly, Yahweh has given us a sharp, two-edged sword—His Word. We must wield this sword effectively if we are to live the victor's life.

Furthermore, God grants us a shield of protection: faith.

Also, Yahweh exercises our gifts so our hands will be strengthened to make war. We can use our "bronze bow" to judge the enemy. Spiritual archers can shoot down the principalities in the heavens!

6. Go to the next level—excellence

> He makes my feet like the feet of deer, and sets me on my high places.
>
> —PSALM 18:33

Boot camp moves us to the next level of battle. We can conquer the mountains before us. Our feet must be strong so we can walk with a sure foot. The feet of deer "track," which means the rear foot will always land where the front foot leaves. Our God allows us to walk in His footsteps, tracking hard after Him.

David's manual, here in Psalm 18, molded the four hundred outcasts into a military machine that would take the kingdom. We too can go to the next level if we become informed and disciplined. The rest of this book will help you know your enemy, understand the battle, equip yourself for the fight, and walk in victory.

SECTION II

TRACING THE HISTORY OF YOUR ENEMY

chapter 5

BATTLE BEYOND THE STARS

SOMETHING IS TERRIBLY wrong in our world that cannot be explained by human reason. Unfortunately, most of the world, especially Western society, has rejected the idea of supernatural evil.

Our own Western culture is the only society both historical and contemporary that has largely rejected the idea of evil spirits. Since the Age of Enlightenment the Western scholar has sought to understand the world through verifiable, rationalistic, and explainable terms. There is no place for good or evil spirit beings in this "scientific" era. While there is much good that has come from the scientific method, there is a large blind spot when it comes to the spiritual side of man.

Christians have no choice but to face the scriptural, historical, and even contemporary fact that there is a supernatural enemy. Because of ludicrous literature and movies, the idea of a supreme evil being is viewed by many as a joke. Satan is caricatured as a red-suited villain with a tail, horns, and a pitchfork. This is a serious underestimation of the enemy.

Sun Tzu, the ancient Chinese philosopher, wrote the now classic *The Art of War* nearly twenty-five hundred years ago. This book has become the classic on how to achieve victory in the battlefield. He said this about the enemy: "If you know the enemy and know yourself, you need not fear the result of a hundred battles. If you know yourself but not the enemy, for every victory gained you will also suffer a defeat. If you know neither the enemy nor yourself, you will succumb in every battle."[1]

This is true of our spiritual warfare. We must have a healthy recognition and knowledge of our enemy combined with a thorough knowledge of our own identity.

The Christian must balance the fierceness of the enemy with powerful resources on our side of this spiritual battle. When this is done, we will exclaim with the prophet Elisha of old, "Do not fear, for those who are with us are more than those who are with them" (2 Kings 6:16).

THE FORMATION OF SATAN

The name Satan appears less than twenty times in the Old Testament. The full revelation of our ancient foe comes in the New Testament. We find Satan already present in the Garden of Eden at the dawn of man's appearance on Earth. The war we are engaged in is the battle beyond the stars, the battle before history begins, indeed, the battle beyond time! We are a part of an intense war that began in the timeless realm we call eternity.

Our universe, with all its galaxies, solar systems, and vast expanses of space, size, and mystery, was created by God before time. There are other realms and dimensions beyond our created universe. In spite of its beauty, there is something wrong in creation! The presence of evil, death, and struggle are evident on our planet. The human race has an enemy who hates and wants to destroy us.

- We find Satan described as a serpent in Genesis 3 tempting our ancient parents and destroying their home.

- We find him testing Job and losing.

- We find Satan provoking David to trust in numbers instead of God: "Now Satan stood up against Israel, and moved David to number Israel" (1 Chron. 21:1).

- We find Satan resisting the ministry of worship in Zechariah's time: "Then he showed me Joshua the high priest standing before the Angel of the LORD, and Satan standing at his right hand to oppose him. And the LORD said to Satan, 'The LORD rebuke you, Satan! The LORD who has chosen Jerusalem rebuke you! Is this not a brand plucked from the fire?'" (Zech. 3:1–2).

Where did this enemy come from? What is the mystery of prehistory called evil? We must piece together several passages from both the Old and New Testaments to understand evil and its origins. In Isaiah 14:12–15, we see a picture of the fall of Satan. We discover that Satan was once known as Lucifer, which means "light" or "daystar."

LUCIFER'S SINS AND FAILURES

Pride brought Lucifer down.

1. He fell from the dimension of glory—the heaven of heavens (Isa. 14:12).

2. He weakens nations (Isa. 14:12).

3. He sought God's place of supremacy. He wanted to be worshiped by the congregation and rise above the Shekinah glory—the cloud of God's presence (Isa. 14:13–15).

WHAT WAS HE LIKE BEFORE HIS FALL?

Far more informative is the passage beginning in Ezekiel 28:11. Like Isaiah, Ezekiel is predicting the fall of earthly kings. Ezekiel's proclamation is against the kings of Tyre and Sidon. Ezekiel also moves beyond an earthly king's description in this prophecy.

There are several reasons why many have viewed him as talking about Satan in this passage. First, there is no historical reference that has been discovered that Tyre ever had a king of this description. During this period there was a prince who ruled over Tyre. He was overthrown. The king of Tyre would be the father of this prince. Second, verse 13 says, "You were in Eden, the garden of God." According to Genesis 3, the only persons in the Garden of Eden were God, Adam, Eve, and the serpent. Since it is obvious that none of these other personages here are being described, we feel confident, along with many other interpreters, that this is a symbolic reference to Satan.

Ezekiel 28:13 says that Satan was created. This reference gives us the opportunity to answer one of the often-asked questions, "Did God create evil?" If this is indeed a description of the formation of Satan, then we can answer resoundingly no! Verse 15 of Ezekiel 28 again refers to his creation: "You were perfect in your ways from the day you were created, till iniquity was found in you" (Ezek. 18:15).

According to this verse, our present-day enemy was created perfect but with a choice that one day he exercised toward evil. God gave the angelic host a will to choose just like man. This gives us a picture of the formation of Satan, but we must turn to the earlier description we find of him in the Scriptures.

THE CHARACTERISTICS AND FUNCTION OF SATAN

Let us look at these ancient texts and imagine what Satan was like before the fall!

He was beautiful!

Look again at Ezekiel's description: "Son of man, take up a lamentation for the king of Tyre, and say to him, 'Thus says the Lord GOD: "You were the seal of perfection, full of wisdom and perfect in beauty"'" (Ezek. 28:12).

He gave off a rainbow of iridescent colors. He was the combined brilliance of every precious stone. He was as valuable as the most costly stones and as beautiful as the colors of the rainbow. The problem was that stones do not give off light of themselves; they only reflect light. He evidently forgot this most important truth as he was puffed up with pride.

He was assigned to cover the angels and the land of Eden.

Eden was part of ancient earth: "You were in Eden, the garden of God; every precious stone was your covering: the sardius, topaz, and diamond, beryl, onyx, and jasper, sapphire, turquoise, and emerald with gold. The workmanship of your timbrels and pipes was prepared for you on the day you were created" (Ezek. 28:13).

The stones indicate that he was a part of a worshiping host. These stones are similar to the stones an Israelite high priest wore. He was musical.

He was also a created being; he was called a cherub.

> You were the anointed cherub who covers...
> —EZEKIEL 28:14

Lucifer's assignment was established by God as guardian over the earth and all its life forms. Also, he was over the land we now know as Israel.

He knew the secrets of creation and life.

> You were on the holy mountain of God; you walked back and forth in the midst of fiery stones.
> —EZEKIEL 28:14

The stones of fire seem to be God's ancient source of creative power. Satan's fall and ultimate judgment are also described by the prophet: "And you sinned; therefore I cast you as a profane thing out of the mountain of God; and I destroyed you, O covering cherub, from the midst of the fiery stones.... I cast you to the ground" (Ezek. 28:16–17).

THE FALL OF SATAN

When did he fall?

Many see the time of his fall as coming between Genesis 1:1 and 1:2. While the scope of this chapter will not allow a lengthy defense of this cosmological view, several key points need to be given as they bear upon our understanding of the origin and function of the enemy. First, there is scriptural warrant that God did not create this earth "without form and void" originally. This designation found in Genesis 1:2 is the Hebrew words *tohuw*, which means "without form," and *bohuw*, which means "void."

We find the same Hebrew word *tohuw* in Isaiah 45:18, but it is translated as "vain": "For thus says the LORD, who created the heavens, who is God who formed the earth and made it...who *did not create it in vain*, who formed it to be inhabited" (emphasis added).

If God did not create the earth this way, then a catastrophe of cataclysmic proportions must have happened between these two verses. Genesis 1:3 and the verses following would indicate a "re-creation" after an undesignated period of time. This is textually possible because the word *created* in Genesis 1:1 is the Hebrew word *bara*. This word stands out as a word meaning "to create something from nothing." The rest of the Hebrew words for "create" (excluding animal life) mean "to create out of existing materials."

Secondly, this would give us an understanding of many other scriptures. Jesus said in Luke 10:18, "I saw Satan fall like lightning from heaven." While many interpret this verse in light of the work of the seventy disciples Jesus had sent out (Luke 10:1–17), there is also strong merit to understand Jesus's statement in light of His preincarnate existence. This would help explain why the enemy in the form of the serpent was already present in the Garden of Eden. The whole idea of Satan as a created angel that rebelled and fell, along with other rebellious angels, fits with this understanding of Bible cosmogony.

Why did Satan fall?

A discussion of why the enemy fell from heaven must follow. Look again at Isaiah 14. It gives insight into the steps that led to the enemy's downfall. Five times in this passage he says, "I will…" Isaiah records them: "For you have said in your heart: '*I will* ascend into heaven, *I will* exalt my throne above the stars of God; *I will* also sit on the mount of the congregation on the farthest sides of the north; *I will* ascend above the heights of the clouds, *I will* be like the Most High'" (Isa. 14:13–14, emphasis added).

When the enemy purposed in his heart to carry out his sin, a terrible thing came to God's domain. There were now two wills in existence. Up until this time there had only been God's will, and everything moved in harmony and peace. God cannot allow any being to oppose His will and continue without punishment. The very essence of sin is to choose our will rather than God's.

What happened? There was an old earth, pristine and beautiful—God was preparing it for human beings so it would have all the resources necessary for us.

Satan was jealous of God's plan to set man into the earth. He and certain angels "covered" the earth. His rebellion was exposed, and he fell to Earth!

This fall was a catastrophe of monumental proportions. Much of the ancient earth and its prehistoric life were destroyed. The earth became void and empty!

God returned to the land of Eden, which stretches from the Mediterranean all the way across the Middle East. This area is the cradle of civilization. He planted a garden in Eden to take back this planet for humanity. This battle began beyond the stars!

In this war one-third of the angels went with the rebel leader, Satan, and are now what we call demons or evil spirits.

God was not surprised, and from fallen humanity He would bring His Son into the world. The battle would rage against Jesus at the cross. And at the cross Jesus would defeat Satan.

Satan is a defeated foe because of the work of Christ on the cross, but he is also a formidable foe. Our struggle with him is likened to the famous battle of New Orleans during the War of 1812. General Andrew Jackson commanded this greatest battle of the war after the papers of treaty had already been signed! Word had not reached them of these events.

We too fight in a battle that has already been decided. Jesus forever sealed the fate of the host of demonic forces and Satan himself when He died on the cross. Yet Satan still "walks about like a roaring lion, seeking whom he may devour" (1 Pet. 5:8).

Thank God Jesus has overthrown Satan. We must put away our pride and bow at Jesus's feet as our Lord and Savior. According to Scripture, one day Satan will be cast down at our feet (Ezek. 28:17). One day he shall be gone forever. "Yet thou shall be brought down to hell, to the sides of the pit" (Isa. 14:15, KJV). Satan is defeated, and you will learn in this study that the victory is already ours.

In January of 1994 the Dallas Cowboys professional football team was preparing to play the San Francisco 49ers for the NFC championship. The coach of the Cowboys, Jimmy Johnson, caused a media uproar when he called into a local radio show the Thursday before the game and boldly asserted, "The Dallas Cowboys will win the game!" When questioned why he would make such a bold statement before playing such a talented opponent, he stated that it didn't matter what team they were playing. He had seen the Cowboys in preparation that week, and they had fire in them. He didn't have to measure their opponent—they were ready.[2] (And by the way, the Cowboys won!) Are we ready?

chapter 6

THE CONTINUOUS
WAR IN EDEN

A FTER LUCIFER'S FALL the earth became without form and void. (See
Genesis 1:1–2.) The Hebrew word translated "was" is often translated
"became." Since Genesis 1:1–2 can be read, "...*became* without form,
and void," it seems obvious that something happened between Genesis
1:1 and 1:2—an earth-shaking, world-destroying catastrophe.

THE OLD CREATION

Lucifer had reigned over the earth from a land called Eden, whose place of
worship was located on the "Mountain of God" in the place the ancients
called Salem ("peace") and that we now call Jerusalem. The world was a
wonder of animate life. It was God's zoo, with strange creatures we call
dinosaurs. From Jerusalem Lucifer led worship and walked in the stones
of fire, which represent healing power. (See Ezekiel 28.)

Lucifer's fall was like the impact of an asteroid. Suddenly all animal
life on the terra firma vanished. It was sudden and catastrophic. When
I visited the Dinosaur National Park in eastern Utah, I was amazed by
two things. First, dinosaurs died with food in their mouth, eggs in the
process of hatching, and were frozen in terror! Second, the river bored
through a solid rock hill like a drill. Under normal circumstances that
river would have gone around the hill. A force not known in geology
drilled through that rock!

I believe this ancient tragedy is the result of Satan's fall to ruin. What scientists call the Cambrian age was caused by the impact of God's judgment on Satan. Here we find the fossils of multitudes of ancient life forms. Though scientists call this time "an explosion of life," it was really an "explosion of death." The aftermath of the death of all these living creatures is the vast deposit of oil and gas that drive the world system and economy even now.

EDEN, A VAST LAND

When we look at the original Eden, we see a vast and beautiful land! In Genesis 2:10–14, we discover that out of the northern part of the land of Eden flowed four large rivers—Pishon, Gihon, Hiddekel (Tigris), and Euphrates. Two of the four rivers are easily recognizable—the Tigris and Euphrates.

The river Pishon is no longer flowing, but its rift has been discovered by land-penetrating satellite technology. Its rift runs through Saudi Arabia all the way to what is now the Red Sea. Some believe that before the continental shifts it flowed all the way to India, to what is now the Ganges River.

The river Gihon is a different matter; it flowed through Israel and Jordan all the way through what is now the Red Sea into Egypt and into the Nile! The Flood made changes in the direction of the rivers.

ANOTHER CATASTROPHE

The big change came in a massive earthquake that was caused when the continental plate of Africa, Europe, and Asia collided. This event is recorded in the Bible during the days of Peleg (101 years after the Flood).

> To Eber were born two sons: the name of one was Peleg, for in his days the earth was divided; and his brother's name was Joktan.
>
> —GENESIS 10:25; SEE ALSO 1 CHRONICLES 1:18–19

This great division created what is called the Africa rift where the Jordan Valley is located today. Before that, the river Gihon ran through Jerusalem. Its remnant is still called the spring of Gihon to this day.

Knowing then that Eden was a huge landmass before the destruction of the old creation, we see that God determined to reclaim the planet and His ancient holy mountain. Many believe that the garden planted as Eden was located in Jerusalem! Genesis 2:8 says that Yahweh planted it in the east of Eden.

In the same place where Lucifer led worship and had been the covering cherub of the old earth, God placed human beings to restore the ruined earth.

As proof of this, a closer examination of Ezekiel 28 will clear up the mystery.

Ezekiel 28:13 declares that Lucifer was in Eden when it was still pristine. The same verse declares that Lucifer was beautiful and musical, giving glory to the Lord. As one of the cherubim, Lucifer was close to the Lord, serving as a traveling throne for God. Psalm 18:10 says, "And He rode upon a cherub, and flew; He flew upon the wings of the wind."

After the fall Lucifer became Satan, a serpent. Fallen from his former glory, Satan lurked in Eden. His desire was to thwart God's plan and dethrone the new king of Eden and of the earth, Adam.

SATAN'S EARLY SUCCESS

The Lord set Adam and Eve in a perfect environment. Made in God's image, they were given a mind to think, a heart to love, and a will to choose. To test the mind, God gave Adam the assignment to name all of the animal life. To prove his heart, God gave Adam his counterpart—the female, Eve. To test his will there were two trees planted—the tree of life and the tree of the knowledge of good and evil. God planted the tree of life, and I believe Satan planted the tree of the knowledge of good and evil! I believe this because God had already given Adam and Eve permission to eat everything except that tree. They could eat of the tree of life, but not of the tree of the knowledge of good and evil. Every day they could choose life or death. God allowed that tree to be there to test the will of Adam. It is this free will that makes us like God. This would be precisely Satan's tactic to tempt our ancient parents. Genesis 3:5 says,

"For God knows that in the day you eat of it your eyes will be opened, and you will be like God, knowing good and evil."

This resulted in man being driven out of the garden east of Eden near what came to be Jericho, Earth's oldest city. Joshua 3:16 speaks of the city of Adam when describing the miraculous parting of the Jordan River. To this day there is a place identified seventeen miles north of Jericho, exactly east of Jerusalem, called the Village of Adam.

It is also interesting that Abel, who was murdered by Cain, is said to have lived in the same region. In fact, "the stone of Abel" mentioned in 1 Samuel 6:18 is cited as the place of Abel's death. There are also four villages named to this day east of Jerusalem connected to Abel (Abel Maim, Abel Meholah, Abel Shittim, Abel Keramim). All of this indicates that the Garden of Eden could have been in Jerusalem.

Perhaps the most telling evidence is the Spring of Gihon. The river of Eden that flowed through the garden was Gihon. It remains an underground water source until this day. Satellite photography shows riverbeds all the way through the Dead Sea into Africa from Syria to the Nile. As we said earlier, the continental shift changed the riverbeds. This shut off the Gihon and created the Dead Sea.

EAST OF EDEN

Adam and Eve continued to worship by returning to the gateway to Eden. There they offered sacrifice and taught their children to do the same.

It is interesting that the presence of God was guarded by other cherubim, Lucifer's replacements! "So He drove out the man; and He placed cherubim at the east of the garden of Eden, and a flaming sword which turned every way, to guard the way to the tree of life" (Gen. 3:24). In man's fallen condition, had he eaten of the tree of life, he would have been condemned to live in an aging body that could never die.

It is interesting that when the tabernacle and later the temple were built, they placed golden images of two cherubim to cover and protect God's throne on Earth, the ark of the covenant! The cherubim still attend and cover the presence of God.

When Genesis 3:8 speaks of the cool of the day when God appeared to Adam and Eve, the word *cool* is *ruwach*, or "spirit." Perhaps when

Adam's fallen family approached the gate of the garden to worship, they could see the glory cloud or Shekinah and feel its cooling breezes.

After Adam and Eve were driven out of Eden, two sons were born to them. The elder one, Cain, killed his brother Abel and was driven away to the land of Nod. This is the land of Iran!

Return to the Garden

The Flood would come, and catastrophe would again touch the whole earth. The land of Eden would disappear, as would the garden. Yet God had chosen Jerusalem to be His point of contact with the earth and mankind! Because of God's love for that land, He called Abraham to leave everything and go there to plant a new nation. Why did God choose that land? I believe it was His mountain! In Psalm 135:21 God is said to dwell in Jerusalem. Jerusalem is mentioned in Scripture more than eight hundred times. The traveling city, which will house the bride of Christ, the church, is called the New Jerusalem. Many believe it will sit in stationary orbit over old Jerusalem.

Abraham returned to Jerusalem, also called Salem, to pay tithes to Melchizedek (Gen. 14). According to the Book of Jasher, which gives us the historical perspective of the Old Testament, Melchizedek was Shem, the son of Noah. Shem lived one hundred years after this visit and talked with Isaac and Jacob.[1] (See Joshua 10:13; 2 Samuel 1:18.) Abraham offered Isaac on the mountain of the Lord.

Later David would take Jerusalem from the Jebusites. From that day until now Satan has hated the Jews and Jerusalem, and he hates the plan of God to save the world through a Jewish Messiah.

Satan's Ultimate Plan

Satan's war against humanity still targets Jerusalem. Here he was humiliated. Here Christ died on the cross and was raised from the dead. Here, in the Middle East, Satan has stirred up war and hatred until this day. Satan hates the Jews, hates Israel, and hates the church.

Adam fell in the Garden of Eden. It is my firm belief that the Garden of Gethsemane is old Eden. Here the Second Adam refused the voice of

Satan and took our cup of death. At the cross Jesus opened the gates of a new paradise and a new Eden.

It is important for you to understand that Satan, through the Muslims, is still trying to conquer Jerusalem. It is also important for you to understand your personal struggles are rooted in an ancient conflict. But you must rejoice in the victory given to us at Calvary; though two thousand years old, this victory is available to you today.

THE TREE OF LIFE

Adam forfeited eternal life by choosing Satan's tree of the knowledge of good and evil over God's tree of life. Because of Jesus we can again taste the tree of life.

> In the middle of its street, and on either side of the river, was the tree of life, which bore twelve fruits, each tree yielding its fruit every month. The leaves of the tree were for the healing of the nations.
> —REVELATION 22:2

And Revelation 22:14 tells us, "Blessed are those who do His commandments, that they may have the right to the tree of life, and may enter through the gates into the city."

chapter 7

WAR ON HUMANITY

I N GENESIS 3:1–15 we read the horrific record of the fall and ruin of humanity. The enemy was present in this most pristine garden.

> Now the serpent was more cunning than any beast of the field which the LORD God had made. And he said to the woman, "Has God indeed said, 'You shall not eat of every tree of the garden'?"
>
> —GENESIS 3:1

Here our enemy questions God's integrity and love. Eve responded to the serpent by repeating God's warning.

> And the woman said to the serpent, "We may eat the fruit of the trees of the garden; but of the fruit of the tree which is in the midst of the garden, God has said, 'You shall not eat it, nor shall you touch it, lest you die.'"
>
> —GENESIS 3:2–3

Clearly she added to the word of God with the phrase "neither shall you touch it."

In verse 4, Satan targets her soul by calling God a liar and then issuing a false promise:

> Then the serpent said to the woman, "You will not surely die. For God knows that in the day you eat of it your eyes will be opened, and you will be like God, knowing good and evil."

Lured by the temptation, Eve bites the poisoned fruit, and Adam does the same.

> So when the woman saw that the tree was good for food, that it was pleasant to the eyes, and a tree desirable to make one wise, she took of its fruit and ate. She also gave to her husband with her, and he ate.
>
> —GENESIS 3:6

They had been clothed in God's glory, and now they are stripped naked by their sin. "Then the eyes of both of them were opened, and they knew that they were naked; and they sewed fig leaves together and made themselves coverings" (Gen. 3:7).

They could not cover themselves, so they hid from God.

> And they heard the sound of the LORD God walking in the garden in the cool of the day, and Adam and his wife hid themselves from the presence of the LORD God among the trees of the garden.
>
> —GENESIS 3:8

Again, the word *cool* is *ruwach* in Hebrew, which means "spirit." God came for communion, and Adam and Eve hid from what they had once enjoyed.

In verse 9, "Then the LORD God called to Adam and said to him, 'Where are you?'" Here is the call of justice and love to fallen humanity. "So he said, 'I heard Your voice in the garden, and I was afraid because I was naked; and I hid myself'" (v. 10). Fear has replaced favor and faith, and God exposes their failure.

> And He said, "Who told you that you were naked? Have you eaten from the tree of which I commanded you that you should not eat?" Then the man said, "The woman whom You gave to be with me, she gave me of the tree, and I ate.
>
> —GENESIS 3:11–12

Adam blamed Eve, and she blamed Satan; yet ultimately they both made the fatal choice.

"And the LORD God said to the woman, 'What is this you have done?' The woman said, 'The serpent deceived me, and I ate'" (v. 13). God pronounced judgment on Satan and issued the great promise of a Seed that would come to be bruised yet would ultimately crush Satan's head.

> So the LORD God said to the serpent: "Because you have done this, you are cursed more than all cattle, and more than every beast of the field; on your belly you shall go, and you shall eat dust all the days of your life. And I will put enmity between you and the woman, and between your seed and her Seed; He shall bruise your head, and you shall bruise His heel."
>
> —GENESIS 3:14–15

Now, having read the story, let's look at the implications for our lives today. As we have seen, there is a basis for the belief that before his fall Lucifer was the principality God had appointed over our created order. At his fall the primeval creation was ruined and enshrouded in darkness. Lucifer, the light bearer, became Satan, the adversary or enemy. The shining cherub became the stalking dragon. Satan thought that he was the source of his beauty, wisdom, and music. He is described as a jewel whose glory can only be seen in pure light. In his pride Lucifer refused to see that his glory was the reflected glory of the Most High God. A diamond in total darkness is no more than a sharp pebble.

Consequently Satan receives the verdict of heaven and is cast out in devastating judgment, losing his position and authority. Creation lies under devastating judgment and darkness. Here are several Scripture verses that confirm his ruin: Job 9:3–10; 38:4–13; Psalm 18:7–15.

The earth bears the scars of two ancient catastrophes: the ancient ruin and the Flood. Our planet has been shaken, its continents torn apart with an age of ice and glaciers having left deep canyons, unstable underground faults, unpredictable volcanoes, and devastating earthquakes testifying to the original ruin.

The preincarnate Christ was the divine creator. John 1:3 tells us, "All things were made by him" (KJV), and in Colossians 1:16–17 we read, "For by him were all things created…and by him all things consist [hold together]" (KJV). Satan's fall from heaven led to the devastation of the ancient creation. It was an attack on Christ before He became incarnate, God in the flesh.

Here the earth remained for an unknown period as a wreck and a ruin. Then God instituted His plan for the ruined creation. He recaptured it through a creature to be known as man.

The state of creation is reset in Genesis 1 and 2; from existing matter God remade the earth and placed it in a paradise called Eden. Out of the chaos God assembled order. In the six-day account of Creation we read that God made, divided, formed, set, and so on. The word *create* is only used in reference to the "breath" of God. He created moving life out of existing materials, but He made it live by His breath. Even man was formed of "dust of the earth" and given life by God's creative Spirit.

So God made man in His own image. This means man was given a spirit, a spirit that has the three qualities of God. Man was given a mind to think, a heart to love, and a will to choose. He was placed in an environment to test all three capacities. He could use his mind to name the animals and govern the earth. He could use his heart to love Eve and God. He could use his will to choose right or wrong.

In the midst of the garden stood the tree of life and the tree of death. God instructed Adam and Eve to eat of all the trees, including the tree of life. The only one forbidden was the tree of the knowledge of good and evil.

At this point Satan embodied himself in a fiery creature called a serpent, or *nachash* in the Hebrew, which speaks of beauty and brilliance. Please note, only three times in Scripture does Satan take a body: the serpent, Judas Iscariot, and the Antichrist. Also notice that Satan is already present on the earth!

THE COMMENCEMENT OF THE WAR

With the stage set, Satan launched his attack on mankind. There are two important things to notice about Satan's attack in the verses we read in Genesis: his motive and his method of attack.

First, the motive of the enemy can be seen. Why did he attack man? Because he viewed the creation of man as a mistake. He was jealous of the future glory God promised man. Psalm 8:5 says, "You have made him a little lower than the angels, and You have crowned him with glory and honor." Satan and his hosts of heavenly beings desired the earth and its glory. They hated man and his position. Hebrews 2:7 states, "You have...set him over the works of Your hands." Satan's motive remains the same—to thwart God's plan on the earth.

Secondly, the method of the enemy's attack is clear. Satan attacked the first human beings in an attempt to get to God through mankind. Satan has a method. Ephesians 6:11 warns us of the "wiles" of the devil. The word *wiles* is the Greek word *methodeia*, from which we get our word *methods*. Satan is deceptive but predictable; he used deception and temptation, methods often repeated since his fall.

THE CASUALTIES OF THE WAR

Satan launched his attack through the woman. The Bible calls woman the weaker sex. That does not mean weaker in mind, body, endurance, or worth. It means more susceptible. While some commentaries may argue this point, Matthew Henry says in his commentary that Satan approached Eve while she was away from her husband. She was completely deceived and thought that she was doing what was best for her husband. First Timothy 2:14 states, "Adam was not deceived..." He knew exactly what he was doing. He chose by his own free will to disobey.

Through this act mankind became lost. (See Romans 5:12, 17, 19; 1 Corinthians 15:21–22.) At one point there had been only two wills: God's and Satan's. Now every man has a will to choose for God or against God. Man is, by fact of nature and by choice of will, a sinner. Man is utterly lost.

THE CONTINUATION OF THE WAR

God announced the continual enmity between man and Satan, our adversary. It would seem as though Satan had won. He had deceived woman. He had succeeded in getting man to doubt the veracity of God's words. He had succeeded in bringing doubt about the goodness of God. But Satan failed at one decisive point. He could not govern the will of man. Isaiah 53:6 states, "We have turned, every one, to his own way." Man now asserts his fallen will. Satan cannot take the chaos of humanity and weld it together for long for his evil purpose.

This explains the terrible tragedies and difficulties of our world. It is a fallen world under the curse of sin. Satan is a rebel against God, and so is every person who chooses his own way. There is a war going on. The very nature of war is to leave tragedy in its wake. Human history is one vast parade of man and Satan trying to do something for man without God. God had permitted the horror of tragedy to convince an unbelieving world it is utterly helpless without Him.

THE CLIMAX OF THE WAR

As we observed in Genesis 3:15, God announced ultimate triumph right from the beginning: "And I will put enmity between you and the woman, and between your seed and her Seed; He shall bruise your head, and you shall bruise His heel." There will be a bruised seed and a crushed serpent. Satan's defeat is to come through man. This is the first prophecy of the decisive battle that took place on Calvary's cross. Satan would vent his anger on the Son of God. Christ died for our sins and destroyed Satan's demand for our souls. Satan held the power of death according to Hebrews 2:14: "Inasmuch then as the children have partaken of flesh and blood, He Himself likewise shared in the same, that through death He might destroy him who had the power of death, that is, the devil."

When we are saved into the family of God, according to Colossians 2:13–15 we rest in the victory of Christ. Christ stripped demonic forces of their authority as well as robbed them of their powers. Satan has already been defeated.

It is our task, then, to enforce the victory of the cross until Jesus returns for us. We do not belong to Satan. He has no authority over us. We are God's property. All we need to do is simply affirm the fact that now all the kingdoms of this world are already overthrown. They are defeated even if they don't know it.

Ultimately all of Satan's invisible forces will be forever confined to the lake of fire. Until that day it is the purpose of God to display His glory in His new people, the church. Ephesians 3:9–11 (NIV) states this ultimate purpose:

> To make plain to everyone the administration of this mystery, which for ages past was kept hidden in God, who created all things. His intent was that now, through the church, the manifold wisdom of God should be made known to the rulers and authorities in the

heavenly realms, according to his eternal purpose which he accomplished in Christ Jesus our Lord.

God was not surprised by the fall of man. His plan is right on schedule. Everyone who surrenders to Him and lays down the weapons of rebellion becomes a part of His new kingdom. We become soldiers as well as saints and servants until that day.

chapter 8

WAR AGAINST THE
PROMISED SEED OF ISRAEL

ONE OF THE key words in Revelation is *overcome*, from the Greek word *nikao*, which means "conqueror." The Nike corporation chose this word to describe their athletic shoes and apparel, implying that the wearers can be conquerors or, better said, "overcomers."

Revelation 12:11 speaks of such a conquest over Satan when it says, "And they overcame him [Satan] by the blood of the Lamb." Satan must be overcome!

That particular word of victory follows some strange battle imagery. In Revelation 12:4–5 Satan is described as a dragon standing before a pregnant woman ready to devour her child as soon as it is born. The next verses describe a war in the spiritual realm between Michael, the prince of the host of righteous angels, and Satan, the fallen prince. This colossal struggle ensues over God's purposes on Earth and culminates in the Incarnation, God coming to Earth in human flesh through "the seed of a woman." This ancient prophecy is found in Genesis 3:15, which declares this seed of woman will crush the head of the serpent while being bruised in the process.

When we look at the prophetic promises of the Messiah, we discover that the Messiah had to be a male descendant of Abraham and Isaac (Gen. 22:18), a Jewish man born from the lineage of Jacob (Num. 24:17). Not only was the Messiah to be Jewish, but He was also to be a descendant of the royal line of David (Matt. 1:6). This prophesied seed had to be born in Bethlehem (Mic. 5:2). This child must be born of a virgin (Isa. 7:14). His arrival must be 450 years after Cyrus's decree and Daniel's seventy weeks of years prophecy (Dan. 9:24). This coming One could only be Jesus Christ, born unto the Virgin Mary.

Satan declared war on the promised seed. He would try to stop the coming of God's Son into the world.

> His tail drew a third of the stars of heaven and threw them to the earth. And the dragon stood before the woman who was ready to give birth, to devour her Child as soon as it was born. She bore a male Child who was to rule all nations with a rod of iron. And her Child was caught up to God and His throne.
>
> —Revelation 12:4–5

Satan's Hatred of Israel

As we turn the pages of Scripture, the struggle unfolds. Satan provoked Cain to murder righteous Abel, yet God sent Seth! Satan corrupted the people of the earth so the judgment of the Flood came. However, Noah and his family were saved, and Noah's son, Shem, became a cousin of the seed. Abraham almost lost Sarah to Pharaoh. Esau sought to kill Jacob (Israel) and destroy the Jewish nation before it could be birthed.

During the Egyptian captivity, Satan stirred wicked Pharaoh to kill the firstborn of Israel and destroy the prophetic line, but Moses was appointed to save the Jewish people once again.

David had to face the giant Goliath and the threats of a demonized King Saul. Furthermore, David's family experienced intrigue, division, and murder.

Later, when King Jehoshaphat died, his son Jehoram murdered all of the royal offspring. Then an Arab enemy attacked Israel while Jehoram was king and killed all his children except for one, Ahaziah. When Jehu slew Ahaziah, Jezebel's daughter Athaliah saw her chance to become queen. In a bloodthirsty rage, she murdered all the children of Ahaziah, again except for one!

A Miraculous Preservation

The wife of Jehoiada, the high priest of Israel, rescued the one remaining child in the royal line of David, Joash, and had him taken away. For a period of six years the entire prophetic promise of the Messiah resided in that one child.

FOR SUCH A TIME AS THIS

The little Book of Esther never mentions God. However, the book's sole purpose is to declare God's victory over another satanic effort to exterminate Israel and stop the advent of the Messiah. The courage of Esther and a king's insomnia exposed the plot of wicked Haman to destroy the Jewish nation.

God's preservation of Israel through the Babylonian captivity and through the murderous scheme of Antiochus Epiphanes is miraculous.

BETHLEHEM BLOODBATH

Finally, the moment came for the promised seed to be born in Bethlehem. Mary and Joseph made the long, arduous journey, and Jesus was born in a cave, swaddled in rags, and laid in a feed trough!

Satan stirred the Edomite Herod, an evil king, to destroy all the babies in the vicinity of Bethlehem. His wish was to destroy any rival for the throne. God sent wise men from Persia (Iran) to bring finances to Mary and Joseph. Once supernaturally warned, Mary, Joseph, and the baby spent seven years in Egypt because of the wealth given them by the wise men.

GOD INCARNATE IN JESUS

When Jesus began His ministry, Satan showed up and tried to get Jesus to kill Himself by jumping from the pinnacle of the temple. Jesus's old friends in Nazareth turned on Him and tried to push Him off a cliff. Satan thought he had finally won when Christ was nailed to a cross and died.

For three days, Jesus faced Satan in the realms of death. Peter declared that Jesus made a proclamation to "the spirits in prison" (1 Pet. 3:18–20). Jesus seized death, Satan's most formidable weapon, and took the keys!

> Inasmuch then as the children have partaken of flesh and blood,
> He Himself likewise shared in the same, that through death He

might destroy him who had the power of death, that is, the devil, and release those who through fear of death were all their lifetime subject to bondage.

—HEBREWS 2:14–15

On the Day of Pentecost Peter, who had been tempted by Satan, declared that death could not hold Jesus: "Whom God raised up, having loosed the pains of death, because it was not possible that He should be held by it" (Acts 2:24).

Satan made the mistake of the ages. In seeking to destroy the seed by killing Jesus, Satan's act of retaliation resulted in the salvation of humanity.

A NEW RACE OF MEN

Jesus was raised from the dead and became the Second Adam, the head of a new race of men not subject to the old division of color and culture.

Romans 5:12–14 declares that a Second Adam has come. A new king has come in Jesus of Nazareth. Jesus has broken the tyranny of Satan, exposed the darkness, and shattered the empire of evil. Jesus has crushed the headship of Satan and rendered sin's dominion powerless. Now grace reigns through Jesus Christ. (See Romans 5:21.)

This "one new man" is the church for whom the Messiah, Jesus, is the head. The reign of grace has resulted in millions becoming Christians. (See Ephesians 2:8–9.) New possibilities appear and are attainable for every obedient believer. God has made a new race of people in the church. We are part of God's new order called "one new man" (Eph. 2:14–15).

THE BATTLE CONTINUES

In the next chapter we will trace the battle lines throughout the history of the church. It is important to note that anti-Semitism is on the rise. The continuing struggles in the Middle East are over Jerusalem. Hitler sought to exterminate the Jewish people. His purposes, if achieved, would have stopped God's chosen people from returning to their homeland and would have thwarted Bible prophecy. Israel survived, and so does the church in spite of two millennia of struggle and strife.

chapter 9

SATAN'S WAR ON
THE CHURCH

THE BOOK OF Revelation is studied and cited for its striking prophe-
cies and thrilling pictures of the coming of the Lord. However, at
the beginning of this important book is a collection of letters directed to
seven churches. Within these letters is a remarkably complete treatment
of problems that face the church in the twenty-first century. Under the
inspiration of the Holy Spirit, John penned warnings about the dangers
of losing their first love (Rev. 2:4), of being afraid of suffering (v. 10), of
doctrinal defection (vv. 14–15), of moral departure (v. 20), of spiritual
deadness (Rev. 3), of not holding fast (v. 11), and of straddling the fence
(vv. 15–16). These problems are just as prevalent in today's church as
they were in the first century.

I believe that the use of the word *overcome* (*nikao* in Greek) (Rev. 2:7,
11, 17, 26; 3:5, 12, 21) used here in the context of Revelation is related to
spiritual warfare. The besetting sins or failures of each of the churches
were caused, influenced, and encouraged by demonic forces that Satan
assigned to attack these churches. Each church had to repent and overcome by recognizing and exposing the demonic force.

If you doubt the operation of Satan in the local church, take a look at
the straightforward references to him in these chapters of Revelation!

> I know your works, tribulation, and poverty (but you are rich);
> and I know the blasphemy of those who say they are Jews and are
> not, but are a synagogue of Satan. Do not fear any of those things
> which you are about to suffer. Indeed, the devil is about to throw

some of you into prison, that you may be tested, and you will have tribulation ten days. Be faithful until death, and I will give you the crown of life.

—Revelation 2:9–10

I know your works, and where you dwell, where Satan's throne is. And you hold fast to My name, and did not deny My faith even in the days in which Antipas was My faithful martyr, who was killed among you, where Satan dwells.

—Revelation 2:13–14

Now to you I say, and to the rest in Thyatira, as many as do not have this doctrine, who have not known the depths of Satan, as they say, I will put on you no other burden.

—Revelation 2:24

Indeed I will make those of the synagogue of Satan, who say they are Jews and are not, but lie—indeed I will make them come and worship before your feet, and to know that I have loved you.

—Revelation 3:9

Although more than one demonic spirit can operate in a single church, each church in these chapters of Revelation manifested one primary satanic influence.

Satan's Plan in the Church

The enemy loves to attend church! Satan has shown his hand clearly through the following methods. These same methods are his *modus operandi*, or mode of operation, in the life of individual believers as well!

- **He attempts to distract your worship.** In the Book of Matthew, we find recorded the temptation of Christ by Satan. The devil tried unsuccessfully to pull our Savior's attention and worship away from God the Father. Jesus told him, "Away with you, Satan! For it is written, 'You shall worship the Lord your God, and Him only you shall serve'" (Matt. 4:10). If the enemy can get your focus off

Jesus and onto yourself, your surroundings, your circumstances, or the people around you, he will gain a foothold. The devil desires to control your worship, knowing that will open the door for his attacks.

- **His goal is to subvert workers**. "And the Lord said, 'Simon, Simon! Indeed, Satan has asked for you, that he may sift you as wheat. But I have prayed for you, that your faith should not fail; and when you have returned to Me, strengthen your brethren'" (Luke 22:31–32). Here the Lord Jesus clearly warns His disciples that Satan attacks those who work for God. To "sift as wheat" refers to the ancient process of separating the wheat kernel from the chaff. The wheat was cast into the air and the kernels were caught in baskets. The heaviest seed would fall, but the lighter and useless chaff would be blown away. Satan wants Christians to be blown off course and find themselves useless for service to the Lord. Yet the prayers of Jesus keep us.

  1.   He is still praying for us, as we see in Hebrews 7:25: "Therefore He is also able to save to the uttermost those who come to God through Him, since He always lives to make intercession for them."

  2.   Satan also tries to take the offerings of God's workers and stop the work of God from going forward. Acts tells the story of Ananias, who decided to keep back some of his tithe to God: "But Peter said, 'Ananias, why has Satan filled your heart to lie to the Holy Spirit and keep back part of the price of the land for yourself?'" (Acts 5:3). Satan is always looking for ways to hinder our witness. We must be on the lookout for his traps "lest Satan should take advantage of us; for we are not ignorant of his devices" (2 Cor. 2:11).

- **Satan tries tirelessly to steal the Word.** "And these are the ones by the wayside where the word is sown. When they hear, Satan comes immediately and takes away the word that was sown in their hearts" (Mark 4:15). Satan goes to church, and when the Word of God is being preached, he works hard to take away the seed. Satan will do whatever it takes to rob you and hide the truth of God from you. He knows the truth is the only way for you to walk in freedom, so he comes to steal the liberating, life-giving Word.

- **Another one of his goals is to inflict wrath.** Scripture tells us that the enemy attacked Paul with blow after blow. Paul himself wrote, "And lest I should be exalted above measure by the abundance of the revelations, a thorn in the flesh was given to me, a messenger of Satan to buffet me, lest I be exalted above measure" (2 Cor. 12:7). God even used the enemy's wrath to bring forth a humble, more powerful servant in Paul. It is clear from the example of Paul's life that Satan can and will buffet even the most upright saints. However, God will also turn sinning Christians over to Satan, removing His protective hedge, in order to bring them toward repentance: "…of whom are Hymenaeus and Alexander, whom I delivered to Satan that they may learn not to blaspheme" (1 Tim. 1:20).

- **Satan will incite wickedness and immorality.** Scripture gives a special warning to married Christians: "Do not deprive one another except with consent for a time, that you may give yourselves to fasting and prayer; and come together again so that Satan does not tempt you because of your lack of self-control" (1 Cor. 7:5). We see here that sexual relations in marriage are approved and encouraged by the Lord. When a married couple refuses to sleep with each other, it can open the door for the enemy to attack the marriage.

- **Ultimately Satan wants nothing more than to hinder God's work on Earth through the church.** Obviously, the enemy will throw up every roadblock he can to stop believers from pursuing the will of God. The apostle Paul faced these roadblocks, as he explained in one of his letters: "Therefore we wanted to come to you—even I,

Paul, time and again—but Satan hindered us" (1 Thess. 2:18). Remember, Satan is not asleep; he is on the prowl to destroy the work of God's children. We must be watchful and ready!

chapter 10

SEVEN DEMONS THAT ATTACK THE CHURCH

W E HAVE EXPLORED many of the ways Satan organizes the demonic forces. We have also exposed many of the demonic strategies against individual believers. When we begin to look at the seven churches described in the Book of Revelation, we discover specific demonic strongholds that can be found at church. Let's take a look at these spirits.

SPIRIT OF RELIGION
(REVELATION 2:4–5, 7)

The church at Ephesus had "left their first love" (Rev. 2:4). They were doctrinally sound and had everything in order, but they had lost their passion for God. When you turn to Acts 19 to look at "first works" and "first love," you discover an astounding truth.

At the birth of the Ephesian church they were baptizing in water, laying hands on the people for the baptism of the Holy Spirit, magnifying God in tongues, casting out demons, healing with prayer cloths, and being evicted from the old order.

The church at Ephesus had every element of church life in order, and they were a hardworking congregation. Yet the fire, the passion, the love had gone out of it. We see now that religion had taken over with its dull duty and tired traditionalism. The power of God was missing; demons were no longer leaving, tongues were absent, and miracles were simply a memory. A loveless routine of religious works had replaced the power and passion of the Holy Spirit.

Who can deny the present reality of this destructive demon of religion? Many churches, like Samson, have been shorn of their power by the Delilahs of religion! Now blind to spiritual things, we grind out our religious activities and traditions with no transforming power. This demon must be exposed and expelled.

SPIRIT OF INTIMIDATION (REVELATION 2:10–11)

The church at Smyrna endured persecution, and many members suffered martyrdom. With this threat Satan tries to strike fear in the hearts of believers by sending intimidation to frighten us away from faithfulness to God and His Word. Remember Simon Peter warming himself by the enemy's fire on the night of Jesus's arrest? This faithful disciple was intimidated by his surroundings and the questioning voice of a little servant girl. Today the church is silent and cowed down before the world and its governments. This demon must be cast down!

SPIRIT OF COMPROMISE (REVELATION 2:12, 14–17)

Pergamos was the capital city of the province of Asia and is mentioned in Revelation as the seat of one of the seven churches of Asia. It was a celebrated city of Mysia in the Caicus Valley, fifteen miles from the Aegean Sea and about sixty miles north of Smyrna. The river Selinus flowed through it, and the river Caicus ran just south of it. This city was rich in historical and literary heritage with a library that boasted well over two hundred thousand volumes, topped only by the library in Alexandria.

The city had a "pet" god in Asklepion, an idol symbolized by a snake who called himself a savior. They believed that their god incarnated into the area snakes, so serpents were allowed to slither freely around the temple. Those who desired healing spent the night in the darkness of the temple, hoping a snake would crawl over them. The city was an outpost to Greek civilization and was home to the temples of many other deities.

Can you see the parallels of the secular plight in America and its churches? Most churches operate in a community or environment that is controlled by Satan rather than God. What can a church do when ministry becomes difficult? Can we allow the snakes of secular humanism to slither through our congregations? Compromise is not the answer. We cannot become comfortable with the sin around us!

The church of Jesus must take active steps to stand strong in our lost and dying world!

- **We must recognize the conflict.** Jesus pointed out that the city was the church's dwelling place or permanent residence. To flee was not an option. Instead, He advised them to settle into service and draw the battle lines. Paul recognized the need for battle readiness when he penned Ephesians 6. The armor of God is needed in the middle of war. Most of all, the church must go forward under the name and banner of Jesus, never operating in their own strength, for in the flesh the enemy could find weakness.

- **We must repent of compromise.** The church at Pergamos had some weaknesses to be dealt with. There were doctrinal problems, along with problems with some of their deacons and leadership. One in particular is mentioned, Nicholas, who began teaching heresy and leading others into sin. How sad when a leader goes bad and quits truly serving the Lord! Oftentimes they lead others astray and take others with them.

    Yet another conflict in the Pergamos church was a discipline problem. They tolerated the mess they were in by overlooking the sin in their own camp. Jesus called them to repentance.

    Another problem that arose was the spirit of Balaam. To give you some history of this, the pagan king Balak literally bought the prophet Balaam's ministry. Balak eventually sent women to seduce the men of Israel, thus bringing judgment upon them. It was Balaam who sold out the people of God. In keeping the spirit of Balaam, too often today money has become the goal and prize of many in the church. Popular preaching has replaced prophetic preaching. Image has replaced anointing, and the church is reduced to no more than a place where pop psychology tickles the ears of its parishioners on Sundays. The image-makers and the politically correct have dulled the sword of the churches and its men of God.

- **We must rely on Christ**. The Pergamos church needed to rely on their Savior, who provided the weapon of the sword of the Spirit, His own Word. This is the weapon we claim as Christians. The popular *Star Wars* phenomenon has had two generations of children captured in imaginative play with light sabers, defending the galaxy as Jedi knights! The movies show the young Jedi apprentice was carefully taught to use his weapon, to guard it, to perfect its use. In the same way, we must cling to the Word of God as our weapon—it has a power that is supernatural and effective against the onslaughts of Satan. Our weapons are not carnal but mighty in God (2 Cor. 10:4), and Satan can be defeated by the power of the Word.

- **Overcomers are promised gifts.** Jesus promised this church that those who didn't succumb to the sins around them—not eating things offered to idols and partaking in sin—would eat hidden manna, the blessing of Jesus Himself. They are promised the presence of Jesus in the barren wasteland of the world's wilderness. He also promised this church that He would set among them a white stone, promising acquittal, acceptance, and acclaim. The new name upon this stone was Jesus!

SPIRIT OF JEZEBEL (CONTROL) (REVELATION 2:18–20, 26)

A war goes on in today's church, and the battle lines are drawn. One of the most powerful spirits at work in this ongoing battle is the spirit of

Jezebel, or control. First Kings tells the story of the woman for whom this spirit is named.

Jezebel was known as the wife of King Ahab and a follower of the false god Baal, and Scripture regarded Ahab's marriage to this woman as a horrible sin: "He not only considered it trivial to commit the sins of Jeroboam son of Nebat, but he also married Jezebel daughter of Ethbaal king of the Sidonians, and began to serve Baal and worship him" (1 Kings 16:31, NIV).

Jezebel ordered a "hit" on the innocent man Naboth so that she could obtain his prize vineyard. Not only was this murder, but it also broke God's land covenant with His people. In addition to her disrespect for ordinary people and their property, she hated the prophets of God. Scripture says, "While Jezebel was killing off the LORD's prophets, Obadiah had taken a hundred prophets and hidden them in two caves, fifty in each, and had supplied them with food and water" (1 Kings 18:4, NIV).

Later, Jezebel pursued the prophet Elijah following the great contest where God sent fire from heaven and defeated the prophets of Baal. Her relentless pursuit drove the prophet into depression and suicidal thoughts.

Jezebel's character was wicked, controlling, sexually immoral, murderous, and demonic! It is astounding that the same strong spirit was still operating in Revelation 2:20 and still operates in today's church. In every congregation we find those who want to control, manipulate, and subvert the men and women of God.

Recognizing the spirit

This spirit is basically the spirit of domination or an unwillingness to cohabit peacefully. This is not about women or liberation, for this spirit can attach itself to a man or a woman. Many may think that this spirit is identified with sexuality, believing that a woman who looks a certain way is a "Jezebel" in her character. But this is not so. A wolf can easily hide in sheep's clothing.

When you find a spirit of Jezebel operating, you will also find an "Ahab" nearby, or someone in leadership who is allowing the spirit access and control.

The strategy of Jezebel

The tool this spirit uses is manipulation. In 1 Kings 21, we learn that King Ahab would pout when he did not get his own way. He had seen a vineyard that he greatly desired, but the owner would not give up his precious property, even to the king. As King Ahab lay on his bed sulking, Jezebel assured him she would get him what he wanted. This powerful woman had introduced pagan worship into her kingdom, and now she was not below killing to obtain the things she needed to gain more power.

The seat of Jezebel

> Nevertheless I have a few things against you, because you allow that woman Jezebel, who calls herself a prophetess, to teach and seduce My servants to commit sexual immorality and eat things sacrificed to idols.
>
> —REVELATION 2:20

When the spirit of Jezebel begins to manifest in the church, it seeks a high seat in the church or a place of dominance. Usually it will manifest in someone who wants to teach or lead, usually leading them astray! To find that place of leadership, Jezebel must look and act in a spiritual manner.

One of these spirits operated in Moses's and Aaron's day. The Book of Numbers tells us:

> Now Korah the son of Izhar, the son of Kohath, the son of Levi, with Dathan and Abiram the sons of Eliab, and On the son of Peleth, sons of Reuben, took men; and they rose up before Moses with some of the children of Israel, two hundred and fifty leaders of the congregation, representatives of the congregation, men of renown. They gathered together against Moses and Aaron, and said to them, "You take too much upon yourselves, for all the congregation is holy, every one of them, and the LORD is among them. Why then do you exalt yourselves above the congregation of the LORD?"
>
> —NUMBERS 16:1–3

Korah was operating in the spirit of Jezebel, with Dathan and Abiram operating as his power core and two hundred fifty other princes as a structure under them. Moses took immediate action—he fell on his face before God and prayed. Following his prayer, he confronted the spirit, saying, "Is it a small thing to you that the God of Israel has separated you from the congregation of Israel, to bring you near to Himself, to do the work of the tabernacle of the LORD, and to stand before the congregation to serve them; and that He has brought you near to Himself, you and all your brethren, the sons of Levi, with you? And are you seeking the priesthood also?" (Num. 16:9–10).

Judgment came to this Jezebel spirit—an earthquake came and took the three evil leaders, and fire consumed all the rest.

Jezebel's targets

The controlling spirit wiggles into the church, bent on destroying and undermining the very things that we hold dear as believers. Through manipulation, domination, and control, the spirit begins its battle against the body of Christ.

First, this spirit hates the prophets, the true leaders of God. She cannot control them, and when she tries to win their approval and fails, she will stop at nothing to try and kill them.

In addition, the spirit of Jezebel hates the preaching of the Word. She can't cope with its message. She will try to either reduce the messenger or the message.

The controlling spirit also hates the praise of the church. During times of true, powerful worship, her carnality is exposed. In 1 Kings when the prophet Elijah prayed fire down from heaven against the prophets of Baal and Jezebel's schemes, praise broke out (1 Kings 18:39). Jezebel had lost, and the praises of God filled the air.

A Jezebel spirit also hates the preeminence of Christ. There is no way to compete against it. The first time *preeminence* is mentioned is in Colossians 1:18: "And he is the head of the body, the church: who is the beginning, the firstborn from the dead; that in all things he might have the preeminence" (KJV). However, the second time we find the word, a Jezebel spirit is attempting to control a body of believers: "I wrote unto the church: but Diotrephes, who loveth to have the preeminence among them, receiveth us not" (3 John 9, KJV).

Banish the spirit

If you sense this spirit is at work in your church, it is important to see the enemy as spiritual, not fleshly. Don't hate the person being controlled by the spirit of Jezebel; recognize that it is a spiritual power—one that God must fight. Let your prayer be, "O our God, will You not judge them? For we have no power against this great multitude that is coming against us; nor do we know what to do, but our eyes are upon You" (2 Chron. 20:12).

SPIRIT OF TRADITIONALISM
(REVELATION 3:1–6)

For centuries the church has been the victim of rumors, hostility, and, what we call in this day and age, negative press. Churches often have to survive this hostile environment; however, outward hostility is not the greatest threat to a local church! Very often the greatest danger comes from within!

The Sardis church lived in a favorable environment with a great reputation. However, in Christ's letter to this church, He ignored their human reputation and told this church they were listed in the obituary!

Environment of death

The city of Sardis was a city of wealth. History tells us that in 550 B.C. King Croesus found gold in the city's river and issued the first gold coins in history. Even in New Testament times, gold could be found all along its rivers.

In addition to its wealth, the city was known for its paganism. The favored idol was Cybele, and worshipers of this pagan god participated in wild, frenzied worship that included sexual immorality.

Remarkably, the community was at peace, for the inhabitants were comfortable in their self-sufficiency. This peaceful self-sufficiency had also invaded the church in Sardis; it became the peace of death. A peaceful coexistence with the city and its wickedness had settled into the church, and all they had left was their reputation.

Evidence of a church's death

Viewers of our television broadcast often write and ask, "How can I find a good church in my area? How can I tell if a church is alive and healthy?" A dead church has some basic characteristics that are spotted easily.

- **It ignores the Holy Spirit.** When the complete work of God's Spirit isn't embraced in a church, that body is already headed for the grave. Jesus told the church at Sardis that they had a spirit of religion and didn't have the Spirit of God. The Holy Spirit will not be managed or controlled by religious tradition or preferences! John 3:8 says, "The wind blows where it wishes.... So is every one who is born of the Spirit."

- **There is a lack of godly leadership.** The "seven stars" mentioned in Revelation 3 stand for the messengers or pastors of the seven churches addressed in the letters. What the church in Sardis needed was a leader who was called by God and who served Him wholeheartedly. Too many churches today fail to get God's man. Several times a month our church offices receive requests from pastor-less churches that have been searching for a replacement. If these churches choose a pastor by his reputation, résumé, physical appearance, or even recommendation, they may find later that they've made a big mistake. As important as background information is, the fruit issued in a pastor's life and his walk with the Spirit of God is what should be investigated. The superficial doesn't matter as much as the supernatural. Hiring solely on superficial facts may result in a short-tenured, flash-in-the-pan, or morally bankrupt leader.

- **It values reputation over reality.** Sardis was a busy, working church with a good name—but it had death upon it. They were an organization but not a living organism. Sadly, they were so caught up in their reputation they didn't even realize that they had died.

  One winter night I noticed our house becoming colder and colder, even though I had turned our heat on full power. I called upon our faithful church grounds supervisor to take a look at the gas-heating unit, and he discovered the pilot light had gone out. The blower was blowing, but the fire was out. Going to church is good if you meet God. Worship is good if it brings on God's presence. Giving is good if we have first given ourselves. Prayer is good, but "if [we] regard iniquity in [our] heart, the Lord will not hear" (Ps. 66:18). Form without force is death to a church. It is like a store window containing lots of fluff and finery but hiding an empty stockroom.

- **There is growth in numbers without growth in people.** The letter to Sardis indicated that even Christians who had life in the Sardis church were dying in the cold environment. Churches must offer ministry that encourages its members to grow in the Lord.

- **Ministry and work were incomplete.** Beginning a new program or outreach is easy; seeing it to completion is much more difficult! A dead church is a graveyard of partially fulfilled goals and half-baked programs. These skeletons are evidence that they went "partway" with the Lord and then backed up and sat down. A church that goes backward is doomed to death.

Escape from death!

To eliminate the spirit of religion from your church, the leadership should gather and repent of religious death. Together they should acknowledge that Jesus's kingdom is coming and there will be an accounting for what they accomplish in His name. In almost any dead church there are a handful of believers who do live in triumph and desire to be alive in God. This team of people should be lifted up and encouraged. Stay with the winning crowd! Finally, rebuke the religious pride that strangles your church. Reject the love of religion and its rules and reputation, and fall in love with Jesus. Determine to listen to the voice of the Holy Spirit in all decision making regarding the church. Let His Word edify, rule, and reign from the pulpit.

SPIRIT OF INFERIORITY
(REVELATION 3:7–8, 12)

Many times a pastor will contact me about a speaking engagement at a church, and he will begin by saying almost apologetically, "We are just a small church…" His tone implies a sense of weakness or inability. But there is nothing little or insignificant in the kingdom of God!

At the other end of the spectrum is the church that thinks they have all the answers, that loves to proclaim their statistics and numbers but are satisfied with mediocre efforts as long as they bring the church notoriety and recognition.

God deals strongly with the church in Revelation 3:

> Because you have kept My command to persevere, I also will keep you from the hour of trial which shall come upon the whole world, to test those who dwell on the earth. Behold, I am coming quickly! Hold fast what you have, that no one may take your crown. He who overcomes, I will make him a pillar in the temple of My God, and he shall go out no more. And I will write on him the name of My God and the name of the city of My God, the New Jerusalem, which comes down out of heaven from My God. And I will write on him My new name.
>
> —REVELATION 3:10–12

Too many churches and individuals use their supposed weakness as an excuse for failing to advance the cause of Christ. Such notions and statements are foreign to the New Testament portrait of the church. I am convinced that such an attitude is not only false and hurtful but also demonic in its origin. There is a stronghold of inferiority, self-pity, and weakness. The enemy deceives those manifesting this spirit by making them think their attitudes are actually meekness and humility. This counterfeit humility is debilitating to the kingdom of God, crippling the advance of the gospel, and it insults the Holy Spirit.

The church at Philadelphia was at risk to be overtaken by such a spirit. If they were ever to become a pillar in the kingdom, they would have to overcome the spirit.

Scripture sets forth the church as a victorious company. Matthew 16:18 declares, "The gates of hell shall not prevail against it" (KJV). In his great prayer for the church in Ephesians 3:14–21, Paul ends with this benediction: "Now to Him who is able to do exceedingly abundantly above all that we ask or think, according to the power that works in us, to Him be glory in the church by Christ Jesus to all generations, forever and ever. Amen" (vv. 20–21).

It is in the church that Jesus looses His divine ability, energy, and glory. The answer to our inferiority is His superiority! It is not in trying harder but in trusting wholly that His work is accomplished.

The church at Philadelphia had "a little strength" (Rev. 3:8). Greek culture, international commerce, and religious diversity dominated them. The pagan god Dionysus was worshiped. This ancient Greek god of wine was credited with inspiring ritual madness and ecstasy. Worship of Dionysus was thought to bring an end to care and worry. The city of Philadelphia was also a center of orthodox Jewish worship.

This small church could have surrendered to the pressures around them. Yet they did not! They received the wonderful encouragement in Revelation, and history tells us that for nearly fourteen hundred years this city stood as a Christian city in the face of Muslim pressure. It was only after centuries of courageous resistance that the city was overthrown by an unholy military alliance of Byzantine and Muslim forces.

How did this church overcome inferiority and have a ministry that would last for fourteen hundred years? They came to know the Lord of opportunity (Rev. 3:7–8). Obedience always leads to opportunity! God promised this church the "key of David." With God's favor and their dependence upon His superiority, nothing could stop this body of believers!

SPIRIT OF PRIDE
(REVELATION 3:14–17, 21)

Revelation 3 also issues a charge to the church at Laodicea. This city was a wealthy and prosperous one. So vast was their wealth that when an earthquake destroyed the city, they required no outside help to recover! The Roman historian Tacitus recorded that Laodicea "was...overthrown by an earthquake, and, without any relief from us, recovered itself by its own resources."[1]

The city was famous for the dark, black wool they produced and was known as the center for fine wool in the ancient world. Laodicea also boasted a famous medical school, having produced two of the most popular medicines for treatment of eye and ear maladies. In short, this city was pompous and full of pride.

But here in Revelation 3, years have passed, and now the church in Laodicea has fallen into a rut of mediocrity. The Lord Jesus Himself renders the verdict on this church. What was His appraisal? This luke-warm church was nauseating Him! What had happened to this church to make it slide into a state of mediocrity?

Lost fervency

Sadly, this church reflects the state of many American churches today. Not too cold…not too hot. Not too bad…not too good. Not too faith-ful…not too unfaithful. The Laodicea church was an ordinary church that had warmth but no fire. If asked about their work, they would say, "We are holding our own."

Jesus is sickened by the mediocre. He would rather a church be as cold as the Arctic or as hot as the Sahara. In God's work, there should be no place for "just getting by."

Elijah recognized this need for commitment when he challenged Israel at the contest of the prophets of Baal in 1 Kings 18. He shouted to the congregation, "If Baal be God, serve him, but if the Lord be God, serve Him!" Standing in the middle was not an option.

A complacent church is a disappointment to Jesus! Laodicea had lost the fire of love for Jesus and for lost souls. The altar fires of prayer were in need of rekindling. It was business as usual week after week. They needed to pray!

The prayer of Amy Carmichael should be the earnest prayer of the church needing a fresh fervency:

O for a passion for souls, dear Lord!
O for a pity that yearns!
O for a love that loves unto death!
O for a fire that burns![2]

Lost faith

The Laodicean church had tried to become self-sufficient. They boasted of wealth, increase of goods, and that they needed nothing, not even the Lord. They were cursed by their wealth.

When the great Thomas Aquinas visited the Vatican, an officer of Pope Innocent the Fourth brought in a bag of money. The pope said to Aquinas, "You see, young man, the age of the church is past, in which she said, 'Silver and gold have I none.'" To which Aquinas replied, "True, holy father, but the age is also past, in which she could say to a paralytic, 'Rise up and walk.'"[3]

A church's reach must exceed its grasp. An ever-enlarging vision must be forged. The challenges we take should be beyond our resources so that our reliance and faith remain upon God. Our dreams and our plans should be God-sized.

When God blesses financially, the church should give more to missions, build a needed building, add another staff member, and have the faith to stretch those resources to their limit.

Unfortunately, the Laodicean church did not really see their true condition. God said they were "wretched, poor, blind, naked"—they were pitiful in the sight of God. They were without riches and spiritually blind in God's eyes. He looked at them and saw them as they really were: spiritually bankrupt.

Lost fear

This church no longer trembled in the presence of a righteous God. There was no remorse recorded for their failures. Jesus warns them by giving three motives to repent: His love, His rebuke, and His chastening rod. These three things could provide the motivation to set this church on the right track.

Lost fellowship

Jesus was standing and knocking outside the door of this church. At one point, He had been shut out; He was no longer the center of things. The church had no basis for fellowship with other churches because Jesus Christ was the only common ground among the fellowship of churches. Without Him, a church can have a "get together" without really being together in unity! "That which we have seen and heard we declare to you, that you also may have fellowship with us; and truly our fellowship is with the Father and with His Son Jesus Christ.... But if we walk in the light as He is in the light, we have fellowship with one another, and the blood of Jesus Christ His Son cleanses us from all sin" (1 John 1:3, 7).

The presence of Jesus Christ is the ground of all true fellowship, but too many churches have shut Him out.

God's promise and plea

Jesus keeps on knocking, hoping that someone in the church will open the door. When that happens, it sets the stage for revival, and fellowship can be restored. A seat at the Lord's table is promised when we welcome Him at ours. We can share in His glorious reign! So, let us blaze and burn for Him until He comes in the blaze of His glory.

SECTION III

UNDERSTANDING THE DYNASTY OF YOUR ENEMY

chapter 11

HOW SATAN OPPRESSES

How DOES SATAN operate? We can trace his career throughout the pages of Scripture. Let's focus on the times in Scripture when *diabolos* is used in reference to Satan.

The first mention of Satan in biblical history is found in Job 1 and 2 when he attacks and accuses of Job. Job's response and subsequent victory silenced Satan for centuries.

Satan then provokes David to number Israel, putting his strength in numbers and not the living God. Satan is a provocateur that will try to move us to actions that do not demonstrate faith (1 Chron. 21:1).

Satan comes to a worship service and opposes the high priest of Israel. He further opposes Jerusalem and Israel (Zech. 3). His next move is to tempt Jesus, the Second Adam, with the same threefold temptation with which he had tempted our ancient father, Adam (Matt. 4). His approach has not changed. Satan still throws before us the lust of the flesh, the lust of the eyes, and the pride of life.

Satan influenced Peter to hinder Jesus's commitment to the cross in Matthew 16:22.

In Luke 10:18, Jesus tells us that He saw Satan fall. He warns us in Mark 4:15 that Satan will try to steal the word of faith from our hearts. Satan crippled a woman for eighteen years (Luke 13:16). Satan entered the heart of Judas to deny Jesus (Luke 22:3), and he sifted and shook the disciple Peter like wheat (v. 31)!

In the early church we see Satan fill the hearts of Ananias and Sapphira, causing them to lie to the Holy Spirit (Acts 5:3). Lost people who come to Christ are said to be delivered "from the power of Satan" (Acts 26:18).

Satan can kill disciplined Christians who embarrass the testimony of Christ and the church by continuous immoral behavior (1 Cor. 5:5). Satan attacks marital fidelity and sexual enjoyment (1 Cor. 7:5). Satan desires to gain an advantage over every believer (2 Cor. 2:11) and can come disguised as a heavenly messenger (2 Cor. 11:14). Satan tries to hinder the work of the church (1 Thess. 2:18). Satan can operate charismatic miracle-working ministries (2 Thess. 2:9). Satan attacks with idleness, gossip, and busybody activity (1 Tim. 5:13). Satan blasphemes, kills, attacks synagogues, and deceives (Rev. 2:9, 13).

Although Satan's methods of oppression are many, do not be discouraged or overwhelmed. Satan can be crushed under the feet of every faithful believer (Rom. 16:20). Remember, Jesus's victory at Calvary assures our victory today. Then one day Satan will be confined to hell, which was prepared for him and all his demons (Rev. 20:10).

THE DEVIL

As the enemy, we find him sowing tares in the good field to deceive (Matt. 13:24–29). He is called the father of those who are not believers in Jesus (John 8:44). The devil causes illness (Acts 10:38). The devil can take over a physical location (Eph. 4:27). The devil has methods and schemes with which to attack believers (Eph. 6:11). The devil instills pride, sets traps, and takes captives (1 Tim. 3:6–7; 2 Tim. 2:26). He has the power of death only with Jesus's permission. The devil desires to devour like a lion and put believers in a prison of spiritual chains (1 Pet. 5:8; Rev. 2:10). As you can see, the enemy is a decisive force on the earth. The devil can be resisted and will flee from believers: "Therefore submit to God. Resist the devil and he will flee from you" (James 4:7). Hallelujah!

chapter 12

THE HIERARCHY OF HELL

I N THE EPIC Star Wars movie series, both evil and good practiced the Force. The Force was an invisible power that had a good side and a dark side. The Force called the dark side was personified in an evil character called Darth Vader. Vader had once been Anakin Skywalker but had turned to evil.

Strangely enough, this scenario mimics what happened before time. In an earlier chapter we learned that Lucifer, an angel of God and a messenger of light, had turned to the dark side and became Satan. In Holy Scripture, evil is never an indefinable force but rather has individuality and personality.

Satan leads the forces of darkness. His former name, Lucifer, means "bearer of light," "daystar," or "right light." His light was a reflection of God's light. He became Satan, which means "accuser" or "adversary." The Hebrew *Ha-Satan* means "the chief adversary." *Satanas* in Greek means "the accuser" (Rev. 20:2). Satan is called a dragon. "Dragon" comes from the Greek word *derkomai*, which means "fearful to look upon." It came to mean a fearful, monstrous creature. In the same verse Satan is called an "old serpent," which in Greek is *archaios ophis* and means "old snake eyes." This is the serpent that has been watching to wound for ages. Finally, Satan is called "the devil," which is *diabolos* in Greek. This means "one who hurls through." The idea is of one throwing a spear or, in our day, shooting a bullet through another body.

Clearly Satan can appear as an angel of light (2 Cor. 11:14), a monstrous creature, a hidden viper, a prosecutor, an assassin, and a deadly enemy. Jesus describes our adversary and his mission when He said, "The thief does not come except to steal, and to kill, and to destroy" (John 10:10).

THE ARMY OF HELL

I believe that Satan is a great imitator, so he patterned his army like the holy angels. The letter to the Ephesians identifies these dark forces in the following flow of authority: "For we do not wrestle against flesh and blood, but against principalities, against powers, against the rulers of the darkness of this age, against spiritual hosts of wickedness in the heavenly places" (Eph. 6:12).

Principalities

Top-ranking demonic beings are called principalities. The word *principalities* is translated from the Greek word *arche*, which means "chief." These are the chief demons, which correspond with the archangels among the holy angels. These princes hold sway over the souls of people (Eph. 2:1–3). A principality is what assigns demonic spirits to operate in the disobedient. Also, these princes rule over continents and nations. In Daniel 10:12–13, the prophet is informed by Gabriel that a principality of Persia had hindered his arrival to Daniel for three weeks. Gabriel had to summon the archangel Michael to take on the archdevil of Persia. These demons are subject to Christ (Eph. 1:20–22). They are also subject to Spirit-filled believers, as we read in Ephesians 2:6; this scripture explains that Christ has "raised us up together, and made us sit together in the heavenly places in Christ Jesus."

Powers

The next rank of evil officers of darkness is called "powers." The word *powers* come from the Greek word *exousia*, which means "delegated authority," like that of a policeman. These demons seem to operate invisibly in governmental centers such as national governments. These powers cannot separate us from the love of God (Rom. 8:38). These powers will be shaken at the end of the age (Matt. 24:29). These powers, like the principalities, are subject to Christ (1 Pet. 3:22).

Rulers of the darkness

This next level of demonic leaders touches the created order. "Rulers of the darkness" is translated from the Greek word *kosmokrator*, which means "to seize and take hold of governments for the sake of darkness and evil." *Kosmas* has to do with "an arrangement or order." These rulers want to take over the offices of government, the legislatures, and the courts.

Spiritual forces of wickedness

Spiritual hosts of wickedness literally means in the Greek "spiritual fakes." The word *wicked* is *poneria*, from which we get *fornication* and *pornography.* These are the unclean spirits we deal with on a daily basis.

Some of these spirits are named for us. *Beelzebub* means "lord of the flies." *Abaddon*, or Apollyon, means "destroyer." *Demon* means "torment the mind." These lower-level spirits are the ones we deal with daily.

Satan's army is well organized, and his legions employ an array of methods and schemes. We must be prepared to face down this infernal enemy and expose his tactics.

chapter 13

UNMASKING THE ENEMY

MAKE NO MISTAKE, there is a real war going on against a real enemy! Once you assume your position in Christ, the next step is to know the enemy so you can be properly equipped. Let us examine the dangerous infernal army at Satan's disposal. Revelation 12:9 reaches back before time, saying, "So the great dragon was cast out, that serpent of old, called the Devil and Satan, who deceives the whole world; he was cast to the earth, and his angels were cast out with him." As we explained earlier, these fallen angels are given many different names in Scripture: demons, principalities, powers, ruler of darkness, wicked spirits, unclean spirits, as well as other descriptions. Also remember that, according to Revelation 12:4, one-third of the innumerable hosts of angels fell: "His [Satan's] tail drew a third of the stars of heaven." "The stars of heaven" refers symbolically to the angels.

THE INFERNAL ARMY ARRAYED AGAINST US

Jesus Christ regularly confronted demons as an integral part of His ministry. Luke records that when Jesus launched His public ministry, He quoted Isaiah 61:1–2: "The Spirit of the Lord is upon Me, because He has anointed me to preach the gospel to the poor; He has sent me to heal the brokenhearted, to proclaim liberty to the captives…to set at liberty those who are oppressed" (Luke 4:18). Obviously Jesus knew His purpose was to rescue humanity from the bondage and oppression of the enemy.

At least nine times in the New Testament Jesus Christ confronts demons. I will give greater detail about demonic operation in later chapters, but let me briefly describe what we learn about demons from one such incident in the life of Jesus. In Luke 8:26–39, we have the beloved physician's version of the demoniac of the Gadarenes's encounter with Jesus.

Then they sailed to the country of the Gadarenes, which is opposite Galilee. And when He stepped out on the land, there met Him a certain man from the city who had demons for a long time. And he wore no clothes, nor did he live in a house but in the tombs. When he saw Jesus, he cried out, fell down before Him, and with a loud voice said, "What have I to do with You, Jesus, Son of the Most High God? I beg You, do not torment me!" For He had commanded the unclean spirit to come out of the man. For it had often seized him, and he was kept under guard, bound with chains and shackles; and he broke the bonds and was driven by the demon into the wilderness. Jesus asked him, saying, "What is your name?" And he said, "Legion," because many demons had entered him. And they begged Him that He would not command them to go out into the abyss. Now a herd of many swine was feeding there on the mountain. And they begged Him that He would permit them to enter them. And He permitted them. Then the demons went out of the man and entered the swine, and the herd ran violently down the steep place into the lake and drowned. When those who fed them saw what had happened, they fled and told it in the city and in the country. Then they went out to see what had happened, and came to Jesus, and found the man from whom the demons had departed, sitting at the feet of Jesus, clothed and in his right mind. And they were afraid. They also who had seen it told them by what means he who had been demon-possessed was healed. Then the whole multitude of the surrounding region of the Gadarenes asked Him to depart from them, for they were seized with great fear. And He got into the boat and returned. Now the man from whom the demons had departed begged Him that he might be with Him. But Jesus sent him away, saying, "Return to your own house, and tell what great things God has done for you." And he went his way and proclaimed throughout the whole city what great things Jesus had done for him.

Now, let's look at the demons and their characteristics in these verses. Demons have personalities, use speed, seem to express the emotion of fear, promote uncleanness, torment, and create mental disorders. Yet the glorious truth is that demons must obey the commands of Jesus Christ!

CAN A PERSON BE DEMON POSSESSED?

The Greek word describing the condition of a person affected by a demon is *daimonizomai*, which was translated as "possessed with devils" in the King James Version of the Bible. According to William Arndt and F. Wilber Gingrich it is a present tense word with an active voice and a passive ending.[1] A person in this condition can be described as in "a demon-controlled passivity." In other words, the person is controlled to a point of passivity by a demon. C. Fred Dickason rightly points out that the term *possession* never appears in the New Testament.[2] A demon can possess an unbeliever. A believer can be demonized by the enemy, which means he or she is controlled but not owned! The degree of demonization is limited in believers.

Demons can use people's voices, confuse, give imaginations, create insanity, appear as multiple personalities, and cause passivity of speech, hearing, and physical movement.

In Luke 8:26–39, which I cited earlier, we observe such feats as unusual physical strength, fits of rage, multiple and disintegrating personalities, resistance to Jesus, clairvoyance (knowing who Jesus was), and occult transference (demons enter swine). Some of these will be discussed in greater detail later.

Prominent German pastor Kurt Koch and German psychiatrist Alfred Lechler researched demonization in Germany. They noted in their findings the following about demonized individuals: resistance to the Bible, falling into a trance-like state, opposition to prayer, and a negative reaction to Jesus's name.[3]

NS AFFECT CHRISTIANS?

gies is to get believers to believe that they are
nce. A Spirit-filled believer walking in obedi-
protected from the enemy. However, while a
rit is protected from the enemy, the mind and
iever can be subject to attack.

ace to the devil" (Eph. 4:27). When a Christian
ibitual sin, the enemy moves into that place
enemy constructs a thought pattern around
d Corinthians 10:4–5 describes that house of
Demons can take up residence in that strong-

ssess the Christian any more than a cockroach
oaches are dirty, can make a mess, and cause
ot own your house. In the same way, demons
s, and suppress the believer. Demons cannot
they can distract the Christian. In the next
ir operation so that as a believer you can be

G DEMONIC OPERATION

ic dynasty in the last section, let us look more
nality and operation. Remember that Satan's
t with the kingdom of God. Though defeated,
g influence in this world. In Matthew 4:8–9
ower, and glory to Jesus. Let's take a look at

lim up on an exceedingly high mountain,
kingdoms of the world and their glory. And
ese things I will give You if You will fall

—MATTHEW 4:8–9

demonic forces at his disposal: "The whole
f the wicked one" (1 John 5:19).

In Luke, Jesus spoke of the operation of these demonic enti
strange passage: "When an unclean spirit goes out of a man,
through dry places, seeking rest; and finding none, he says, 'I wi
to my house from which I came.' And when he comes, he finds
and put in order. Then he goes and takes with him seven othe
more wicked than himself, and they enter and dwell there; and
state of that man is worse than the first" (Luke 11:24–26).

I believe this is the clearest picture of demonic thinking and
in all of Scripture. Look carefully at these verses, and you will
following disturbing facts about demonic operation.

First, demons can exist both inside and outside human being

Second, demons travel at will. The verse says that they go "
dry places, seeking rest" (v. 24). They seem to prefer traveling o
rather than water. In Mark 5 Jesus dispatched the demons into
swine and sent them into the Sea of Galilee. Demons can move
the atmosphere of this planet.

Third, demons need a human host in order to rest: "…goes
dry places, seeking rest." It seems that demons are weary until
a human to embody.

Fourth, demons can communicate using the vocal apparatus
host. On many occasions in Scripture demons spoke from the
their host. Luke 11:24 makes it clear that demons can speak. In
they speak to Jesus through the human host, saying, "Do not
me."

Fifth, demons have individual personalities and identities. I
Luke 11:24 when the demon says, "I will…" Demons are not im
forces, but like the angels, they have names and personalities.

Sixth, demons consider the body they live in to be their h
Luke 11:24 the demon says of his former human host, "I will
my house from which I came." Demons are possessive and see
ownership of the human life they invade. Think of it—a demon
to his cohorts that your body is his house. That is why Paul v
in Ephesians 4:27, "Nor give place to the devil." If you give the
foothold, he will put up a mailbox and declare your body his ac

In the movie *Pacific Heights* a young couple purchases a lar
and remodels it. In order to meet the mortgage, they rent out pa
a man. He refuses to pay rent, harasses the couple, sues them, ar

their life a living hell. The house was possessed by a madman who took over their lives.

That story graphically illustrates the strategy of demons. A demon will come in quietly to live in that little area of your life you refuse to surrender to Jesus. From that stronghold he will try to rule and ruin your life.

Seventh, demons can plant thoughts and influence mental health. In Luke 11:25 we find a reference to the human mind: "And when he comes, he finds it swept and put in order." The demon returns to the person who has been set free. He finds the mind clean and in order. Yet this person has no spiritual fullness. The Holy Spirit is either not present in the life or is in the spirit of the person and not filling the mind and controlling the body. This person has gone back to the same sin. Perhaps anger was the stronghold from which they had been delivered, and instead of growing in the Lord, filling the mind with Scripture, and living in praise, this individual falls into the same pattern as before. The demon can see the emptiness in that individual and attack the mind that is devoid of the Holy Spirit.

Eighth, demons can remember, think, and plan. Notice in all these verses the strategies employed by these entities. They are not stupid and must not be regarded lightly.

Ninth, demons can communicate with each other. In Luke 11:26 this demon communicates with seven others. When one gives place to a demonic entity, that entity will often bring compatible demons. The Bible speaks of the "spirit of fear" (2 Tim. 1:7), and in 1 John 4:18 Scripture speaks of love as a weapon that "casts out fear." Then it adds, "Fear hath torment" (KJV). Jesus speaks of "tormentors" in regard to those who will not forgive: "And his master was angry, and delivered him to the torturers until he should pay all that was due to him. So My heavenly Father also will do to you if each of you, from his heart, does not forgive his brother his trespasses" (Matt. 18:34–35).

So a demon of fear can bring demons of torment. Unforgiveness can invite tormentors into a person's life. Demons are like cockroaches, as we said before; they tend to increase in number if not evicted by the power of God.

Tenth, levels of evil exist within the demonic hierarchy. Luke 11:26 says that the demon "takes with him seven other spirits more wicked than himself." Demonic entities live in various levels of wickedness.

Here a demon enlists seven more to occupy his host. If a person tolerates a little evil, then more evil comes.

Eleventh, demons are a problem to Christians today. Ephesians 6:12 says that we are in a hand-to-hand wrestling match "against principalities, against powers, against the rulers of the darkness of this age, against spiritual hosts of wickedness." Though these spirits cannot possess a Christian in his spirit, they can afflict the body and oppress the mind. We must be very vigilant to enforce the victory of the cross on these evil forces.

Twelfth, demons are involved in deceiving believers by teaching false doctrine. First Timothy 4:1 says, "Now the Spirit expressly says that in the latter times some will depart from the faith, giving heed to deceiving spirits and doctrines of demons." In these last days demons are seducing and deceiving many through false teaching. Just because a person waves a Bible and acts spiritually does not mean that their ministry is anointed by God. Religious deception is the worst of all demonic control.

In concluding this chapter let it be clear that ignoring the truth about the demonic forces is frivolous and perilous. By not facing the truth about our enemy we leave ourselves and the church ill prepared for the battle that rages. How many spiritual casualties will it take before the church wakes up to the reality of spiritual warfare?

chapter 14

DEMONIC PROTOCOLS

IN THE GOVERNMENTS of the world, there are the visible armies and strategies of war. A more hidden and subtle form of warfare is called covert operations. These are undercover strategies executed by every branch of the military; plus, special operations and agencies such as the FBI and CIA have covert operatives.

Satan uses covert operations as well. Much of what he does is masked and hidden from view.

SATAN'S WILES

The word *wiles* comes from the Greek word *methodeia*. Our English word *method* comes from this word also. It is derived from two Greek words: *meta*, which means "in the midst," and *hodos*, which means "to travel a road or to journey." Satan wants to interrupt your journey, kill your vision, change your route, and move you off center! How does he do that?

Satan uses temptation to lure people away from God's best. *Temptation* is *peirasmos*, which means to "solicit" or "lure to action." Satan uses this tool to draw us away from God and cause us to do evil. Satan may tempt us, but the human will must participate and agree.

> Let no one say when he is tempted, "I am tempted by God"; for God cannot be tempted by evil, nor does He Himself tempt anyone. But each one is tempted when he is drawn away by his own desires and

enticed. Then, when desire has conceived, it gives birth to sin; and sin, when it is full-grown, brings forth death.

—James 1:13–15

Jesus Christ was tempted, yet He did not sin. We must never confuse temptation with sin. All of us must resist temptation by not allowing wrong desires to take over our thinking and move us away from God. The Bible teaches us that temptation is our common lot as human beings (1 Cor. 10:13). It also teaches that wealth affords a greater problem of temptation (1 Tim. 6:9). We are to pray, "Do not lead us into temptation, but deliver us from the evil one" (Matt. 6:13).

It is interesting that our English word *piracy* comes from the Greek word *peirasmos*. Temptation is Satan's way of stealing your precious life.

Satan uses perversion to destroy that which is good. The word *perverse* (used in Isaiah 19:14) comes from the Hebrew *avah*, which means "to make crooked." It is sometimes translated "iniquity." The Greek word is *diastrepho*, which means "to twist through" or "to distort." Satan takes good things and makes them ugly. For instance, sex in a heterosexual marriage is a gift from God. Satan can twist it into homosexuality, pornography, and abuse.

Satan uses imitation to draw people away from the true God. Most religions are bad copies of God's teachings. Satan's greatest imitation will be the Antichrist, who will imitate the miracles of Christ. He will even be raised from a deadly wound and will be worshiped as God. (See 2 Thessalonians 2:9; Revelation 13:13–18.)

Satan can still counterfeit worship and ministry (2 Cor. 11:14). That is why we must test those who claim to have the Holy Ghost and not be led away by the false (1 John 4:1–3).

Demons Use Deception

Revelation 12:9 declares that Satan has deceived the whole world. The word *deceive* pictures a person who believes a lie to be the truth. A deceived person is one who is utterly convinced that right is wrong and wrong is right. Satan is a deceiver. He practices his deception in many realms. Basically, deception is practiced in the area of the Word of God. If Satan can convince a person that God is a liar, then he can get that person to violate God's principles of living. The other area of deception is on the person and work of Christ.

Demons use perversion to distort the plan of God. Satan is a perverter of all the physical appetites that God has given us. The appetite for food may be perverted into gluttony. Alcohol given by God as a medicine has been perverted into the worst social problem in America. (See Proverbs 20:1; 23:1–3, 20–21, 29–35.) Sex is God's gift to a man and woman in the bond of marriage. Now this gift has been perverted into every wickedness imaginable. Scripture forbids premarital sex and homosexual acts; Satan says they are acceptable. The world calls it "sexual preference."

Satan perverts the plan of God. Satan produces imitators who misuse the plan of God and lead people astray. When Moses stood before Pharaoh and his rod became a serpent, Pharaoh's magicians did the same thing (Exod. 7:11–22). There have been and will be many wolves in sheep's clothing until the return of Christ. Satan will ultimately produce the Antichrist, who will be an imitation of Jesus.

Therefore it is necessary to test the spirit that speaks out of a man. Test it by the Word of God. "Beloved, do not believe every spirit, but test the spirits, whether they are of God; because many false prophets have gone out into the world" (1 John 4:1).

Satan's greatest device against Christians is that which he used against Job: namely, accusation. Satan will accuse us of sin that God has forgiven. He is a slanderer and a liar. He accused Job of serving God for material blessings. Job was vindicated, and God was victorious. Satan used the weather, death, family, disease, and false friends. Through it all, Job neither cursed God nor charged God wrongly.

Satan will tell you that God is to blame for your troubles. He will tell you sin is to blame. He will accuse you and try to defeat and destroy your faith. Our defense is confession of sin according to 1 John 1:9. We are not condemned; we are forgiven.

Perhaps one of the greatest ways Satan operates in the world is through rebellion against authority. Human government was permitted in order to thwart Satan's purpose of lawlessness. When rebellion and anarchy overthrow a government, it always brings a more repressive regime. The breakdown of authority in the nation, home, and church will bring a harsher government or total destruction. The bombing of New York City's World Trade Center in 1993 and the tragic bombing of the federal building in Oklahoma City in 1995 are clear examples of demonically inspired rebellion.

The Bible warns us of the sin of rebellion. Saul's rebellion is described as witchcraft and his stubbornness as iniquity and idolatry (1 Sam. 15:23). Satan destroyed Saul by rebellion. Living out from under authority is dangerous! God-given authority must be established and honored in our churches.

Other methods Satan uses include temptations of the flesh, occult involvement, religious charlatans, fear, and intimidation.

The victory is won by the believer who will utilize the weapons provided by God. Only the unarmed will know defeat! When Eliot Ness and the Treasury Department first began fighting the Capone mob in Chicago, the FBI was not allowed to carry weapons. Only after a number of agents were killed did the government finally agree to arm them.

Our king has permitted us to bear arms! Let us clothe ourselves with God's armor and live in victory!

chapter 15

SYMPTOMS OF DEMONIC OPERATION

THE SUBJECT OF mental illness is very controversial in Christian circles. Inside the extreme schools of thought we find balance and a scriptural viewpoint. First, let me say clearly, all mental illness is not the result of demonic attack. Further, good psychological care from Christian professionals is vital and in order when an individual is struggling. Also, professionally administered medication may be necessary when chemical imbalances occur. When normal medicine and therapy do not result in a cure, then it is possible that these symptoms could point to demonic operation.

Let me list for you fourteen symptoms of demonic operation. As these symptoms are listed, realize that some of them could also be caused by something other than demonic oppression. The first six symptoms on this list are extreme and are drawn from the account of the demoniac of Gadara in Mark 5. This man had been chained in a cemetery because of his erratic and violent behavior. When you look at Mark 5:1–15, you can see clear symptoms of demonic activity.

Symptom 1: Incapacity for normal living (Mark 5:1–5)

Just as the actions of Legion made him unsuitable for normal social interaction with friends and family, an unusual desire for solitude, accompanied by a deep loneliness, will often set in. The person will often become very passive with no desire to change.

Symptom 2: Extreme behavior (Mark 5:4)

Violence will often be evident in the victim's life. An explosive temper and extreme, uncontrollable anger are dangerous behaviors that control the individual and the people who love him or her.

Symptom 3: Personality changes (Mark 5:9, 12)

Multiple personalities exist in some of the most serious cases of demonic control. This man had a "legion" of spirits within his life. All cases of multiple personality may not be demonic, but in most cases demon activity is involved. Changes in personality, extreme or mild, may be evidence of demonic activity.

Symptom 4: Restlessness and insomnia (Mark 5:5)

In verse 5 we see this man crying in the tombs "night and day." He could not sleep. Insomnia can be a sign of a physical problem or a sign of a spiritual problem. God has gifted His children with sleep (Ps. 127:2). So when you cannot sleep night after night and there is no medical reason for this disturbance, the devil maybe tormenting you. Don't forget; you have the right to rest in Jesus!

In Psalm 3 we see a picture of warfare. Here David was hounded by his enemies. In verses 3 and 4, he cried to the Lord, "You…are a shield for me." In verses 5 and 6, he cried, "I lay down and slept; I awoke, for the LORD sustained me. I will not be afraid of ten thousands of people who have set themselves against me all around." He also said in Psalm 4:8, "I will both lie down in peace, and sleep; for You alone, O LORD, make me dwell in safety." Sleep is God's gift to all who trust in Him.

Symptom 5: A terrible inner anguish (Mark 5:5)

This man was deeply tormented in mind and heart. Various levels of anguish are evident in those who are afflicted by demons. Grief and anguish are normal emotions for us all. Yet, persistent, unresolved anguish that will not leave after normal therapies of counseling, encouragement, and prayer could well be demonic.

Symptom 6: Self-inflicted injury and suicide (Mark 5:5)

Here we see the demonic man was cutting himself. If you read Mark 9:14–29, you will see the story of the man whose son was both deaf and mute because of a demon: "Wherever he [the evil spirit] seizes him, he throws him down….Often he [the demon] has thrown him [the boy] both into the fire and into the water to destroy him" (vv. 18, 22). Jesus cast out the demon. "The spirit cried out, convulsed him greatly, and came out of him. And he became as one dead....But Jesus took him by the hand and lifted him up, and he arose" (vv. 26–27). Demons can cause people to injure themselves. They even incite suicide.

Symptom 7: Unexplained illness with no obvious medical cause

When medical testing produces no physical cause for an illness, then we should look to the mind and spirit for answers. Sometimes illnesses are psychological, and good counseling can result in a cure. Other times the battle is with demons.

A scriptural example of this is found in Luke 13:11–16, the story of a woman afflicted by a "spirit of infirmity" (v. 11). Jesus called her "a daughter of Abraham, whom Satan has bound" (v. 16). Obviously she was a child of God and faithful to her synagogue, with a desire to know more about the Lord. "Jesus...said to her, 'Woman, you are loosed from your infirmity.' And He laid hands on her, and immediately she was made straight, and glorified God" (vv. 12–13). There are physical illnesses caused by a class of demons known as "spirits of infirmity."

Symptom 8: Addictive behavior

Addiction to alcohol, drugs, sex, food, gambling, and other things opens the door to demonic influence and control. I am not saying demons cause all of these problems; certainly people are responsible for their own wrong choices. But anything that causes one to be out of control opens that person to infernal control.

Symptom 9: Abnormal sexual behavior

When Jezebel's son inquired about peace, Jehu responded, "What peace, as long as the harlotries of your mother Jezebel and her witchcraft are so many?" (2 Kings 9:22).

In Ezekiel 16:20–51 the spirit of harlotry is mentioned several times. This spirit infected the nation of Israel with the sins of Sodom (vv. 49–50). They even sacrificed their own children (vv. 20–21).

Homosexuality, adultery, fornication, and even infanticide are all inspired by the spirit of harlotry. Hosea 4:12 says, "The spirit of harlotry has caused them to stray, and they have played the harlot against their God." Look at Hosea 5:4: "They do not direct their deeds toward turning to their God, for the spirit of harlotry is in their midst, and they do not know the Lord."

A nation and a people given over to sexual sins and abominations is governed by this spirit of harlotry. Look at Nahum 3:4: "Because of the multitude of harlotries of the seductive harlot, the mistress of sorceries, who sells nations through her harlotries, and families through her sorceries."

Nations and families are sold into spiritual bondage by the witchcraft of the spirit of harlotry. When we play around with sexual sin, we open ourselves to this demonic spirit. We must battle this principality that dominates our nation.

Symptom 10: Defeat, failure, and depression in the Christian life

Paul wrote in 2 Corinthians 2:14, "Now thanks be to God who always leads us in triumph in Christ." Notice this verse is preceded by an exhortation from Paul to forgive others "lest Satan should take advantage of us; for we are not ignorant of his devices" (vv. 10–11). It is Satan's purpose to take advantage of our situations and to rob us of the victorious life that is ours in Christ. The psalmist cried out, "By this I know that You are well pleased with me, because my enemy does not triumph over me" (Ps. 41:11).

This symptom is often manifested by an inability to praise and worship. Psalm 92:1–4 is a testimony to the power of praise. It culminates in verse 4, where David said, "For You, Lord, have made me glad through Your work; I will triumph in the works of Your hands." Again he said, "Save us, O Lord our God…to give thanks…[and] to triumph in Your praise" (Ps. 106:47).

Symptom 11: Occult involvement and behavior

Deuteronomy 18:9–12 catalogs the works of the occult and witchcraft, including child sacrifice; fortune-telling; soothsaying; interpreting omens; sorcery; and the work of those who conjure spells, mediums, spiritists, and those who call up the dead. Then verse 15 instructs the people to hear the word of God from the prophet of God and order their lives accordingly. Occult involvement is clearly a symptom of demonic control.

Symptom 12: Speech difficulties

In Matthew 9:32–33 Jesus rebuked a demon, and the mute man was able to speak. Speech difficulties may be physical, emotional, mental, and, in some cases, demonic. Extreme language and cursing may be prompted by the enemy.

Symptom 13: Doctrinal error

In 1 Timothy 4:1 we receive a warning that in the last days deceiving spirits will teach the doctrines of demons. Today, religious cults and charlatans abound. The reason these deceivers draw many people is the power of the demonic that teaches them.

Symptom 14: Religious legalism

Galatians 3:1 says to the believer who is in danger of going back under the Law, "Who has bewitched you that you should not obey the truth?" The church at Galatia had forsaken a faith ministry that resulted in the miraculous (v. 5) for a law ministry of rules and regulations. Paul classified this error as witchcraft.

Some deeply religious people are under the bondage of tradition, man-made rules, and outward appearances. Demons thrive in this kind of environment, especially demons of control. It is a lot easier to keep a ritual or list of rules than it is to walk by faith. Wherever there is any substitute for faith in the finished work of Christ, it is a doctrine of demons.

SECTION IV

KNOWING THE STRATEGIES OF YOUR ENEMY

chapter 16

THE STRATEGY OF FEAR

IN JOB 3:25, we find these words: "For the thing I greatly feared has come upon me, and what I dreaded has happened to me." Satan came to Yahweh and said, "I want permission to touch Job," and God gave him permission. However, the only reason the enemy had any access whatsoever to Job—even though he had permission—was because Job gave him ground.

I believe two sins of fear existed in Job's life. Job was a man who lived in fear of something happening to his children, and he lived in fear of something happening to his money. He lived that way all his life.

Fear is a magnet to demons. Fear will draw in the enemy and will bring to pass the thing you have spoken out of your mouth. You need to understand that not only is fear an emotion, but it is also a spirit. In 2 Timothy 1:7 we read, "For God has not given us a spirit of fear, but of power and of love and of a sound mind."

I believe that spirits of timidity and cowardice come in and paralyze us and keep us from moving as God wants us to move. This is not simply a "little" problem; I believe that fear is actually killing people: "Men's hearts failing them from fear and the expectation of those things which are coming on the earth, for the powers of heaven will be shaken" (Luke 21:26). Fear is a deadly magnet that will destroy you and drive happiness from your life. In the Bible, the opposite of fear is not courage; it is faith and hope.

Recognize Your Fears

What specific fears flood and bring failure to your life? It is time to examine yourself and see what fears exist in your thought processes.

Fear of life

Every day I meet people who are afraid to live life to its fullest. This fear is one of the first to ever show its face in this world. Right after Adam and Eve fell into sin, God showed up to speak to them. Adam admitted to God, "I heard Your voice in the garden, and I was afraid because I was naked; and I hid myself" (Gen. 3:10). Adam couldn't even go through his normal routines there in the garden!

Perhaps you're afraid that people will find out who you really are and then shun you. You are afraid that some of the things you've done, things that are between you and God, may come out. You live in fear of the truth. However, if there is any place in this world where you should be able to live a transparent life, it is the church! You should be able to share your difficulties and your failures and have them safely dealt with.

God judges fear as harshly as any sin discussed in the Bible. Matthew 25 contains the parable of the talents. One fellow gets five talents, another gets two, and one gets a single talent. The one with five invested and doubled his money, as did the one who was given two. God expects something out of His investment! He wants to see results from what He sows. However, the fellow who was given one talent simply hid his. Look at his reasoning: "Lord, I knew you to be a hard man, reaping where you have not sown, and gathering where you have not scattered seed. And I was afraid, and went and hid your talent in the ground" (vv. 24–25). This nervous fellow didn't truly know the God we serve; he had the wrong perception of God. What was the master's response? He didn't say, "Poor little old frightened fellow!" Rather he said, "Take the talent from him, and give it to him who has ten talents" (v. 28). You see, if you don't use it, you lose it.

The impact of fear reaches beyond spiritual issues; it can also affect your job. Perhaps you are afraid to take the next step for advancement. Maybe you fear going into management because you're afraid the responsibility will be bigger than anything you've ever known. The comfort zone is preferred over progress. Someone reading this book may have birthed a wonderful idea, but you won't take a risk because you so deeply fear failure.

History tells us that Abraham Lincoln lost every election he ran in except for when he ran for president! What if he had quit? We would not have had one of our greatest presidents. There are those who are paralyzed by the fear of getting up in the morning and going about the routines of life. I want to challenge you to break this spirit and believe that you can be everything God has created you to be.

Fear of death

> He Himself [Jesus] likewise shared in the same, that through death He might destroy him who had the power of death, that is, the devil, and release those who through fear of death were all their lifetime subject to bondage.
>
> —HEBREWS 2:14–15

Many people sustain a powerful fear of dying. I believe that's why so many of our hospital dollars are going to give people tests for diseases they don't have. Many people wake up nightly short of breath. They actually could be suffering from night terrors, a demonic attack on basic health.

If you are saved, why should you be afraid of dying? Shouldn't every Christian boast, "To live is Christ, and to die is gain" (Phil. 1:21)? Heaven is not a destination to be feared! I've heard people say, "You know, I want to go to heaven, but I'm just not ready." Well, I'm ready to go today! I would miss my family, and they would miss me terribly. But after Jesus died on the cross and then arose from the tomb, He lit up the corridors of death forever! I will not be afraid! "Yea, though I walk through the valley of the shadow of death, I will fear no evil; for You are with me" (Ps. 23:4). Even in death we are not alone.

Fear of the enemy

Here is the proper response when you are facing the enemy: "For I hear the slander of many; fear is on every side; while they take counsel together against me, they scheme to take away my life. But as for me, I trust in You, O LORD; I say, 'You are my God.' My times are in Your hand; deliver me from the hand of my enemies, and from those who persecute me" (Ps. 31:13–15).

I don't have to be afraid of the devil or his emissaries that are embodied here on the earth. Jesus spoiled principalities and powers! He ripped the astro-deities from their thrones and exposed the enemy. I don't have to be afraid of a tarot card or a horoscope. I don't need to call a psychic to find out what is going to happen tomorrow. I boast with the psalmist David, "My times are in Your hands."

Fear of man

> The fear of man brings a snare, but whoever trusts in the LORD shall be safe.
>
> —PROVERBS 29:25

This fear is a powerful fear for many in our world today. Is there someone in your life who causes fear to rise in your spirit? Is there something within you that causes you to agree with people or even go along with them when they are wrong simply because you are afraid of what they will think of you?

This fear of man is something that really grips our young people today. Peer pressure, a fear of what friends think, can take over their lives. The fear of being different, the fear of what other people will think—these can be so strong. I'm not telling you to be obnoxious, but here's the honest truth: it doesn't matter what anybody thinks but God! Young people and adults alike need to quit allowing the fear of man to hinder what God wants to do in their lives.

Fear of insignificance

People are so afraid that their lives won't count for anything. I think of the story of Abraham. Here's old Abram. He left fame and fortune in Ur of the Chaldees, left his beautiful home, and is living in a tent. Out here, nobody knows who he is. "After these things the word of the LORD came to Abram in a vision, saying, 'Do not be afraid, Abram. I am your shield, your exceedingly great reward'" (Gen. 15:1).

You say, "Well, I didn't win Employee of the Month even though I deserved it." But God saw it, and He took account of your stewardship. You say, "Nobody has ever given me a plaque. Nobody appreciates what I do." I want to tell you, your greatest reward is God.

Let me remind you of the story of the woman who broke the alabaster box and wept over Jesus's feet. Nobody really knows her name; some scholars believe it was Mary. What we do know for sure is that Jesus appreciated what she did! No one knows the name of the widow who gave all she had to the temple offering, but Jesus knows her name. She is significant to Him.

If you experience feelings of inferiority, you must embrace the understanding that Jesus Christ is the One who can bring significance and importance to your life. Then one day when you arrive in heaven, you will see that everything you sowed into this life is still over there!

One night I was watching TV with friends when an award show extravaganza came on. A friend said, "Look at that, catering to the flesh. It's all so worldly!" I couldn't help but say in response, "Leave them alone. That little gold statue may be all they ever get in recognition for this life."

But you know, I have something more laid up for me—a crown in glory. My Savior knows my name and the number of hairs on my head, and He has ordered my life. I don't have to be afraid of feeling insignificant or lost in the crowd!

Fear of the future

> For I know the thoughts that I think toward you, says the LORD,
> thoughts of peace and not of evil, to give you a future and a hope.
> —JEREMIAH 29:11

You don't have to be afraid of what is going to happen tomorrow. Once you know the Lord Jesus Christ, fear of the future can leave.

When my son, Ronnie Jr., was a little boy, he loved to go with me on errands. Even when he was four or five years old, he would eagerly jump into the passenger seat even if it was a quick trip. Looking back, I think it is significant that not once did he say, "Daddy, do you have enough gas in the car?" "Daddy, do you have any money with you?" "Daddy, do you really know the directions to where we're going?"

You see, he didn't have to ask those questions. He put his little hand in my hand, and that was all he needed. He was ready to go because he trusted me. He knew that if he was with me, his needs would be met in abundance. Whether it was a soda from the gas station or a quick trip through a fast-food drive-through, he knew he wouldn't go hungry on our trip. If he needed a restroom, Daddy would find one. And he could trust that Daddy would know the way back home when it was time.

I can't predict to you what will happen in your future. But I can tell you this: as a believer, what is waiting for you in eternity is wonderful, and you don't have to worry.

FACING PRIVATE STRONGHOLDS OF FEAR

If you have an inordinate fear, such as fear of an animal, the dark, crowds, shortages, certain places, or times of the day, please understand that these fears just won't go away. They must be dealt with. First Peter 3:14 says, "If you suffer for righteousness' sake, you are blessed. 'And do not be afraid of their threats, nor be troubled.'" And 2 Timothy 1:7 says, "For God has not given us a spirit of fear, but of power and of love and of a sound mind." The Bible says that fear has to be cast out.

Fear is a magnet for demons.

> And we have known and believed the love that God has for us. God is love, and he who abides in love abides in God, and God in him. Love has been perfected among us in this: that we may have boldness in the day of judgment.
>
> —1 JOHN 4:16–17

Verse 18 continues this thought: "There is no fear in love [*agape*]; but perfect love casts out fear." This spirit won't simply just leave. You can take all the Valium and Zoloft you want. You can get drunk, smoke, take sleep aids, or go to the movies or a comedy club. You may temporarily forget your fear. But when you wake up or sober up, that fear is going to be staring you in the face.

FEAR'S FRIGHTENING COHORTS

When you engage the spirit of fear, he brings along his tormenting buddies. Fear never comes alone. Fear's best friend is torment. Torment involves sleepless nights…or thinking your husband is having an affair when he is not…or the inability to speak the truth out of your mouth. It's all of these torments and more.

Fear and torment gain access into your life through wrong relationships. Some of you may harbor fear because of something from your past that has never been death with. In Matthew 18, Jesus told a parable of a man who forgave someone who owed him a lot of money. However, that forgiven man then remembered a debt that someone owed him. He refused to forgive the little debt and harassed the indebted man.

Soon the master found out and called him to task, saying, "'You wicked servant! I forgave you all that debt because you begged me. Should you not also have had compassion on your fellow servant, just as I had pity on you?' And his master was angry, and delivered him to the torturers until he should pay all that was due to him" (Matt. 18:32–34). The story closes with a warning: "So My heavenly Father also will do to you if each of you, from his heart, does not forgive his brother his trespasses" (v. 35).

The reason why some of you are tormented by fear is because something happened to you. Maybe you were abused or hurt. Maybe you were lied to or suffered rejection from someone significant. It could be physical or verbal abuse, but either way, you are still tormented because you have never let the pain go and forgiven those who hurt you.

What's the point of the parable of the wicked servant? Simply this: God knows the heart. He is looking at you and saying He knows everything you have ever thought or ever done. He sent His Son to Calvary to shed His blood and forgive you all of your debt. Therefore, no matter who has hurt you or how deeply you may have been hurt—whether they have ever asked you to forgive them or not—just like the servant, you must forgive them! Otherwise you will be chained to them for the rest of your life, and tormenting demons will drive the sleep and peace from your life.

I don't have an easy, quick fix for you. You simply must deal with your hurts. Perhaps you have knelt a hundred times at a church altar but only felt temporary relief because you picked up that grudge and walked out the door with it. Or the next day somebody else said something harmful to you, and right then all the old pain rushed back in. Fear and torments gain access when you have unforgiveness toward others. I was ministering at the altar during a series of meetings when a lady stood before me for prayer. The Holy Spirit showed me immediately what her need was. I spoke forth the Spirit's prompting and told her, "You have to forgive your daddy." She bent over, fell down on her knees, and said, "No!" It wasn't her crying out. It was that tormenting spirit that had invaded her life twenty-two years ago. All her makeup, her beauty, and her money (and she had plenty) didn't help her, because she was tormented by the fact that her father had wronged her deeply, and she had never settled it.

God provided not only for our forgiveness but also for those who wrong us. Maybe you think that isn't fair, but fairness isn't what we need in life—we need mercy! In the Spirit, I see the blood of Jesus showering down upon you as you read this and chains falling off. Old fears are leaving, and new life is beginning even as you hold this book!

Casting Out Fear

How do you cast it out? The apostle John gave the answer when he wrote, "Perfect love casts out fear" (1 John 4:18). Jesus lives in our hearts, and His perfect love is in us. He has poured out His love in us by the Holy Ghost. You ask, "How does fear leave?" You tell it to leave! Why don't you forgive the one who hurt you and say, "Now, you lousy, sorry spirit of fear and all of your tormenting spirits, I have forgiven the ones who hurt me. You are trespassing. Get out!" They have to go. Love is the antidote to fear. Let go of the hurt, and grab on to God's love.

Retaining Your Freedom

Once you've uprooted your fear, how can you stay free of it? Look again at what God says to us: "For I know the thoughts that I think toward you, says the Lord, thoughts of peace and not of evil, to give you a future and a hope" (Jer. 29:11). Imagine God thinking about us! That blows me away. Even when you are not thinking about Him, He's thinking about you. And his thoughts are not thoughts of malice or judgment, but they are thoughts of peace. *Shalom* in the Hebrew means not only "good feelings," but it also means "prosperity." When Jeremiah wrote this, he was writing to a people who were being taken captive to Babylon for seventy years. Many of them would never live to get back to their homes. They were going to a place they had never seen, and it was a place where there had to be fear. But God wanted them to know hope stood strong in the future.

LIVE IN FREEDOM

How do you live in the face of such turmoil? How do you live in hope and not in fear, even when it seems there are things in your life that you can't do anything about?

> Thus says the LORD of hosts, the God of Israel, to all who were carried away captive, whom I have caused to be carried away from Jerusalem to Babylon: Build houses and dwell in them; plant gardens and eat their fruit. Take wives and beget sons and daughters; and take wives for your sons and give your daughters to husbands, so that they may bear sons and daughters—that you may be increased there, and not diminished. And seek the peace of the city where I have caused you to be carried away captive, and pray to the LORD for it; for in its peace you will have peace.
>
> —JEREMIAH 29:4–7

Let me tell you another antidote to fear: just enjoy what God has given you and quit feeling guilty about it. Perhaps when you buy something new, you always feel like you have to explain it to others. You may be afraid people will think, "Boy, they are pretentious. Look at that extravagance!" But God said, "Enjoy what I've blessed you with."

TURN A DEAF EAR TO THE NEGATIVE

Quit listening to negative people. "For thus says the LORD of hosts, the God of Israel: Do not let your prophets and your diviners who are in your midst deceive you, nor listen to your dreams which you cause to be dreamed. For they prophesy falsely to you in My name; I have not sent them, says the LORD" (Jer. 29:8–9).

If God has given you a dream, you can almost count on someone coming along to speak gloom and doom over it! A sure way to look to the future with hope is to ask God what He wants to do in your life, get a sure word from Him, and then hold on to your dream. Refuse to listen to dream killers!

TRUST HIS GOOD WORD

To keep fear away, you must anchor your hope to the Word of God. Jeremiah 29:10 promised, "For thus says the LORD: After seventy years are completed in Babylon, I will visit you and perform My good word toward you and cause you to return to this place.'" That word *good* in the Hebrew literally means "beautiful." God basically said, "I have spoken a beautiful word. You go on and live your life. You go on with your dream. It may not get here in your timing, but I have spoken." It took seventy years for Israel's dream to happen, but God did perform everything He spoke.

You need to quit being afraid of what your family thinks and what others think. That doesn't mean to be obnoxious. Just keep His promises firm in your mind and tell yourself, "I don't really care if others speak negatively about my dream—God has spoken!"

DAILY KNOWING GOD

Truthfully, I'm not much of a morning person, but my wife and I have set up a routine. Paulette will call, "Honey, I've got the coffee ready." About 6:30 a.m. with coffee in hand, we will slip in front of the TV and watch one of our favorite devotional programs together. About five minutes into the broadcast, I'm ready to charge hell with a water pistol!

How do you keep hope alive? View every tomorrow as a gift from God. When you get up tomorrow, even if it is a Monday, open your eyes and say, "Good morning, Lord. How are You doing? What are we doing today, Lord?" Even though you are going to that secular job, you are on duty for Him. God knows us. He has a plan for our lives.

In addition, you will find that prayer keeps fear from returning. Look at Jeremiah 29:12: "Then you will call upon Me and go and pray to Me and I will listen to you." So first He told us, "I'm thinking about you!" and now He says, "I'm going to listen to you!"

We also must nurture our passion for God. Look at Jeremiah 29:13: "And you will seek Me and you will find Me, when you search for Me with all your heart." Verse 14 tells us that God is a God of hope. He says, "I will be found by you." It may seem sometimes that God is playing hide-and-seek with you, but eventually He's going to say, "I'm over here! If you will just come after Me with all of your heart, you will find Me."

In this relentless pursuit of the glory of God, you will find that He is in the midst of every circumstance in your life.

I used to tell Paulette that our courtship can be summed up this way: I chased her until she caught me! It is comforting to know that you can chase God until He catches you. Perfect love casts out fear. A joyful and confident future can be yours.

Right now you can ask God to apply what is needed in your life. Fear is about to leave forever:

> *In the name of Jesus, I command the spirit of fear to come to attention. I command you to loose your hold according to the Word of God. I hold you before the Lord Jesus, who said, "Fear not," whose birth heralded a new day. I command your power to be broken and that you will leave in the name that is above every name. Now, Holy Spirit, come and replace fear with fruit—love, joy, peace, longsuffering, gentleness, meekness, kindness, and self-control. Come, fullness of power. Come, peace of God and a sound mind. Come, Jehovah, and touch my life. In Jesus's name, amen.*

chapter 17

THE STRATEGY OF DEPRESSION

I S THERE A permanent cure for depression? Statistics show that multitudes of Americans are hoping for the quick cure. In 2001, it was estimated that 28 million Americans were taking antidepressants. Some studies show that at least one in four Americans are on some kind of psychiatric drug, but experts believe that number is low.[1]

Our Lord Jesus, when He began His ministry, knew what kind of world He was coming into. His very first sermon was preached from the passage of Isaiah 61. Jesus began His ministry by saying:

> The Spirit of the Lord GOD is upon Me, because the LORD has anointed Me to preach good tidings to the poor; He has sent Me to heal the brokenhearted, to proclaim liberty to the captives, and the opening of the prison to those who are bound; to proclaim the acceptable year of the LORD, and the day of vengeance of our God; to comfort all who mourn, to console those who mourn in Zion, to give them beauty for ashes, the oil of joy for mourning, the garment of praise for the spirit of heaviness; that they may be called trees of righteousness, the planting of the LORD, that He may be glorified.
>
> —ISAIAH 61:1–3

This passage is literally the liberator speaking liberation. It is the voice of your Savior issuing freedom's call to your spirit! Then why is the number-one complaint among confessing Christians in America the problem of depression?

Depression is the state of being depressed—a feeling of letdown, of hopelessness. It can affect the body. It can cause an overwhelming sense of fatigue to come upon a person. In fact, there are studies that indicate that many psychological neuroses, as well as some fatigue diseases, are the results of living with depression.

The Bible doesn't call it depression. The Bible calls it the spirit of heaviness. There is a demon involved here. David called it "being cast down." Depression is a state of mourning in your life, a state of heaviness over circumstances. You are under the circumstances of your life.

OPEN DOORS TO DEPRESSION

A great many things can open your life to the spirit of depression. Let us look at a few of them briefly.

Circumstances

In Isaiah 61, Jesus said, "I've come to preach good news." One of the obvious causes or triggers of depression is negative circumstances, or bad news. Johnny Cash used to sing a song about bad news traveling like wildfire; in fact, in the lyrics of that song he said they called him "Wildfire."

That's just like the devil—he would be thrilled to be known as "Old Wildfire"! But Jesus isn't like that. He didn't come to give you bad news. Even the word *gospel* means "good news." Jesus came to tell you that the dark night is over. He came to set you free! Many of you are living with a spirit of heaviness because of negative circumstances that have come into your life.

Illness

In addition, physical or mental sickness can make you depressed. If you are physically sick for a prolonged time, sometimes that can bring on a spirit of depression. The doctor bills that come with a prolonged sickness are yet another negative circumstance! Sometimes mental problems truly are the cause of a depressed soul. It is important to remember that not all mental problems are demons.

Thought patterns

Sometimes wrong thinking just takes over your life. It becomes hard to look at life through the clear lenses of reality. You look through the sunglasses of your own circumstances, and everyone and everything seems tainted by your own experiences. That's why sometimes a woman whose daddy was an adulterer and was unfaithful will look at every man as if he's an adulterer or unfaithful. It is time to get rid of those old glasses of the past.

Chains of habit

Demonic bondage and habits can chain you down. Isaiah 61 tells us that Jesus came to proclaim liberty to captives. God doesn't want you to live as the captive of the enemy with depression. He came to console those who mourn.

Rejection

Rejection may have you deep in depression. If I may, let me paraphrase Isaiah 61:2 to read, "He came to declare the year of the Lord's acceptance." Jesus came to tell you that God has not rejected you; you have rejected Him. He has come to make you accepted. Maybe you are depressed because the enemy of rejection has come, and you have believed the devil's lie about yourself. Let me tell you a secret: God loves you just the way you are!

Death and loss

Perhaps you are depressed because you have lost someone. You need to know Jesus said He came to comfort all those who mourn in Zion. He came with the oil of gladness.

Understand this: there is nothing wrong with legitimate mourning. If you have had a death in your family, you are not demon possessed or demonized just because you are sad about your loss. It is human to feel sadness when somebody dies. Too often some well-meaning person tries to comfort those who have lost a mate or loved one, and he or she says, "Well, Jesus knows what's going on. You're really blessed to know they are in heaven." While their words may be true, at that moment of grief you don't feel blessed. It takes time to work through loss.

When my daddy died, my mother had a significant time of adjustment to go through. She loved Jesus with all her heart, but here on Earth, Daddy was everything to her. I mean, Mama even ironed Daddy's socks! She laid his clothes out. She loved him, and he loved her. When he was gone, Mama didn't know what to do with herself. She had to find another outlet for her service, and she didn't get there the next day.

Everyone should go through the stages of grief at their own pace. However, if more than a year has passed since your loss and you are still mourning, it is time for you to put off the mourning garments and put on the garment of praise. Do not allow the enemy to carry you away into dark depression.

No direction

You may be depressed because you lack direction in your life. Isaiah 61:3 reads, "To appoint unto them that mourn in Zion" (KJV). *Appoint* is the same word used for enthroning a king. You need to know that God has a place for you. If you will come to Him and let Him get rid of this depression in your life, God Almighty is going to put you in the place of His appointment. When you are in the center of His will, with His direction, the reason for your depression will leave!

Failure

Jesus said, "I've come to give them beauty for ashes" (Isa. 61:3). God is waiting for you to give Him your failure. God can use your failures much more than He can ever use your successes, if you trust Him with those failures. Bill and Gloria Gaither wrote the song "Something Beautiful," which talks about God taking our failures and turning them into something beautiful. Find this song, and listen to it; it will bless you as much as it's blessed me.

You may feel like a failure. Just wrap that failure up and bring it to Jesus. He knows how to raise visions and dreams from the dead. He can bring life out of ashes.

Loss of passion for God

Perhaps you are depressed because you have lost touch with God. Jesus said, "I'll give you a garment of praise for the spirit of heaviness" (Isa. 61:3). You know you have lost touch with God when you don't praise Him anymore. We must praise Him not only when things are going great but also when everything goes wrong! When you don't feel like singing, that's the time to sing.

The jailers had beaten Paul and Silas nearly to death. It was midnight. What do you do at midnight in a jail when you've been beaten half to death? Curse the jailer? Scripture tells us that at midnight they began to sing, and God showed up and lifted them. You may feel as if you've been beaten and jailed, but it is time to sing.

DEPRESSION'S SYMPTOMS

In Psalms 42 and 43 we see a clear picture of what it feels like to be depressed.

Running in a panic

"As the deer pants for the water brooks, so pants my soul for You, O God" (Ps. 42:1). Here is a hunted animal. Depression sometimes feels as if you are being chased by something. You are so tired of running from what you are afraid of that you don't know where to go. That's one of the symptoms. David is talking about his cast-down soul. He said, "I feel like a deer, and a hunter is right on my trail."

Dissatisfaction

You may be thirsty and unsatisfied in your soul: "My soul thirsts for God, for the living God. When shall I come and appear before God?" (Ps. 42:2). Jesus said in the Sermon on the Mount, "Blessed are those who hunger and thirst for righteousness, for they shall be filled" (Matt. 5:6). I get so excited in my spirit when I visit a church and sense they are hungry and thirsty. They don't know it all. There is something in their soul crying out. They are not satisfied with where they are. Depression will put a thirst in you. It will cause you to say, "Lord, I have to get out of this. I can't stand this. I don't care what it takes. I'm thirsty for You, God. I need You to show up in my life."

Unstable emotions

"My tears have been my food day and night, while they continually say to me, 'Where is your God?'" (Ps. 42:3). These are questions thrown at any believer who suffers from depression: "I thought you were a Christian. I thought you had some help. I thought you knew something about God. What's wrong with you?"

I speak as a man who suffered with depression for twelve years. A lot of the reason for it was the daily grind of ministry. I had reached point where I didn't trust anybody, didn't want to hear anybody, and didn't believe anybody. I know what it's like to want to quit. I know what it's like to soak a pillow with tears every night but still have to stand up and smile behind a pulpit when everything in you is torn completely apart.

I also know what it is like to just want to die. Much earlier in life, at the tender age of fourteen, I stood on a railroad trestle and told God, "I don't want to live any longer. Either let the train run over me, or give me courage to jump." But I heard a voice out there on that trestle. I had a friend out there with me, and He didn't come and lecture me on being depressed. He simply pulled me away. I know what it is like to have to fight those unstable emotions and to "take every thought captive."

Feeling forgotten

Have you ever felt like crying out, "God, I don't know where You are; I'm looking, but I just can't find You"? Welcome to the real world. Even Jesus cried out, "My God, my God, why hast Thou forsaken me?" (Matt. 27:46). I'm talking about the Son of God. Of course, God had not abandoned His Son. But even Jesus, as He took on our sin and drank our cup, felt that overwhelming flood, and for a moment He felt like God had forsaken Him.

David also felt far from God at times. The Book of Psalms is full of his cries: "God, where are You? Have You forgotten me? It's David, Lord. I'm here. My enemies are around me. I'm sick. Lord, I don't know what to do." Please understand the Bible isn't full of "super-saints"; Bible heroes are ordinary people, just like you and me.

Feeling overwhelmed

"Why are you cast down, O my soul? And why are you disquieted within me? Hope in God, for I shall yet praise Him for the help of His countenance....Deep calls unto deep at the noise of Your waterfalls; all Your waves and billows have gone over me" (Ps. 42:5, 7). Do you ever feel like you are drowning, but you can't drown? You aren't quite water-logged, but you can't keep your head above water either. That's how it is to be depressed.

Oppression

"I will say to God my Rock, 'Why have You forgotten me? Why do I go mourning because of the oppression of the enemy?'" (Ps. 42:9) The devil doesn't cause depression. When you allow the circumstances in life to drive you away from God, when you quit praising Him, and when you quit going to church, you become open to this spirit. Verse 4 tells us, "When I remember these things, I pour out my soul within me. For I used to go with the multitude; I went with them to the house of God, with the voice of joy and praise, with a multitude that kept a pilgrim feast." Too often this is how we react under pressure; the very place we need to be is the place we avoid.

Your road to recovery

In order to be healed from depression, you must experience a fresh work of the Holy Spirit in your life! Isaiah 61:1 tells how Jesus would come to the depressed, enslaved, and the broken: "The Spirit of the Lord GOD is upon Me, because the LORD has anointed Me..." Jesus came with an anointing—a yoke-breaking, depression-crushing, life-giving, freedom-announcing anointing. All you need to do is ask Him for it.

Then ask for a fresh word from the Lord. He says, "I've come to proclaim. I've come with a word." He is our help and our salvation!

The third thing you need is a fresh worship offering to God. "Therefore by Him let us continually offer the sacrifice of praise to God, that is, the fruit of our lips, giving thanks to His name" (Heb. 13:15). Remember, Jesus says to put on a garment of praise. Don't be afraid to let God do something different in your worship life. You say, "Well, Pastor Phillips, I'll just praise Him in my heart." I can guarantee that when you get up tomorrow morning at 6:00 a.m., no matter how tired you are, you will get dressed for work! You can't walk into your workplace with no clothes on, saying, "I didn't feel like getting dressed; I thought I'd just skip that today!" God said, "I'll give you a garment of praise." You put on a garment whether you feel like it or not! Your heart may be heavy. You may have experienced insurmountable pain, but shout to the Lord anyway!

The devil can't take away the blood of the cross. Satan can't take away the resurrection of Jesus. He can't take away your salvation. Proclaim along with Job, "Though he slay me, yet will I trust in him" (Job 13:15, KJV). "For I know that my Redeemer lives, and He shall stand at last on the earth" (Job 19:25).

This devil of depression must be rooted out, or its impact will be devastating. If the depressed father doesn't take these steps to overcome it, it could take his wife and his children. Grandmother, it could take your grandchildren. You had better get rid of it.

I used to fight this spirit of depression every Christmas due to the difficulties in my youth. The memories would haunt me every year. I could actually feel myself begin to withdraw from family and friends as the celebration of Jesus's birth intensified. God used my children to pull me out of this seasonal attack of depression. I tell you this to be on guard and ever watchful of these attacks.

Demons can't possess Christians, but they can obsess, compress, and depress you. They can live in you like a rat or a cockroach. You have to drive them out. I didn't get rid of them by telling them, "Well, I'm just so sorry you're here." I just told them where to go: "Get out of my life, heaviness!" And by the power and blood of Jesus, those spirits must flee!

chapter 18

THE STRATEGY OF AFFLICTION

L UKE TELLS THE story of a woman, a child of God, who suffered from an attack of Satan upon her physical body:

> Now He was teaching in one of the synagogues on the Sabbath. And behold, there was a woman who had a spirit of infirmity eighteen years, and was bent over and could in no way raise herself up. But when Jesus saw her, He called her to Him and said to her, "Woman, you are loosed from your infirmity." And He laid His hands on her, and immediately she was made straight, and glorified God. But the ruler of the synagogue answered with indignation, because Jesus had healed on the Sabbath; and he said to the crowd, "There are six days on which men ought to work; therefore come and be healed on them, and not on the Sabbath day." The Lord then answered him and said, "Hypocrite! Does not each one of you on the Sabbath loose his ox or donkey from the stall, and lead it away to water it? So ought not this woman, being a daughter of Abraham, whom Satan has bound—think of it—for eighteen years, be loosed from this bond on the Sabbath?" And when He said these things, all His adversaries were put to shame; and all the multitude rejoiced for all the glorious things that were done by Him.
>
> —LUKE 13:10–17

This woman had all the physical symptoms of a crippled back, yet Jesus clearly states that Satan himself had this woman bound for eighteen years. Satan was the culprit who made this woman's life a living hell.

The woman's background showed that she was a God-fearing, upright believer. She faithfully attended church, for she was present in the synagogue where Jesus was teaching. She came from a good family—"a daughter of Abraham," says the passage. But as a daughter, she was living beneath her privilege.

While some people assume that the enemy cannot affect believers, clearly this woman was a faithful believer, and yet she was almost incapacitated by her affliction.

Verse 16 tells us that this daughter of Abraham was "bound" by Satan. In the Greek, the word *bound* means to "fasten by chains" or "to put under obligation." You see, this woman was married to her sickness. She was imprisoned and incapacitated by it. She was under its legal authority. A spirit of infirmity sent by Satan caused the bondage.

This poor woman was unable to function and serve due to her bent condition. You can imagine her inability to be an effective wife and mother. Satan wanted to keep her from doing and being all she could be for the kingdom of God.

Medical authorities are fully aware today that much physical illness is a result of poor mental health. People may present multitudes of symptoms, yet no disease or physical cause can be found.

The woman in our passage received no help from her church. She came week after week, but they seemed powerless to help her. Even when Jesus touched and healed her, the church leaders criticized Him because He did not do it in their "accepted" manner.

But healing was on its way! "And when Jesus saw her, he called her to him, and said unto her, Woman, thou art loosed from thine infirmity. And he laid his hands on her: and immediately she was made straight, and glorified God" (Luke 13:12–13, KJV).

I believe that all sickness caused by spirits of infirmity can be healed through deliverance. Luke's account of Jesus's healing ministry strongly indicates this, for he wrote, "God anointed Jesus of Nazareth with the Holy Ghost and with power: who went about doing good, and healing all that were oppressed of the devil; for God was with him" (Acts 10:38, KJV).

Luke's insight tells us many things about Jesus. First, Jesus operated under the anointing of the Holy Spirit. This same Holy Spirit can equip, empower, and enable us today!

Secondly, the anointing and power of the Holy Spirit is released "to do good." Deliverance ministry is a life-giving work that ought to be a part of every church's ministry. Too many churches have substituted dead religious activity for the mighty power of the Holy Ghost.

Thirdly, disease can be caused or worsened by the devil. Make no mistake: the enemy of your soul desires to render you ineffective, just as he did the woman in Luke 13. These diseases will leave when the demonic power is broken.

As you decide what church to attend, you must determine if there is an authentic work of God's kingdom in that place. Jesus said, "But if I cast out demons by the Spirit of God, surely the kingdom of God has come upon you" (Matt. 12:28). When we take on the forces of darkness and win, it becomes evident that God has extended His realm and reign over the church.

God's Word reveals other examples of infirm spirits:

> Now there was a man in their synagogue with an unclean spirit. And he cried out, saying, "Let us alone! What have we to do with You, Jesus of Nazareth? Did You come to destroy us? I know who You are—the Holy One of God!" But Jesus rebuked him, saying, "Be quiet, and come out of him!" And when the unclean spirit had convulsed him and cried out with a loud voice, he came out of him.
> —MARK 1:23–26

Yet another occasion is recorded in Luke's Gospel:

> Suddenly a man from the multitude cried out, saying, "Teacher, I implore You, look on my son, for he is my only child. And behold, a spirit seizes him, and he suddenly cries out; it convulses him so that he foams at the mouth, and it departs from him with great difficulty, bruising him. So I implored Your disciples to cast it out, but they could not." Then Jesus answered and said, "O faithless and perverse generation, how long shall I be with you and bear with you? Bring your son here." And as he was still coming, the demon threw him

down and convulsed him. Then Jesus rebuked the unclean spirit, healed the child, and gave him back to his father.

—LUKE 9:38–42

The spirits of infirmity and uncleanness, and deaf and dumb spirits, manifest in illness.

STEPS FOR DELIVERANCE HEALING

Believers can be healed, especially when their infirmity is caused by a satanic attack or bondage. Seven steps are necessary for healing.

1. **Make sure you have a clear medical appraisal**. Be certain your condition is not physical in origin. I knew a man suffering from depression. His antidepressants seemed to be having the opposite effect; his depression only increased. Checking with a doctor, he learned that he had diabetes! Once his sugar was under control, his depression left! If indeed medical practices and tests find no injury or cause, then proceed in the steps for deliverance. Furthermore, if doctors find a diagnosis but cannot seem to find a cure, also proceed through deliverance.

2. **Make sure you are right with God**. All sins must be confessed and put under the blood of Jesus. Any hidden sin will give the enemy a place to hide in your body.

3. **Be filled with the Holy Ghost**. Submit yourself to the Holy Spirit for a fresh filling, and be sure those assisting you in deliverance have done the same.

4. **Put on the armor of God (Eph. 6:10–18)**. Every believer must suit up daily for the battle, for God says, "Put on the whole armor of God, that you may be able to stand against the wiles of the devil" (v. 11).

5. **Pray and speak the Word of God, specifically His promises about freedom and healing.** I have found ten healing

vehicles in Scripture that are available to the Christian! God may choose to use any of these to touch your life with His healing: (1) the presence of the gifting and anointing to heal in a church or individual (1 Cor. 12:9); (2) the laying on of hands by other believers (Mark 16:18); (3) the elders of the church praying and anointing with oil (James 5:14); (4) speaking the word to your sickness (Mark 11:23); (5) coming into agreement through prayer with other believers (Matt. 18:19–20); (6) your own faith (Mark 11:24); (7) partaking of the Lord's Supper (Luke 22:14–20); (8) the name of Jesus (John 14:13); (9) praying for others (Job 42:10); (10) the faith of others moving on behalf of your healing (Mark 4:40).

6. **Command the spirit of infirmity to leave.** After taking authority, take deep breaths until you feel rest in your body and soul.

7. **Rejoice in your deliverance.** Deliverance must be maintained by a proper walk with God. Demons desire to return to their hosts, and they will come back with a vengeance if given a place. Turn your heart toward God in worship and devotion, and allow Him to fill up the empty places in your life.

chapter 19

THE STRATEGY OF ERROR

M ANY CHRISTIANS ARE not walking in freedom. Before we uncover some of the spirits that are plaguing the church today, let us set the foundation.

REMEMBER THE BASICS

Spiritual warfare involves some basics. First, you must know when it is time to fight. You must fight when there is a just cause. When obvious conflict and oppression are in the air, you must act!

Second, use the proper spiritual weapons—prayer and the Word of God. The minute you step away from the Word of God and prayer, you will likely get whipped! You may appear to win a temporary battle here or there, but you are going to lose the spiritual war unless you are armed with God's Word and bathed in prayer.

Lastly, you must maintain a will to fight and carry knowledge of the enemy you face. When you know it is the devil behind the conflict, you can hit him a lot harder and a lot quicker and get rid of him. Many of us are battling the people around us, but they are not our enemy. We must never forget who it is we are truly fighting. In this sense you unwittingly embrace the first enemy spirit—the spirit of error.

Recognize Error and Deception

Once the foundations are laid, you must move on to becoming a discerning warrior.

> And every spirit that does not confess that Jesus Christ has come in the flesh is not of God. And this is the spirit of the Antichrist, which you have heard was coming, and is now already in the world. You are of God, little children, and have overcome them, because He who is in you is greater than he who is in the world. They are of the world. Therefore they speak as of the world, and the world hears them. We are of God. He who knows God hears us; he who is not of God does not hear us. By this we know the spirit of truth and the spirit of error.
>
> —1 John 4:3–6

This invading spirit is possibly the number-one bondage in the church. It is not simply a bad habit. Believing a lie, repeating a lie, gossiping about a lie, and embracing a lie open you up to a demon named the spirit of error. You open your life up to the control of the enemy!

As I've traveled to churches across this country and meet with people, I'm amazed at the strange, mutated doctrines that people have embraced and cling to stubbornly. They have been captured by a lie.

The devil is a liar, and it is in his nature to lie. That's why embracing only truth is so important to the Christian. Dr. Neil Anderson began his splendid best seller *The Bondage Breaker* with this statement: "Freedom from spiritual conflicts and bondage [spiritual warfare] is not a power encounter; it's a truth encounter."[1] We must understand that most spiritual warfare is over the moment the truth is embraced by the individual. This is why it's important to face the fact that we are engaged in warfare and that the enemy's greatest weapon against us is a lie.

Almost, but Not Quite

Imagine you were the stationmaster of a state-of-the-art railroad. Your job is to see that the computers and train schedules run perfectly. What would be more dangerous—a clock that was five hours off or a clock that was thirty seconds off? Of course, if a clock were five hours off, any one of your employees (and customers!) would notice the error, and it would be corrected. However, a thirty-second error could cost hundreds of lives in a fast-paced, busy switching station!

Something that looks awfully close to the truth is more dangerous than a blatant, obvious lie. I find this to be all too true in the framework of church life, both through doctrinal error being taught and in the poor judgment of those who listen to and embrace this error. Believing something "nearly true" has opened too many believers up to evil strongholds in their lives.

Paul speaks of this: "Though we walk in the flesh, we do not war according to the flesh" (2 Cor. 10:3). It is too easy to blame a fellow Christian if you have personal struggles and conflict. However, most often your problem is with the enemy: "We wrestle not against flesh and blood" (Eph. 6:12, KJV). Although it seems we spend so much of our time fussing, fighting, talking, griping, grunting, running, arguing, and discussing problems of the flesh, we are not in a battle against each other in the church!

A half-truth is a lie; telling part of the story is a lie. There are no gray areas with God: "Casting down arguments and every high thing that exalts itself against the knowledge of God, bringing every thought into captivity to the obedience of Christ" (2 Cor. 10:5). I believe every stronghold in a person's life begins with a lie.

THE ROOT OF ERROR

Jesus said, "You are of your father the devil, and the desires of your father you want to do. He was a murderer from the beginning, and does not stand in the truth, because there is no truth in him. When he speaks a lie, he speaks from his own resources, for he is a liar and the father of it" (John 8:44). Whether it is the New Age movement, humanism, or whatever the source may be, lies and error are birthed from Satan, who is the father of all lies. Make a note of this—there is no innocent lying, no innocent gossiping, no innocent whispering! These things open the door to the enemy. If you participate in them, your old nature, your flesh, is still being governed by Satan, the father of lies.

The words of James are very bold concerning our use of our tongues: "But no man can tame the tongue. It is an unruly evil, full of deadly poison" (James 3:8). You can easily picture the image of a lying tongue as a flaming inferno, destroying everything in its path! When you put a lie on your lips and begin to communicate that lie, at that moment you have "brimstone breath"! You will likely injure not only yourself but also those around you.

Christians often get sucked into the most simple half-truths and doctrines of error. Have any of these examples crept into your life and conversation?

- Old wives' tales and superstitions
- Friday the thirteenth
- Not walking under a ladder
- "Lucky" rabbit's foot
- Wearing crystals
- Reading horoscopes
- Watching or listening to talk shows or "reality" shows (blindly listening without verifying the truth)

You don't need a rabbit's foot or a good luck charm to have a blessing. "My God shall supply all your need according to His riches in glory by Christ Jesus" (Phil. 4:19). Some Christians have told themselves that simply reading their horoscope every day is an innocent practice, but they open themselves up to the lies of the enemy. We receive a clear warning to "reject profane and old wives' fables, and exercise yourself toward godliness" (1 Tim. 4:7).

More lies run rampant in our entertainment culture today. While recreation is a good thing, many Christians spend their movie dollars on movies that contain questionable content. Over time they find it doesn't make them as uncomfortable as it once did. The fornication, the sodomy, the vulgar talk, the extreme violence...before long you have been softened up to the lie.

Then there is the "respectable" sin of gossip. Watch out when someone begins their conversation with "I'm not gossiping, but..." or "Have you heard about so-and-so? Let me tell you so you can pray..." You had better watch it when you hear that! This has its roots in the spirit of error also. If you indulge yourself and encourage such gossip, you are immediately open to a stronghold. By listening, you take up that other person's offense. Soon you continue the cycle by spreading it to family and friends. The original ones offended are still not speaking to each other, and now peripheral people are involved. What's happening? Strongholds—of bitterness, anger, rage, and division—are rising in the minds and hearts of others around you!

So what do you do when someone comes to you with a tale of someone who's wronged them? Simply this: "Dear friend, Matthew 18 says if you have an offense against someone, go to them. Try to restore the fellowship with that brother or sister!" In my experience, most reasonable people can work out their conflicts if they will just sit down together and give that a try. When no attempt at reconciliation is made, all kinds of anger and imaginations occur. Paranoia and despair can creep in.

We are all going to get offended at one time or another. The interesting thing is that most of the time the offense isn't worth fretting about! When a situation or conflict worries you, consider if you were told you had an inoperable tumor tomorrow. Would the conflict still seem as huge and pressing? Sometimes when we are so close to something it looks like it is the end of the world, but in God's perspective, it's not worth losing fellowship with a brother!

Of course, if you and a brother aren't able to work through a problem one on one, then the Bible says you should take a mutual friend and sit down together. If that doesn't solve it, then you ask the church to assist you with it. Until those steps are followed, nobody else needs to hear about the problem, talk through it, or send it through the gossip vine!

THE STRENGTH OF ERROR

Error is a pervasive disease. So much of what we see and hear through media is nothing but out-and-out lies. That's why we need to be zealous for the truth in living it as well as embracing it and preaching it to those who are around us. Those in the grip of error often do not see it. We must bring them to the light of truth. Those who are growing in the Lord will be able to discern error.

The spirit of the Antichrist is at work in our nation. This spirit denies the deity of Christ and stands against everything we believe in. It breeds lawlessness and the breakdown of society. Secular humanism is the polite name we give to this spirit of error.

Dr. Bill Bright, the late director of Campus Crusade for Christ, once said, "Have you ever wondered why our society is becoming more secular, why prayer and Bible reading are no longer welcome at our public schools? The religion of humanism is largely responsible. Have you ever wondered why Americans are much more tolerant today of sexual freedom, homosexuality, incest, and abortion? The religion of humanism is largely responsible."[2]

James 5:19–20 warns us that error leads to death: "Brethren, if anyone among you wanders from the truth, and someone turns him back, let him know that he who turns a sinner from the error of his way will save a soul from death and cover a multitude of sins." The moment we correct a lie or refuse to embrace one, we are fighting against sin multiplying. However, if we allow the lie to run rampant, we are going to see corpses falling, spiritually, all around us.

I think of the childhood story of the scorpion and the frog. The scorpion asked the frog to carry him across the river. The reluctant frog, fearing the death-dealing sting, tried to politely decline, but he was finally convinced by the eloquent words of the scorpion. In the middle of the river, the scorpion stung the frog. "Why did you do that? Now we will both die!" cried the frog as he felt the poison sear through his body. The scorpion answered, "But it is in my nature to sting."

It is the nature of Satan to destroy. Perhaps you are reading this book and have even refused the gift of salvation that Christ freely gives. Perhaps you have lived for years proclaiming yourself to be a Christian, but inwardly you know there has never been a true change in your life. If this is you, pray this prayer now:

> *Lord, forgive me for believing a lie for so long. I now believe that without Christ I am lost. I receive His death and resurrection as my only hope. I accept Jesus as Lord and Savior of my life. In Jesus's name, amen.*

Others reading here may be feeling the temptations offered in the infectious pull of error. Do not listen to that scorpion! Allow yourself to embrace only the truth. Stand on the living Word of God and the righteous truths it contains—you can live and love life on its principles! Let your prayer be this:

In Jesus's name I bind the spirit of error, and I command you to leave my mind. I refuse and reject all lies and twisted thoughts you have brought to me. I here and now loose in my life the Spirit of truth. I love You, Jesus, and thank You for helping me be free from the lies.

chapter 20

THE STRATEGY OF PERVERSION

THE SPIRIT OF whoredom and the spirit of perversion often work hand in hand. These demons, or strongmen, lead to sexual immorality. These demons hate humanity and are attacking today's youth with great force. In America, these spirits have taken over the entertainment media on every level. Our nation of young people idolizes and applauds the entertainers, many of whom are demonized by these entities.

Tiger Woods, golf pro and no doubt the greatest golfer to ever play the game, had it all. Just a few months ago the entire world envied Woods. It seemed as if Tiger had everything—money, fame, influence, and a beautiful wife and children. But after a simple one-car accident we learned that Tiger Woods had a sex addiction. This addiction cost him millions of dollars in endorsements, and now his popularity is limited to the scope of the recent scandal and tabloid speculation.

Michael Jackson, celebrated as the King of Pop, died last year after a decade or more of extreme controversy over having questionable relationships with children. In some of the suits against Jackson the evidence was so overwhelming that he settled out of court, claiming that he didn't want the public exposure. The exposure came nonetheless, and Jackson's financial kingdom crumbled in front of our eyes.

Still, the public raced to buy tickets to Jackson's "This Is It" tour. Even in death the movie/documentary of this final concert made millions of dollars, which, of course, is useless to Jackson now.

American college student Amanda Knox was found guilty of murdering her British roommate in Italy and was given a twenty-six-year prison sentence. Knox seemed to have everything any young woman could desire, including intelligence and beauty. After a demonic night saturated in the deepest perversion, Knox and her boyfriend sexually assaulted and killed Meredith Kercher.[1] Amanda Knox's life is over, and all she could do when the verdict was read was weep and murmur, "No, no!"[2] But it was too late.

I've personally seen the massive AIDS graveyards in third-world countries, testifying to the death-dealing results of trafficking with demons of perversion. Often people never expect these sins to be their problem, yet they end up trapped.

You may have settled into a comfort zone as you saw the heading to this chapter, thinking, "I don't have problems with sexual sins. I've never been a prostitute or visited one. I've pretty much stayed away from pornography and cheap novels. Surely this chapter doesn't have application for me."

However, the spirit of whoredom has at its core the problem of idolatry. Anything that takes over your life can become an idol. This includes career, sports, a person, a worthy cause or project, food, TV, hobbies, or sex. First Corinthians 6:12 puts it plainly: "All things are lawful for me, but all things are not helpful. All things are lawful for me, but I will not be brought under the power of any." Those controlled by whoredom and perversion have more than simply a sexual problem; there are always root causes in the mind and spirit of a person that lead to these outward actions.

THE FORMING OF IDOLS

In the Ten Commandments, God began with a fundamental instruction: "Thou shalt have no other gods before me.... I the LORD thy God, am a jealous God" (Exod. 20:3, 5, KJV).

Manifestations of the spirits of whoredom and perversion begin when you give yourself over to anything above the Lord. When you sell out your heart's devotion to anything less than the Lord Jesus Christ, you prostitute your life. You are selling out for less than God's best. The Bible reveals many reasons why whoredom and perversion gain entry into one's life.

Parental failure

Abuse in any form has tragic results that can later cause a child to form wrong attachments, even into adulthood. For this reason let's define child abuse as, "Any recent act or failure to act on the part of a parent or caretaker which results in death, serious physical or emotional harm, sexual abuse or exploitation; or an act or failure to act which presents an imminent risk of serious harm."[3]

We have led former prostitutes to deliverance through our ministry and discovered that most were victims of sexual abuse at the hand of their father, stepfather, or some other authority figure. Others were victims of date rape at one time or another. Satan gained entry through that abuse. Most homosexuals that I have counseled were also victims of early sexual encounters and abuse. Others simply had no male role model or were emotionally abused by fathers. Generational curses follow bad parental behavior.

Sexual problems in marriage

If a couple is not enjoying a healthy sex life, the deprived mate is placed under the attack of the enemy. Temptation can follow to draw the flesh into sin. The Bible says, "Do not deprive one another except with consent for a time, that you may give yourselves to fasting and prayer; and come together again so that Satan does not tempt you because of your lack of self-control" (1 Cor. 7:5).

There is a progression that occurs: wrong desires, enticement, wrong acts, sin, and then death. "But each one is tempted when he is drawn away by his own desires and enticed. Then, when desire has conceived, it gives birth to sin; and sin, when it is full-grown, brings forth death" (James 1:14–15).

Today we can find sexual opportunity everywhere. The Internet has become a new place to solicit evil. Pornography is readily available, and chat rooms can be a breeding ground for illicit affairs.

Early exposure to sexually explicit material

The enemy wants to pollute the mind, and the younger the person, the better. Even children can access the worst of materials, and this early exposure can open the door to demonic spirits. Television, movies, and the Internet are portholes into the minds of both young and old, and there's no escaping the necessity of each in our age of information. Students are assigned homework on the Internet, and their entire educational and social structure is built around information technology. Workers in every arena are working via the Internet. In other words, hiding from technology is not the answer.

Technology is not evil; it's neutral. Obviously we don't want to turn the clock back to 1955 when a lot of people refused technology, seeing it as a source for potential evil. But we must stand guard against the enemy, realizing that Satan wants to utterly destroy our families and our lives.

We need to be accountable to our wives and husbands. Parents must set parental controls on their computers, monitor television programs and movies, and guard against any temptation. Grandparents must consider their influence, as more grandparents are serving as surrogate parents. Something as innocent and even helpful as social networks on the Internet can create avenues for sexual perversion to infiltrate our homes. Consider this personal example from a dear friend of mine:

> A few nights ago my young son was visiting his grandmother. One of his favorite activities is playing an online video game. A friend at school, who we now know suffered from abuse at home, told my son to go to a Web site. This name of the Web site sounded harmless to my son (as it would to anyone), but when he visited this Web site (unsupervised and without security controls), he was shocked at what he saw. He ran to his grandmother crying and confessed. This incident could have been prevented with parental controls and better monitoring. After rewarding my son for his confession, we all confessed that there had been a breakdown in our monitoring system and prayed with my son.

An undisciplined devotional life

Those who are committed to Jesus Christ and seek Him daily will likely remain untouched by spirits of perversion. Believers must live a life of self-control and stay away from things that tempt the flesh. Seeking God daily means an active prayer life that includes thankfulness and praise. Angels inhabit the praises of God, and in our daily devotion to God there is protection! Seeking God daily also means an active study life. The Bible illuminates our world and exposes the enemy.

Occult involvement

This is a doorway into whoredoms. Jezebel was deeply into occult practices although she sat on the throne of Israel, a nation founded by God. She seduced God's servants and usurped the kingdom from its proper leadership. Those whom we have counseled into freedom from occult practices and witchcraft have all told me of sexual encounters that were a part of their initiation.

There is a connection between spiritual rebellion and whoredom. Many ministers and church members fall victim to the spirit of whoredom when they rebel against God's will. By stepping outside of God's protection because of our disobedience, we hand demons the keys to our self-control and eventually our reputation.

Society is extremely interested in the occult. It seems like on every television channel ghost hunters and witch doctors are studied, believed, and even imitated. In southeastern Tennessee there are several groups that now call themselves ghost hunters who go everywhere there is said to be a haunting.

Consider this definition of *the occult*: "A twisted draconian knowledge of the paranormal opposed to the knowledge of God through Christ Jesus."

LESSONS FROM HOSEA

The Book of Hosea is an unusual book. The entire story of this prophet's life is framed around his marriage to Gomer, a harlot and a prostitute. Hosea endured the agony of loving a woman who was controlled by such a spirit. Gomer gave Hosea three sons, the last of which was named "not mine." Gomer was sexually addicted and left him to become a temple prostitute to the god Baal; she would have probably died in her life as a slave had Hosea not mercifully and lovingly bought her and brought her back to him. Her life of adultery was a picture of Israel's unfaithfulness to God.

You see, when a person walks away from God, it becomes easy to walk away from every other important commitment in life. The Book of Hosea marks the course of one taken in the spirit of whoredom. Notice the seven steps downward:

    1. The person taken in this spirit doesn't know God
       (Hosea 5:4).

2. He or she violates His laws (Hosea 4:2–3).

3. Destruction comes upon him or her (Hosea 4:6).

4. Prosperity becomes a means to evil instead of to blessing (Hosea 4:7).

5. People idolize things other than God (Hosea 4:12).

6. Church becomes hypocrisy (Hosea 4:15).

7. God then punishes the one controlled by the spirit of harlotry and whoredoms (Hosea 4:9).

The New Testament also relates this downward course of the sinner. A clear path toward judgment is evident in those who follow whoredom and perversion. Romans 1:17–32 lists them this way:

1. Refusal to live by faith (v. 17)
2. Rejection of God (vv. 18–22)
3. Exchanging God's glory for an idol (vv. 21–23)
4. Exchanging God's truth for lies (vv. 24–25)
5. Embracing sexual perversion (vv. 26–27)
6. Being released by God to their devices (v. 28)
7. The destruction of society (vv. 29–32)

Those who fall into this destructive path make a huge exchange. This exchange is mentally justified based on instant gratification and temporary emotional and physical pleasure that cannot and will not last. The judgment of God upon them is threefold. He gives them up to uncleanness, vile passion, and a reprobate mind.

The ramifications of these destructive strongholds reach into two areas. First, a person opens up his or her life to destruction. This is followed by moral failure, mental anguish, and emotional hell. Physical and mental dangers such as disease, depression, and AIDS can even bring death.

It was Lord Byron, the great poet, who wrote of his own moral failures and their consequences:

My days are in the yellow leaf;
The flowers and fruits of love are gone;
The worm, the canker, and the grief,
Are mine alone![4]

The basic tenets of society disintegrate following moral reprobation. The demons of whoredom undermine family and societal norms, causing havoc. What are social norms? Social norms are no longer clearly defined for *anyone* unplugged from the church body. Our television and our government are redefining social norms with clever and entertaining marketing. Even unfaithful Christians are finding themselves believing perpetuating lies at church and at work because their sense of social norms is skewed. The latest example of this is Cindy McCain posing for a photography shoot wearing duct tape over her mouth in support for gay marriage and NOH8, a photographic protest against Proposition 8, which bans gay marriage and was passed in California in 2008.[5] Despite all of the PR cleanup by the Republican Party, it sent shock waves through the GOP.

Divorce rates are as high inside the church as they are outside the walls of our often-gated city. This only further proves the influence of the twisted media and current governmental vision of what it means to be a family. Crumbling marriages and broken children testify to the destructive power of perversion.

BINDING THE IDOLATRY

To overcome this evil stronghold, you must first be certain Jesus is Lord of your life. Examine your heart and determine if He reigns on the throne of your life. Have you withheld any desires or areas of your heart and mind from Him? Yield them to His will.

Secondly, tear every idol out of your heart. If there is anything that you invest more time, talent, and passion in than you do in your love for God, consider its place as an idol and deal with it immediately!

Lastly, bind the spirits of harlotry and whoredoms that may have taken root in your life. Take a moment and pray:

Lord Jesus, forgive me for allowing anything or anyone but You to rule over my life. I confess that You alone have the right to be Lord. I reject every lie of Satan and every idol he has brought into my life. In Jesus's name, I bind these destructive spirits and ask You to cleanse my life of every wrong they have brought. Thank You for freedom. In Jesus's name, amen.

chapter 21

THE STRATEGY OF
CONFUSION

THE PROMISE TO all of us in the church is the flow of God's presence. This flow is pictured by river and streams.

> On the last day, that great day of the feast, Jesus stood and cried out, saying, "If anyone thirsts, let him come to Me and drink. He who believes in Me, as the Scripture has said, out of his heart will flow rivers of living water." But this He spoke concerning the Spirit, whom those believing in Him would receive; for the Holy Spirit was not yet given, because Jesus was not yet glorified.
>
> —JOHN 7:37–39

> There is a river whose streams shall make glad the city of God.
>
> —PSALM 46:4

When we gather in unity and worship, streams flow together from our hearts and ministry power flows. There should be a flow in your spirit, yet often the flow is hindered by hidden spirits. Let's look at the spirit of Leviathan and learn to deal with his snare of confusion.

Leviathan is first mentioned in the Book of Job.

> May those curse it who curse the day, those who are ready to arouse Leviathan.
>
> —JOB 3:8

> Can you draw out Leviathan with a hook, or snare his tongue with a line which you lower? Can you put a reed through his nose, or pierce his jaw with a hook? Will he make many supplications to you? Will he speak softly to you? Will he make a covenant with you? Will you take him as a servant forever? Will you play with him as with a bird, or will you leash him for your maidens? Will your companions make a banquet of him? Will they apportion him among the merchants?
>
> —JOB 41:1–6

Then we see Leviathan mentioned again in the Book of Isaiah.

> In that day the LORD with His severe sword, great and strong, will punish Leviathan the fleeing serpent, Leviathan that twisted serpent; and He will slay the reptile that is in the sea.
>
> —ISAIAH 27:1

And again in the Book of Psalms: "There the ships sail about; there is that Leviathan which You have made to play there" (Ps. 104:26).

Here is an animal that is symbolic of evil. This Leviathan is a giant spirit that blocks the flow of God's purpose, power, and prosperity in your life. The name literally means "to twist." He is the monster demonic force that twists everything to hinder the flow of God. He is called the twisting serpent. According to *Easton's Illustrated Bible Dictionary*, Leviathan is used figuratively for a "cruel enemy."[1] *Brown-Driver-Briggs Hebrew Lexicon* says that this is a dragon not unlike a dinosaur, a beast that is hostile to God's people.[2]

For us, Leviathan and his characteristics are a picture of a large but hidden enemy in the church that chokes off the flow! Let's take a closer look at what Job tells us about a hidden spirit, taking a minute to read the first nine verses of Job 41. Here Scripture tells us the strong characteristics of Leviathan. Scripture speaks of a formidable, frightening spirit, one who is not easily detected or caught through natural means. In the flesh, no human can do battle with him.

HERE IS CHURCH ENEMY #1!

Why do I say he is the number-one enemy of the church? Look closer. He is hidden: can you "draw out...with a hook, or snare...with a line"? He hides underneath the water. Water in the Bible represents several things:

1. The Word
2. The flow of God's will
3. The mass of humanity

Leviathan tries to hide where the Word and the flow of God's Spirit are moving among people. We often do not observe his work until many are hurt. He is hidden until exposed by God.

Another reason he is our number-one enemy is that he will not live in covenant. When someone is affected by this spirit, it destroys covenant relationships. This spirit breaks up marriages, business partnerships, friendships, and, worst of all, churches. If you cannot get along, it may be Leviathan. Now stay with me. I will show you in a moment that this is nobody's fault.

This coiling serpent twists the truth. Look again at Isaiah 27:1: "...that twisted serpent..." Here is how this deceiving spirit operates. Something is said from the Word, and before you hear it, he twists it! You hear it wrong. Maybe you speak to your mate about an issue meaning good, but he or she is angered by it. Some decision is made in church, and "it is what it is"; yet you feel there must be more. Or someone infected with Leviathan twists what has been said and creates division. (Remember Adam and Eve.) This serpent gets between you and me and twists the truth. He gets between friends and marital partners and twists. He gets into church life and twists.

Perhaps Leviathan is similar to the crocodile. A crocodile is dangerous as the water rises, but during droughts a crocodile may change locations to find water. The crocodile is cold-blooded, so its metabolism is partially based on its environment; therefore, for the crocodile to cool itself it must be in the water or cake itself in mud.

If water in this example symbolizes the move of God's Spirit, then let's examine how frightening Leviathan can be when compared to a crocodile. The crocodile knows that its potential prey will always follow the water, so the crocodile's entire economy is based on hiding and feasting in and around its food, often appearing harmless for many days.

But in an instant the crocodile takes its prey and twists it around until it takes the life out of it. The strike is extremely fast. After the crocodile twists its prey, it drowns its victims underneath the muddy waters. The enemy will take good people and twist them until confusion comes, then he buries them in the abyss, leaving no chance for escape.

We also see in Isaiah 27:1 that he attacks first, then flees. This is why people will often leave a mate, leave a church, and leave a friendship. He puts a spirit of fleeing in them or, better said, a quitting and running attitude in people. Because most people are unaware of this choking, strangling spirit, they often feel as if they have no choice other than to leave the dreadful situation. So in a state of panic and confusion, they run in an attempt for clarity.

Leviathan has attacked motherhood. A twisted form of feminism through the media appears to empower women innocently, but in reality women are shunning the responsibility of child rearing in the name of freedom. Women are escaping motherhood either altogether with the diabolical practice of abortion or simply giving their kids to ex-husbands and grandparents to raise. America's young women, thanks to examples like Britney Spears, are being twisted and confused.

The previous generation has often been labeled "fatherless" because of millions of fathers who walked away from their responsibilities. We can only assume that this next generation has a potential of being both motherless and fatherless—spiritual orphans who can naturally be the easiest prey for demonic forces.

Leviathan is attacking our schools. Even after prayer was taken from school and a misunderstood interpretation of the separation of church and state was implemented, parents could rest knowing that our children would be taught basic freedoms and the values that made this country great.

Instead, even in the Bible Belt, a precedent is being set for sex education to include teaching homosexuality as an alternate lifestyle. As Christians, our freedom to disagree has been stripped.

The great minds that once led our educational institutions live in fear of being ostracized by the media or losing government funding if they disagree.

Leviathan begins to twist historical records, twists testimonials from professing homosexuals, and twists community support until a school is buried beneath the waves of so-called tolerance. It is evident that Leviathan is alive and well as test scores continue to plummet and our high school students are less educated now than at any other time in history.

THIS ENEMY CAN BE DEFEATED

In that day the LORD with His severe sword, great and strong, will punish Leviathan the fleeing serpent, Leviathan that twisted serpent; and He will slay the reptile that is in the sea.

—ISAIAH 27:1

Leviathan is defeated by the sword of the Lord, which is severe, great, and strong. The Lord's sword is the Word and Spirit, as we see in Ephesians 6:17: "…the sword of the Spirit, which is the word of God." Also we find in Hebrews the sword is discerning: "For the word of God is living and powerful, and sharper than any two-edged sword, piercing even to the division of soul and spirit, and of joints and marrow, and is a discerner of the thoughts and intents of the heart. And there is no creature hidden from His sight, but all things are naked and open to the eyes of Him to whom we must give account" (Heb. 4:12–13).

This sword helps you recognize Leviathan; you cannot without the Holy Spirit and the Word. When the church is determined to let Jesus speak, this sword will operate, and Leviathan will flee!

What must we do? Realize our pride is from the enemy. Look at the last scripture about Leviathan: "He beholds every high thing; he is king over all the children of pride" (Job 41:34). He is king of all pride? Pride keeps us away from God. Pride causes us to be offended easily. Pride causes us to fall. Pride keeps us from God's plan.

As also in all his epistles, speaking in them of these things, in which are some things hard to understand, which untaught and unstable people *twist* to their own *destruction,* as they do also the rest of the Scriptures. You therefore, beloved, since you know this beforehand, beware lest you also *fall* from your own steadfastness, being *led away* with the error of the wicked; but grow in the grace and knowledge of our Lord and Savior Jesus Christ. To Him be the glory both now and forever. Amen.

—2 PETER 3:16–18, EMPHASIS ADDED

One final thought. Notice these words—*twist, destruction, fall, led away.* That is the work of Leviathan! How do we defeat him? You just read the answer—grow through Scripture, grow in grace (love and forgiveness), and grow in knowledge (intimacy with Jesus).

chapter 22

THE STRATEGY OF BITTERNESS

B ELIEVERS LIVING FULL of the Spirit and in unity flow together like a mighty river of God's power: "There is a river whose streams shall make glad the city of God" (Ps. 46:4).

However, in Revelation we have a description of a specific End Time disaster: "Then the third angel sounded: And a great star fell from heaven, burning like a torch, and it fell on a third of the rivers and on the springs of water. The name of the star is Wormwood. A third of the waters became wormwood, and many men died from the water, because it was made bitter" (Rev. 8:10–11). The Holy Spirit revealed to me that this event has a spiritual application.

Here is a "falling star" that defiles the rivers and the springs of water! The river is God's flow, and the springs represent the Holy Spirit in God's people: "But whoever drinks of the water that I shall give him will never thirst. But the water that I shall give him will become in him a fountain of water springing up into everlasting life" (John 4:14).

Wormwood is the Greek word *absinthos*. Here is a demon fallen to the earth to poison the water and to spread death over God's life-giving rivers. In the Old Testament we find this same demon mentioned: "So that there may not be among you man or woman or family or tribe, whose heart turns away today from the LORD our God, to go and serve the gods of these nations, and that there may not be among you a root bearing bitterness or wormwood" (Deut. 29:18).

Let's look at the words *bitterness* and *wormwood*: bitterness, originally *rosh*, means "head of poison"; it was used for venom from a snake or poison from the head of a plant. *Wormwood*, originally *laanah*, refers to a poison that curses!

When *absinthos* comes, it makes a person bitter, and the results are horrific!

Absinthos Starts Small

> Where do wars and fights come from among you? Do they not come from your desires for pleasure that war in your members? You lust and do not have. You murder and covet and cannot obtain. You fight and war. Yet you do not have because you do not ask. You ask and do not receive, because you ask amiss, that you may spend it on your pleasures. Adulterers and adulteresses! Do you not know that friendship with the world is enmity with God? Whoever therefore wants to be a friend of the world makes himself an enemy of God. Or do you think that the Scripture says in vain, "The Spirit who dwells in us yearns jealously"?
>
> —James 4:1–5

Notice, it is words that engender bitterness. We learned that Leviathan, that twisting spirit, can cause confusion. When confusion comes, bitterness follows.

> You are snared by the words of your mouth; you are taken by the words of your mouth.
>
> —Proverbs 6:2

> A worthless person, a wicked man, walks with a perverse mouth; he winks with his eyes, he shuffles his feet, he points with his fingers; perversity is in his heart, he devises evil continually, he sows discord. Therefore his calamity shall come suddenly; suddenly he shall be broken without remedy. These six things the Lord hates, yes, seven are an abomination to Him: a proud look, a lying tongue, hands that shed innocent blood, a heart that devises wicked plans, feet that are swift in running to evil, a false witness who speaks lies, and one who sows discord among brethren.
>
> —Proverbs 6:12–19

Absinthos Spreads Quickly

Bitterness spreads quickly from one person to the next; just as a small spark in the woods can kindle a forest fire, so does *absinthos* do her work. Notice that bitterness defiles the entire body; a little bitterness can poison and weaken the entire church body. "The roads to Zion mourn because no one comes to the set feasts. All her gates are desolate; her priests sigh, her virgins are afflicted, and she is in bitterness" (Lam. 1:4).

Absinthos Hinders Blessing and Brings Curses

Absinthos stops the flow of blessing that we should be releasing on each other. That's right. We should be releasing blessing on each other! We are accustomed to sitting in our sanctuaries like babies in a high chair crying, "Feed me, Daddy." We place the responsibility of our spiritual nurturing on our pastors, teachers, and church leadership. We fail to see the tremendous blessing in engaging, learning, fellowshiping, and blessing those sitting next to us because we are too busy trying to figure out if they are in the same sphere of influence or maybe their socioeconomic status. Or maybe we are holding their past over their head.

Jealousy in the churches between worship leaders, pastors, life-group teachers, and deacons creates bitterness and reduces the flow of God's Spirit from a river to a trickle. A life-group leader was encouraging a minister from another local ministry who was full of bitterness. The bitter minister was bad-mouthing that the number in their meeting place was low. The life-group teacher offered some administrative advice based on the success of his life group. The minister full of bitterness barked, "I don't teach some little life group. I have a ministry." He failed to see the value or receive the blessing from a fellow combatant!

Bitterness stemming from jealousy and pride prevents us from hearing the ways to improve our lives, businesses, and ministries.

> Therefore submit to God. Resist the devil and he will flee from you. Draw near to God and He will draw near to you. Cleanse your hands, you sinners; and purify your hearts, you double-minded. Lament and mourn and weep! Let your laughter be turned to mourning and your joy to gloom. Humble yourselves in the sight of the Lord, and

He will lift you up. Do not speak evil of one another, brethren. He who speaks evil of a brother and judges his brother, speaks evil of the law and judges the law. But if you judge the law, you are not a doer of the law but a judge. There is one Lawgiver, who is able to save and to destroy. Who are you to judge another?

—JAMES 4:7–12

Absinthos is poison that is deadly to your spiritual life and hinders you from bringing forth the fruit from God. You cannot curse and bless at the same time. We come to church and say the repetitive "God bless you," then go home and verbally murder fellow co-workers, church members, teachers, students, and even our spouse, subliminally teaching our children the art of murder. And sometimes in this same moment we bless our food. Consequently, constant reports of food tainted with disease find their way into our homes and restaurants, and stomach and intestinal medication is prescribed now more than ever. Meanwhile, our murderous conversations reverberate off the walls and back into our lives.

Another exhausted but popular Christian saying if someone asks how you are doing is to say, "I'm blessed and highly favored." A murderous tongue is not blessed or favored, and God hates a lying tongue! Next time you hear "God bless you" or "I'm blessed and highly favored," do not judge the statement but ask yourself, "Is my mouth allowing me to be blessed, and do I have God's favor based on my conversation?"

ABSINTHOS IS THE WISDOM FROM HELL UNLEASHED

Now we see the source of this spirit more clearly. It is:

- Earthly (*epigeios*)—that which is on the whole earth

- Sensual (*psache*)—this came from your soul and emotion, not your spirit

- Demonic (*daimonia*)—this comes from demonic oppression! This spirit opens the door to envy, self-seeking, confusion, and every evil thing, which now have access

HOW CAN WE WALK IN FREEDOM
FROM *ABSINTHOS*?

First, we must walk in the Spirit using pure, peaceable wisdom from above.

> Who is wise and understanding among you? Let him show by good conduct that his works are done in the meekness of wisdom. But if you have bitter envy and self-seeking in your hearts, do not boast and lie against the truth. This wisdom does not descend from above, but is earthly, sensual, demonic. For where envy and self-seeking exist, confusion and every evil thing are there. But the wisdom that is from above is first pure, then peaceable, gentle, willing to yield, full of mercy and good fruits, without partiality and without hypocrisy. Now the fruit of righteousness is sown in peace by those who make peace.
>
> —JAMES 3:13–18

We need God to speak to our bitterness. He will bring forgiveness and release blessing in our lives. The fruit of the Spirit will flow.

To walk in freedom, we must put away wrong words as instructed in Ephesians 4:31: "Let all bitterness, wrath, anger, clamor, and evil speaking be put away from you, with all malice."

Also, we must show forgiveness and pardon others. I like the word *pardon* because when one is pardoned, his or her crime is no longer subject to further inquiry, scrutiny, discussion, or explanation. If someone is pardoned from a prison sentence, he or she was once in jail and now is out of jail. It's that simple. In today's English, we allow others "off the hook." Ephesians 4:32 says it this way: "And be kind to one another, tenderhearted, forgiving one another, just as God in Christ forgave you."

Finally, we must pursue peace—run after it, chase it down, use all our resources to live in peace with each other. The word *peace* means that everyone in a society or relationship operates harmoniously. Notice that it doesn't mean we operate the same. We celebrate our godly differences in our common pursuit of righteousness instead of demanding cookie-cutter Christians who look, act, and think exactly the same way.

> Pursue peace with all people, and holiness, without which no one
> will see the Lord: looking diligently lest anyone fall short of the
> grace of God; lest any root of bitterness springing up cause trouble,
> and by this many become defiled.
>
> —Hebrews 12:14–15

This means we do not let bad talk, unforgiveness, or poison take root in our lives. Get rid of it and choose peace! Notice the phrase "cause trouble." The word *trouble* in the Greek is *enochleo*, which means "to be harassed by a mob."

When the Church Becomes a Mob would be a great title for a different book altogether. How many ministers have suffered at the hands of a tyrannical mob? Even our American forefathers feared the tyranny of uncontrolled masses with misinformation as much as they feared the tyranny of kings. In fact, our governmental structure is partially based on such fears.

In revolutionary France, King Louis XVI and his wife, Marie Antoinette, were beheaded in part because of unabated tabloids that exaggerated the monarch's personal lives. The next four years were some of the bloodiest in French history, as more than forty thousand people died at the guillotine.[1] Each following French government failed, again, partially due to rumors and exaggerations, murderous whispers that created death and chaos. Finally, instead of king, instead of a democracy, the French allowed themselves to be placed under the boot of Napoleon Bonaparte, who is considered by some historians a despot.

There is nothing peaceful about a rumor-filled mob. How many churches have exchanged peace for the despotic Satan?

So the bottom line is, partake, put away, pardon, and pursue; then your life will know peace!

chapter 23

THE STRATEGY OF DEATH

L ET US CONTINUE exposing some hidden spirits that hinder the flow of God. In this chapter we will focus first on Cain, the firstborn of Adam and Eve; though a gift from God, he turned to the enemy: "Not as Cain who was of the wicked one and murdered his brother. And why did he murder him? Because his works were evil and his brother's righteous" (1 John 3:12). As in the case of Jezebel, we find the demon spirit on him still operating in the New Testament.

> But these speak evil of whatever they do not know; and whatever they know naturally, like brute beasts, in these things they corrupt themselves. Woe to them! For they have gone in the way of Cain, have run greedily in the error of Balaam for profit, and perished in the rebellion of Korah.
>
> —JUDE 10–11

There are those who choose "the way of Cain." Cain is known for murdering his brother Abel in a worship war!

> By faith Abel offered to God a more excellent sacrifice than Cain, through which he obtained witness that he was righteous, God testifying of his gifts; and through it he being dead still speaks.
>
> —HEBREWS 11:4

Abel was a man of faith, while Cain operated in his own strength. Today the killing is done by words, not weapons. Hate is not an emotion; it is an action. Wrong words and false reports can kill others. Look again at the ancient account in Jude, and examine if this spirit has attacked you and your church.

This spirit characteristically operates within families: "Now Adam knew Eve his wife, and she conceived and bore Cain, and said, 'I have acquired a man from the LORD.' Then she bore again, this time his brother Abel. Now Abel was a keeper of sheep, but Cain was a tiller of the ground" (Gen. 4:1–2). Cain had issues not with those outside of his family but with those of his own house. How often has the flow been hindered because of conflict in the family? When I say "family," I am referring as well to the church, which is God's family.

This spirit also rejects leadership and believes it has a better way of doing things.

> And in the process of time it came to pass that Cain brought an offering of the fruit of the ground to the LORD. Abel also brought of the firstborn of his flock and of their fat. And the LORD respected Abel and his offering.
>
> —GENESIS 4:3–4

God had clearly instructed the early family that He could only be approached by a blood sacrifice. At the gate of Eden between the cherubim who guarded its gate, Jehovah shed the blood of animals to clothe our ancient parents. Cain rejected the instruction of his authority, Adam and Eve, and thought he had a better way.

In the church family there are always "Monday morning quarterbacks" or "second guessers," people who are quick to criticize decisions. Honest disagreement is welcomed if offered in the right spirit; however, rebellion that attacks and undermines leadership is witchcraft. Witchcraft, as we've discussed, is a part of the occult that carries a host of other demonic strongmen.

Notice this spirit expresses anger and sarcasm: "But He did not respect Cain and his offering. And Cain was very angry, and his countenance fell" (Gen. 4:5). This killing spirit will not receive correction, as was displayed by Cain. Knowing he was wrong, Cain did not repent. Instead he got angry, and it showed on his face.

This same spirit can be seen in the story of the prodigal son: "And he said to him, 'Your brother has come, and because he has received him safe and sound, your father has killed the fatted calf.' But he was angry and would not go in. Therefore his father came out and pleaded with him" (Luke 15:27–28). When the prodigal came home, it was the older brother who got angry and cut off fellowship. In our local church, hundreds have been baptized, and thousands have received Christ's salvation; yet there are those who will not rejoice because of the spirit of Cain.

As we read further in Genesis, we see that this spirit will not listen to the Word of God: "So the LORD said to Cain, 'Why are you angry? And why has your countenance fallen?'" (Gen. 4:6). Here God's Word came directly to Cain. God told him that all could be remedied, but this spirit cannot receive the Word.

This spirit opens the door to more disastrous spirits: "If you do well, will you not be accepted? And if you do not do well, sin lies at the door. And its desire is for you, but you should rule over it" (Gen. 4:7). God warns us that, like Cain, if we refuse to change, the door will be opened to sin. The Hebrew text indicates that sin is like a ferocious beast ready to leap through the open door. If you as a parent live in this spirit, you will open a door to disaster on your children!

This spirit blocks life: "Now Cain talked with Abel his brother; and it came to pass, when they were in the field, that Cain rose up against Abel his brother and killed him" (Gen. 4:8). Cain murdered Abel, who had done nothing but worship and serve God! This spirit blocks the worship of the church. This is why music ministers struggle.

This spirit strikes at harvest time to disrupt God's plan. Look at verse 8 again: "Now Cain talked with Abel his brother; and it came to pass, when they were in the field, that Cain rose up against Abel his brother and killed him." Cain struck his brother in the field during the harvest. Discord often rises in churches when it is time to harvest. The spirit of Cain not only kills its desired target, but in killing the tiller of the ground, it also kills those who are dependent on the harvest. The spirit of Cain in this sense is a spiritual mass murderer.

During the Great Depression, Joseph Stalin's brand of tyranny dominated Russia, then known as the Soviet Union. During a famine, Stalin was facing assassination attempts and rumors that he might be removed from power. Stalin's paranoia focused on the once politically powerful farming community known as the Kulaks. Stalin sent a small army into the farming community and raided the storehouses of seed for the next spring.

In doing so, Stalin was able to falsely accuse the farmers of hoarding grain. Thousands (later millions) of these farmers were executed. The

Russian people ate a little for a season, but the real famine came later, as there was nothing to plant in the spring.[1]

This spirit brings a curse on the carriers: "Then the LORD said to Cain, 'Where is Abel your brother?' He said, 'I do not know. Am I my brother's keeper?' And He said, 'What have you done? The voice of your brother's blood cries out to Me from the ground. So now you are cursed from the earth, which has opened its mouth to receive your brother's blood from your hand'" (Gen. 4:9–11). When you kill the worship, harvest, and leadership in the church with gossip, talk, and rebellion, you will answer! It will curse you, your family, and your finances.

Is it possible that our national economic woes and wants are due to the attack on the leadership of churches nationwide? Historical precedent seems to indicate that every major attack on the church and leadership results in an economic downturn and even war.

This spirit creates spiritual vagabonds:

> And He [God] said…"When you till the ground, it shall no longer yield its strength to you. A fugitive and a vagabond you shall be on the earth." And Cain said to the LORD, "My punishment is greater than I can bear! Surely You have driven me out this day from the face of the ground; I shall be hidden from Your face; I shall be a fugitive and a vagabond on the earth, and it will happen that anyone who finds me will kill me." And the LORD said to him, "Therefore, whoever kills Cain, vengeance shall be taken on him sevenfold." And the LORD set a mark on Cain, lest anyone finding him should kill him.
>
> —GENESIS 4:10, 12–15

This spirit will not let you find a church home. You will wander around, and wherever you go, you will end up with the same crowd. Your life will be marked by an unsettling spirit.

A spiritually marked person is recognized at every church he or she attends by those with the ability to discern spirits. This mark may also extend into one's professional life outside the walls of the church. Someone with this murderous mark loses friends and family as well, as the spirit of Cain cannot be trusted.

GETTING SET FREE FROM THE SPIRIT OF CAIN

How do you live in freedom from the control and effects of this killing spirit?

Admit your need to harness your tongue.

> Death and life are in the power of the tongue, and those who love it will eat its fruit.
>
> —PROVERBS 18:21

> But I say to you that for every idle word men may speak, they will give account of it in the day of judgment. For by your words you will be justified, and by your words you will be condemned.
>
> —MATTHEW 12:36–37

> If anyone among you thinks he is religious, and does not bridle his tongue but deceives his own heart, this one's religion is useless.
>
> —JAMES 1:26

Ask God to get your heart and thinking right.

> Brood of vipers! How can you, being evil, speak good things? For out of the abundance of the heart the mouth speaks.
>
> —MATTHEW 12:34

> I beseech you therefore, brethren, by the mercies of God, that you present your bodies a living sacrifice, holy, acceptable to God, which is your reasonable service. And do not be conformed to this world, but be transformed by the renewing of your mind, that you may prove what is that good and acceptable and perfect will of God.
>
> —ROMANS 12:1–2

Ask God to cleanse your tongue with fire.

> In the year that King Uzziah died, I saw the Lord sitting on a throne, high and lifted up, and the train of His robe filled the temple. Above it stood seraphim; each one had six wings: with two he covered his face, with two he covered his feet, and with two he flew. And one

cried to another and said: "Holy, holy, holy is the LORD of hosts; the whole earth is full of His glory!" And the posts of the door were shaken by the voice of him who cried out, and the house was filled with smoke.

So I said: "Woe is me, for I am undone! Because I am a man of unclean lips, and I dwell in the midst of a people of unclean lips; for my eyes have seen the King, the LORD of hosts." Then one of the seraphim flew to me, having in his hand a live coal which he had taken with the tongs from the altar. And he touched my mouth with it, and said: "Behold, this has touched your lips; your iniquity is taken away, and your sin purged."

Also I heard the voice of the Lord, saying: "Whom shall I send, and who will go for Us?" Then I said, "Here am I! Send me." And He said, "Go, and tell this people: 'Keep on hearing, but do not understand; keep on seeing, but do not perceive.'"

—ISAIAH 6:1–9

After this encounter Isaiah was ready for service!
Now pray this prayer:

Lord, forgive me for demonstrating the spirit of Cain, the spirit of murder, in my life. I admit that I have been wrong in my attitude toward others, and I repent of all the negative words I have spoken about them.

I commit to You today that with Your help I will change the words I speak from words of cursing to words of blessing. Thank You for giving me the gift of speech that allows me to bless those in my life.

Lord, with Your help I will strive to be a blessing to my family, my church, those in authority over me, and all the others You have placed in my life. Amen.

chapter 24

The Strategy of Pressure

ONE OF THE dangers in spiritual warfare is giving the enemy a way back into your life. In the Old Testament these ways are called "cords of the wicked."

> The LORD is righteous; He has cut in pieces the cords of the wicked. Let all those who hate Zion be put to shame and turned back.
> —PSALM 129:4–5

Here the cords are coiled around the wicked like a snake.

> His own iniquities entrap the wicked man, and he is caught in the cords of his sin. He shall die for lack of instruction, and in the greatness of his folly he shall go astray.
> —PROVERBS 5:22–23

The New Testament identifies the coiling spirit that wraps around us like a rope as "python": "Now it happened, as we went to prayer, that a certain slave girl possessed with a spirit of divination met us, who brought her masters much profit by fortune-telling" (Acts 16:16). Here is a young woman who is being squeezed to death by "python." The enemy desires to coil around you and squeeze the life out of you!

PYTHON—THE VOICE OF THE PAST

The word for this spirit in the Old Testament is '*owb*, which is also "familiar spirits." This girl spoke by demons to consult people who were dead. This manifested in modern day is generational sins, tendencies, failures, and curses.

> You shall be brought down, you shall speak out of the ground; your speech shall be low, out of the dust; your voice shall be like a medium's, out of the ground; and your speech shall whisper out of the dust.
>
> —ISAIAH 29:4

There are entities that try to track through your family history! Let me make it clear that the "pythons" spoke out of the dust or ground. Simply stated, the past wraps around you and tries to squeeze the life out of you.

Our past is dead! Often our past represents death, destruction, and despair. At times we are infected with a nostalgic attitude that strangles the hopes and dreams of tomorrow. This nostalgic attitude infects the church, and we cling to styles of worship and traditional points of view instead of allowing God to do a "new thing." There is a healthy way to build from our past to gain a perspective of our present circumstances in order to build our future.

Let's examine a conversation between God and Moses so that we might catch a hidden glimpse of God's view of a healthy past, present, and future. Moses desperately wanted to see the face of God:

> But He said, "You cannot see My face; for no man shall see Me, and live." And the LORD said, "Here is a place by Me, and you shall stand on the rock. So it shall be, while My glory passes by, that I will put you in the cleft of the rock, and will cover you with My hand while I pass by. Then I will take away My hand, and you shall see My back; but My face shall not be seen."
>
> —EXODUS 33:20–23

It was Moses who chronicled the birth of Planet Earth, the fall of man, and the lives of Abraham, Isaac, and Jacob. No human understood the past better than Moses, and yet Moses wanted to see the face of God because he knew that the only hope of leading God's people to the Promised Land was if God was with him on his journey. Moses knew and understood the triumphs and debacles of the human condition because of his knowledge of the past. Moses's promise was only secured if God's favor was upon him.

As Moses learned, our God is always on the move. Maybe God could have drawn a picture of Himself for Moses or given a written description of His glory. God could have said no to Moses's request. But God gave Moses a certain place at a certain time to show Moses a glimpse of where He'd been.

There is no future in your past because God is always moving forward. We can only linger in halls of our past visiting triumphs and failures to learn from our mistakes, or we will miss what God is doing now and His promise for our future.

Python—the Piling Up of Bad Circumstances

> Terrors overtake him like a flood; a tempest steals him away in the night.
>
> —Job 27:20

In football a team can be penalized for "piling on" after the tackle. The worse "pile on" takes place after a team fumbles the ball. Satan knows no rules. When we make mistakes or spend too long celebrating a victory of the past, he will pile on. The word *flood* in Hebrew means "to be surrounded by waters." The enemy will try to surround you.

Python—the Power of Wrong Relationships

> Do not be deceived: "Evil company corrupts good habits."
>
> —1 Corinthians 15:33

There is something called peer pressure that is no more than a cluster of demons that come together around those who are not living right.

Also, in your own family there can be dream killers. Sometimes the cords of the enemy are momma's apron strings. Sometimes the cords are controlling family members.

Python loves worn-out cultural theology and spends a lot of time surfing apologetic Web sites, debating and arguing, strangling young and insecure Christians with doubt and unbelief. With this, accompanied with peer pressure and dream killers, it's no wonder that python can feel like "a flood." And unless you are grounded in the Word of God, you'll be swept away in a torrent of destruction.

> Now the LORD had said to Abram: "Get out of your country, from your family and from your father's house, to a land that I will show you. I will make you a great nation; I will bless you and make your name great; and you shall be a blessing. I will bless those who bless you, and I will curse him who curses you; and in you all the families of the earth shall be blessed."
>
> So Abram departed as the LORD had spoken to him, and Lot went with him. And Abram was seventy-five years old when he departed from Haran. Then Abram took Sarai his wife and Lot his brother's son, and all their possessions that they had gathered, and the people whom they had acquired in Haran, and they departed to go to the land of Canaan. So they came to the land of Canaan.
>
> —GENESIS 12:1–5

Abraham had to get away from his family and culture to find his true purpose. Paul had to leave the suffocating spirit of the Pharisees.

BREAKING FREE FROM THE PYTHON SPIRIT

How then can you cut the snake in half and get his coils off you?

1. **We must pray and fast.** "For this cause everyone who is godly shall pray to You in a time when You may be found; surely in a flood of great waters they shall not come near him" (Ps. 32:6). "Is this not the fast that I have chosen: To loose the bonds of wickedness, to undo the heavy burdens, to let the oppressed go free, and that you break every yoke?" (Isa. 58:6). As we pray and fast, that which surrounds us is broken. We can hide.

2. **We must seek His presence.** "You are my hiding place; You shall preserve me from trouble; You shall surround me with songs of deliverance" (Ps. 32:7). We find His presence in the gathered church. In the congregation God unwraps python and wraps us in songs of deliverance.

3. **We must experience the power of the Holy Spirit.** "So shall they fear the name of the Lord from the west, and His glory from the rising of the sun; when the enemy comes in like a flood, the Spirit of the Lord will lift up a standard against him" (Isa. 59:19). The Holy Spirit lifts up a banner against the enemy. Here is *Jehovah Nissi*—our flag of victory.

4. **We must confess the promise of the Word.** "'As for Me,' says the Lord, 'this is My covenant with them: My Spirit who is upon you, and My words which I have put in your mouth, shall not depart from your mouth, nor from the mouth of your descendants, nor from the mouth of your descendants' descendants,' says the Lord, 'from this time and forevermore'" (Isa. 59:21). Instead of this coiling spirit of python coming out of your past, releasing bad circumstances and rotting every relationship, you can change your destiny and the destiny of your descendants forever. How? By saying the Word of God! Put the Word in your mouth and in the mouths of your children. God covenants to change your family forever!

Say to the spirit of python, "Today you leave!"

chapter 25

THE STRATEGY OF POVERTY

THE OPPOSITE OF a curse in the Bible is a blessing. A curse is when difficulties, distress, illness, shortage, or other negative issues rest continually on an individual or family. Blessing is when the presence of God releases health, abundance, favor, and contentment in an individual or family.

In many families and in the church there has been a curse of poverty. The spirit of poverty operates by using unexpected shortages to generate fear. This fear will often bring tormenting spirits, including depression, lack of motivation, quarreling, and despair. Even people of wealth are afraid they will lose their wealth, so they do not tithe and give as they should. But the Bible says, "Command those who are rich in this present age not to be haughty, nor to trust in uncertain riches but in the living God, who gives us richly all things to enjoy" (1 Tim. 6:17).

I am to speak a command or warning to everyone whom God has blessed.

1. Don't be proud of your accomplishments. The Lord "gives you power to get wealth," and "the blessing of the LORD makes one rich, and He adds no sorrow with it" (Deut. 8:18; Prov. 10:22).

2. Don't put your faith in your wealth or your possessions.

3. Trust the "living God" to provide for your future.

4. Enjoy what you have, but don't hoard!

5. Share what you have with others.

6. Remember to lay up treasure in heaven.

GETTING FREE FROM THE SPIRIT OF POVERTY

Now, to those who feel cursed, whether of shortage or fear of losing what you have, what is the way out? How can the curse be reversed and cast down and blessings come? God has revealed to me that Psalm 112 is the positive response we can make. This response will stop the negative forces of the enemy and release the positive flow of blessing from God.

Reverential awe before the covenant Lord

> Praise the LORD! Blessed is the man who fears the LORD.
> —PSALM 112:1

Fear is not cringing but a reverence for Yahweh, the great I AM. This is the name God spoke to Moses at the burning bush. It is His covenant name as provider and protector of His people. Are you submitted in reverence to the Lord who keeps covenant? Say, "I am in awe of the covenant-keeping God!"

Joyful obedience to the Lord's commands

> Praise the LORD! Blessed is the man…who delights greatly in His commandments.
> —PSALM 112:1

This person does not cringe before the commands of God. He knows when God says, "You shall not," it means, "Don't hurt yourself." When God gives a positive word, it means, "Help yourself to happiness!"

In the area of giving, the command to tithe and its promise is the most disobeyed commandment in all of Scripture by believers: "'Bring all the tithes into the storehouse, that there may be food in My house, and try Me now in this,' says the LORD of hosts, 'if I will not open for you the windows of heaven and pour out for you such blessing that there will not be room enough to receive it'" (Mal. 3:10).

Expectation of a better future—hope

> Wealth and riches will be in his house, and his righteousness
> endures forever.
>
> —PSALM 112:3

1. *Strength.* Here is a promise for your descendants: the
   generations to come will be mighty on the earth, if they
   are upright.

2. *Supply.* As your descendants walk in righteousness, God
   will continue to multiply what you leave behind.

Perception of God's guidance in the darkness

> Unto the upright there arises light in the darkness.
>
> —PSALM 112:4

Here is promised revelation when darkness hides direction. God promises wisdom to make right decisions at difficult moments. Jehoshaphat
said, "Lord, we know not what to do, but our eyes are on Thee" (2 Chron.
20:12, author's paraphrase).

Gracious and generous spirit

> He is gracious, and full of compassion, and righteous. A good
> man deals graciously and lends; he will guide his affairs with
> discretion.... He has dispersed abroad, he has given to the poor; his
> righteousness endures forever; his horn will be exalted with honor.
>
> —PSALM 112:4–5, 9

This person is blessed and not cursed by the spirit of poverty because
he has a generous spirit. He lends to those in need. He gives by dispersing
abroad to the needy of the kingdom. The word *disperse* is a word used
for sowing. He is honest and careful in all his financial dealings. He
works hard.

Here is the key that unlocks the flow of heaven in your life: "Give, and
it will be given to you: good measure, pressed down, shaken together, and

running over will be put into your bosom. For with the same measure that you use, it will be measured back to you" (Luke 6:38).

Live by faith, not fear

> He will not be afraid of evil tidings; his heart is steadfast, trusting in the LORD. His heart is established; he will not be afraid, until he sees his desire upon his enemies.
>
> —PSALM 112:7–8

This person does not check with Wall Street or operate based on the report of men! When tough times come, he trusts in the Lord and proves it by not withholding tithes and offerings. He refuses to allow the enemy to intimidate and block the work of God. He knows that all that the enemy does, God will turn for his good.

Allow God to be glorified

> He has dispersed abroad, he has given to the poor; his righteousness endures forever; his horn will be exalted with honor.
>
> —PSALM 112:9

The word *horn* represents position. God will put His glory on the blessed and release honor and favor in their lives. This is God's promise.

We are here to break the spirit of poverty, to cast it down, and to demonstrate our faith, not fear. Today God will break the spirit of poverty in you and in the church.

chapter 26

THE STRATEGY OF LEGALISM

I T IS EASIER to live by someone's set of rules than to obey and follow the Holy Spirit! I am grieved to have to report that throughout my nearly forty years of ministry I have been both the initiator and the victim of legalism.

I first experienced church legalism as a high school student in the mid-1960s. While the war raged in Vietnam and Dr. Martin Luther King Jr. was marching to my hometown of Montgomery, Alabama, our preacher was warning us of the insidious dangers of the prom!

When I came to Chattanooga in 1979 to minister at Central Baptist Church, a war raged in conservative churches over women wearing slacks and the length of men's hair. Even wire-rimmed glasses were supposedly banned in some circles, with the reasoning that they marked you as a liberal!

Going from one Christian circle to another can be a literal culture shock due to issues of legalism. I will never forget hearing the report from a friend visiting Christians in a European country. At a Christian fellowship, women were overheard sadly discussing the American women who wore excessive makeup. As they grieved over the decline of the standards of Christianity in America, these European women wept great tears into their glasses of beer!

Have we cluttered up our message with our own tastes and cultural preferences? Where do we draw the line at what God requires and what man prefers? And how can we prevent our churches from tainting the message of God with pharisaical rules that only hinder the work of God?

One of the most insidious demons warring against the church, dividing the church, and hindering revival is legalism. It can be most simply defined as the substitution of man's works for God's plan of salvation. It can be related to the laws of the Old Testament.

Some want to add something to the simple gospel of Christ's death and resurrection and our own faith in that act. This is the heart of legalism. Others want to add cultural norms to the practice of the Christian life that may not have biblical foundation. Others want to add denominational distinctives to the definition of spirituality. Still others want to add their own personal likes, tastes, or dislikes to what is proper for a godly Christian.

Anything that is added to the gospel is another gospel and is unacceptable in God's eyes. I believe the world has not rejected our message, but they have rejected our caricature of the message.

Looking at the excesses of legalistic Islam and the bondage it creates ought to be a wake-up call to the Christian church. If we truly have a burden to touch one billion Muslims with the gospel of Christ, then we better have more to offer them than a long set of rules and guidelines to live by.

PAUL ADDRESSES LEGALISM

When Jesus came into the world, the Jewish faith had disintegrated into extreme legalism. Rules had replaced a relationship with God. Legalism had made slaves out of the people. Jesus came to set them free.

Galatians 3 is Paul's key argument contrasting law and faith. Many of the Galatians who had come to Christ were falling back into Judaism. They were going back under the Law. Galatians 3:7 states, "Know ye therefore that they which are of faith, the same are the children of Abraham" (KJV). A "true Jew" who is a part of God's family is one who is "of faith." In that sense all who believe are sons of Abraham. Paul appeals to the Galatians from two bases.

1. The spiritual appeal
Paul appeals to the Galatians on the basis of their personal experience.

> O foolish Galatians! Who has bewitched you that you should not obey the truth, before whose eyes Jesus Christ was clearly portrayed among you as crucified? This only I want to learn from you: Did you receive the Spirit by the works of the law, or by the hearing of

faith? Are you so foolish? Having begun in the Spirit, are you now being made perfect by the flesh? Have you suffered so many things in vain—if indeed it was in vain? Therefore He who supplies the Spirit to you and works miracles among you, does He do it by the works of the law, or by the hearing of faith?

—GALATIANS 3:1–5

Three times we find their experience with the Holy Spirit mentioned. Paul uses the word *foolish*, which in the original language is translated literally "without sense." These Christians had lost their common sense! You can see why legalism makes the Christian "senseless" when you study its spiritual implications.

Legalism is demonic deception.

"Who has bewitched you…" The Greek here is *baskaino* and means "to cast a spell." It is an obvious reference to a deceiving spirit that had led these Christians into error. Much of the extraneous trappings that men have added to the practice of Christianity are there because of Satan's deception or "spells."

Legalism disobeys the truth.

"…that you should not obey the truth…" These believers had followed blind deception right into a path of disobedience. The truth of God was changed into a lie that they followed, and thus they lived a life of disobedience to God's will for them.

Legalism dishonors the cross.

"…before whose eyes Jesus Christ was clearly portrayed among you as crucified?" Paul declared that Jesus had been "placarded" or put on display. It seems the crucifixion of Christ had been preached in such a way that they had very dramatically been saved by its message. The crucified Christ had affected the church at Galatia, but they foolishly turned their back on the cross to return to the Law. In doing so, they dishonored the sacrifice Jesus made for them on the cross.

Legalism disclaims the Spirit.

"Did you receive the Spirit…" These believers had received the Holy Ghost, and He had begun a work in them. But now they were attempting to try to live by the Law and according to the flesh.

The Holy Spirit makes possible the offering of one's life as a sacrifice to God. We cannot compete with the flesh with what is begun in the

Spirit. It is amazing how many Christians are saved by the work of God's Spirit, but then go on to try to live the Christian life according to what man says is proper.

Legalism disregards the miraculous.

Paul ministered to the Galatians by the Spirit. Miracles were manifested by that same power. The Law has no supernatural power. Miracles happen when the Word of God is preached under the power of the Spirit and the people receive it in faith.

In this passage we learn that preaching will only be effective if it receives the "hearing of faith." Some Christians listen to preaching only critically. Others listen intellectually. Still more listen prejudicially. Others don't listen at all! But if you listen with ears of faith, the Word of God can translate into the practice of life.

Hebrews chapter 3 warns us about refusing to hear, admonishing us that if we don't hear by faith we will be hardened. Hebrews 4:2 gives yet another admonition: "For indeed the gospel was preached to us as well as to them; but the word which they heard did not profit them, not being mixed with faith in those who heard it." If the preaching is not mixed with faith, it will be unprofitable.

The church at Galatia had lost its senses. Faith had been replaced by works, and grace by Law. The next appeal Paul would make would come straight from the pages of the Old Testament.

2. The scriptural appeal

Paul felt he needed to underline the doctrine of salvation by grace with proof from Old Testament scriptures. In Galatians 3:6–7, Paul cites Abraham's conversion as the Old Testament proof of salvation by faith. In Genesis 15:6 we read of Abraham, "And he believed in the LORD, and He accounted it to him for righteousness." By this we see that God saved people then in the same way He saves us now.

Galatians 3 continues this theme by moving from the conversion of Abraham to the covenant God made with him: "And the Scripture, foreseeing that God would justify the Gentiles by faith, preached the gospel to Abraham beforehand, saying, 'In you all the nations shall be blessed.' So then those who are of faith are blessed with believing Abraham" (Gal. 3:8–9). This covenant included both Jews and Gentiles. The whole world is promised blessing through the seed of Abraham.

Paul goes on to say, "For as many as are of the works of the law are under the curse; for it is written, 'Cursed is everyone who does not continue in all things which are written in the book of the law, to do them.' But that no one is justified by the law in the sight of God is evident, for 'the just shall live by faith.' Yet the law is not of faith, but 'the man who does them shall live by them'" (Gal. 3:10–12).

The Law cannot save; it can only curse. If one cannot keep all the Law, he falls under the curse of the Law. The only way out of that curse is the life of faith. We do not live under the restraint of the Law but under the power of grace. Galatians 3:11 quotes from Habakkuk 2:4. If a man chooses the Law, he lives under both the blessing and the curse of the Law. Since all men have sinned, we rest under the curse of the Law until we receive Christ, who bore our curse.

Christ came to set us free, or to redeem us, from the awful curse of bondage to sin.

> Christ has redeemed us from the curse of the law, having become a curse for us (for it is written, "Cursed is everyone who hangs on a tree"), that the blessing of Abraham might come upon the Gentiles in Christ Jesus, that we might receive the promise of the Spirit through faith.
>
> —GALATIANS 3:13–14

Paul quotes Deuteronomy 21:23, reminding us that hanging on a tree was an outward sign to the Jew that a man was cursed before God. Christ took that curse for us: "Who Himself bore our sins in His own body on the tree, that we, having died to sins, might live for righteousness—by whose stripes you were healed" (1 Pet. 2:24).

When Christ cried out, "My God, my God, why hast thou forsaken me" (Mark 15:34. KJV), He was bearing our curse that we might go free. It was through the death of Christ that God's promise of blessing the world through Abraham was fulfilled. When we believe on Him, we receive the promise of the Spirit, and we can live in the freedom of faith.

At the close of Galatians 3, Paul sums up his argument by contrasting the Law and promise. First, he emphasizes that the Law came *after* the promise. God made a promise to Abraham four hundred years before God came to Moses and gave the nation of Israel the Law. The Law did not cancel the promise.

Paul also reminds us that the Law was added because of wickedness: "What purpose then does the law serve? It was added because of transgressions, till the Seed should come to whom the promise was made; and it was appointed through angels by the hand of a mediator. Now a mediator does not mediate for one only, but God is one" (Gal. 3:19–20).

The Law came through a mediator to the people. Salvation promised through Abraham was brought in person by Jesus Christ! As we further study Paul's argument, we learn that the Law exposes sin: "Is the law then against the promises of God? Certainly not! For if there had been a law given which could have given life, truly righteousness would have been by the law. But the Scripture has confined all under sin, that the promise by faith in Jesus Christ might be given to those who believe.... Therefore the law was our tutor to bring us to Christ, that we might be justified by faith" (Gal. 3:21–22, 24).

The Law can display sin, but it cannot deliver us from sin. Other translations use the word *schoolmaster* to describe the role of the Law in our hearts. The Greek word used was *paidagogos*. In Bible days this referred to a slave who was assigned to a boy to train him to be a man. In ancient artwork, this unique tutor is depicted with a rod in his hand. The *paidagogos* were generally harsh, much like the drill sergeants of the Marine Corps.

The Law's purpose was to bring us to terms with our lost condition, to force us to face and confess our utter helplessness and inability to save ourselves. We are literally both imprisoned and guarded by the Law. But it brings us to Christ, who then frees us and makes us His family.

As believers, we stand together in Christ in full equality of fellowship. We are sharers of the promise given to Abraham. We are God's heirs. Let us not divide over cultural preferences, denominational distinctives, or millennial positions. Let us celebrate the fact that all of us are saved by the blood of Jesus!

ENFORCING THE VICTORY OVER YOUR ENEMY

chapter 27

THE VICTORY AT CALVARY

A BIBLICAL UNDERSTANDING OF spiritual warfare begins at the end and not at the beginning. This is correct because it is ever important to keep our focus on Christ and not on the power of the enemy. Satan has no rightful authority over any believer. He is a usurper and a trespasser on God's earth. We cannot even acquiesce to his proud claim to the kingdom of this world. This would be treason to Christ, who refused to avoid the cross by bowing to the enemy at the wilderness temptation.

We must go right to the heart of spiritual warfare: the battle has already been won! Satan has lain under judgment since Eden. We must never forget that judgment was announced in Eden and implemented on Calvary! We must proclaim that the sentence handed down upon Satan in Eden has been executed: "And I will put enmity between you and the woman, and between your seed and her Seed; He shall bruise your head, and you shall bruise His heel" (Gen. 3:15). Strong man that he is, he has been dispossessed by one stronger.

In John Bunyan's classic *The Pilgrim's Progress*, Timorous and Mistrust turn back from their journey to God's city when they see two lions. The narrator says, "The Lions were chained, but he saw not the Chains."[1] Satan and the forces of hell are on a short leash since Calvary. We are not fighting for victory but rather from victory. The bottom line of spiritual warfare is applying and enforcing the victory of the cross upon the enemy. We cannot overestimate him; neither can we underestimate him.

We are not duelists who believe that God and the devil are equal and struggling for control of man. Satan does not coexist with God. The powers of darkness were conquered at the cross. This tremendous passage in Colossians chapter 2 reaches its climax in verse 15 with a victorious affirmation of Christ's victory: "Having disarmed principalities and powers, He made a public spectacle of them, triumphing over them in it."

Most of us see in the cross the sacrifice of Christ for our forgiveness. We see the ultimate example of unconditional love. We see the demonstration of God's love to us. This is certainly true, but there is an unseen truth about what took place on the cross. There was a cosmic spiritual war waged that day.

This day was the culmination of all of Satan's hatred of Jesus. Satan tried to kill Jesus at His birth using the tyrant Herod. He tempted Jesus in the wilderness to stray from the Father's plan. He set before the Lord the lust of the flesh, the lust of the eye, and the pride of life. He tempted Jesus's body, soul, and spirit. Jesus defeated Him with the Word of God.

We should make no mistake about what the clear purpose of Jesus was in coming into the world. He came to do battle with Satan. The Lord Jesus Christ left heaven and invaded Satan's sphere. He came unwelcomed by the masses and hated by Satan. In Jesus's inaugural address at the synagogue in Nazareth He quoted Isaiah 61:1: "The Spirit of the Lord GOD is upon Me, because the Lord has anointed Me to preach good tidings to the poor; He has sent Me to heal the brokenhearted, to proclaim liberty to the captives, and the opening of the prison to those who are bound." Jesus saw our world as bound, blind, brokenhearted and bruised; here were the disastrous effects of Satan's control.

Throughout His ministry Jesus confronted the forces of hell and cast them out. Many times He opened the eyes of the blind—and He still opens the eyes of those blinded by Satan. He still sets the captive free. Jesus saw the destructive work of Satan and did something about it.

The Bible is replete with verses that reveal these truths. In one of the many statements given as to the purpose of the Lord coming into the world John tells us, "For this purpose the Son of God was manifested, that He might destroy the works of the devil" (1 John 3:8).

Shortly before the cross Jesus said, "Now is the judgment of this world; now the ruler of this world will be cast out" (John 12:31).

When He was arrested, Jesus said to His arresters, "When I was with you daily in the temple, you did not try to seize Me. But this is your hour, and the power of darkness" (Luke 22:53).

The world in which He ministered was a world dominated by Satan: "We know that we are of God, and the whole world lies under the sway of the wicked one" (1 John 5:19).

Again His purpose is stated by the writer of Hebrews: "Inasmuch then as the children have partaken of flesh and blood, He Himself likewise shared in the same, that through death He might destroy him who had the power of death, that is, the devil" (Heb. 2:14).

The apostle Paul had no room for doubt about what took place in the spiritual realm on the day Jesus was crucified. In specific detail the passage in Colossians 2:6–15 gives us a spiritual picture of the cosmic war that raged on Calvary that day and demonstrates to us our victory. Paul says three main things happened at the cross that the natural eye could not see.

THE CROSS DISARMED SATAN

Hostile spiritual powers had reigned over man and the world. This reign had its origin in sin and the Fall. Now Jesus had come to spoil them: "Having disarmed principalities and powers, He made a public spectacle of them, triumphing over them in it" (Col. 2:15). The word translated "disarmed" means "to spoil," "to strip," or "to rob." It is in the Greek aorist tense in the original, which means it was a once-and-for-all disarming.

There will not be a rematch; the battle has forever been decided. The word picture is that of a fallen enemy who has been stripped of his sword, armor, shield, position, and wealth. The Scripture teaches us that Satan has been stripped of his right, power, and authority over all those who have bowed at the foot of the cross and received the precious blood of Christ as atonement for their sin.

What did Jesus rob Satan of? We see in Romans 8:33–34 that He robbed him of the right to accuse us: "Who shall bring a charge against God's elect? It is God who justifies. Who is he who condemns? It is Christ who died, and furthermore is also risen, who is even at the right hand of God, who also makes intercession for us." Satan has been robbed of his right to kill us. We are no longer guilty. He has been robbed of his ownership of us. He has no weapon and no way to keep us.

The Cross Displayed Satan

Christ made a "public spectacle of them." Someone might object to this passage and say, "Wasn't it Christ who was made a public spectacle that day?" Indeed He was. He was stripped of His garments and made a public spectacle before men who cried, "If You are really God, then come down off the cross." But we must remember there was another public spectacle going on in the unseen spiritual realm.

In the spiritual realm Christ made a public spectacle of Satan and all of the demonic forces. Jesus displayed him before the angelic world, the demonic world, the spiritual world, and before "just men made perfect." They saw him not as an angel of light, as he so often would make himself appear, but rather they saw his true nature. They saw him as a rotten, filthy, lying thief. Satan and all of the demonic forces were viewed in their true nature.

Satan and all of his host flurried themselves in full fury against the seemingly helpless Son of God. Satan came as Apollyon the destroyer. When the smoke of the battle had lifted, there was an empty cross and an empty tomb. Jesus defeated Satan on Satan's home field. He was put on display as the defeated foe he really is. The word picture is of a billboard. They were put on display for everyone to see.

Satan is forever a public spectacle of defeat when God's people enforce Calvary's victory. At His ascension Jesus passed through the atmosphere, declaring that neither the laws of gravity nor the powers of hell could hold Him back.

The Cross Defeated Satan

Dr. James S. Stewart, Scottish preacher and former chaplain to the queen of England, stood for the fundamentals of the faith in the Anglican church when it was not popular to do so. Dr. Stewart called for a return to the truth, stating that a cosmic battle took place at the cross. Behind the cross we see the fallen design of man. Human sins such as pride, jealousy, greed, self-righteousness, religion, political injustice and human apathy brought our Savior to the cross. Yet behind these stood principalities and powers of evil. The people were driven by forces beyond themselves.[2]

Jesus chose to die for His people because He knew the enemy as a strongman had a death grip on them. He came as one stronger to set the captive free. Jesus acted in history not only to reconcile sinners but also to expose the error of dualism. People everywhere feared the gods of superstition. Jesus not only defeated them but also announced that they would bow before Him and acknowledge him as Lord.

> Therefore God also has highly exalted Him and given Him the name which is above every name, that at the name of Jesus every knee should bow, of those in heaven, and of those on earth, and of those under the earth, and that every tongue should confess that Jesus Christ is Lord, to the glory of God the Father.
>
> —PHILIPPIANS 2:9–11

The power of Satan was shattered at the cross. Triumph over Satan has come at last. The verb translated "triumph" means "a complete and irretrievable subjugation."

However, the question remains, "If Satan has been disarmed, displayed, and defeated at the cross, why is my life so far from victorious?" Number one, if you have not been saved, then you are fair game for the attacks and residency of Satan in your life. You cannot have victory over Satan apart from the application of the blood of Jesus to your sins.

Secondly, if you are a believer, then the only way Satan can attack you is if you have given him the right. The Bible warns, "Nor give place to the devil" (Eph. 4:27). If you have given place to the devil by living in rebellious sin, then you have put out a welcome mat for the enemy to come and enslave you. Many believers live such defeated, depressed lives that they neither bring honor to the Lord nor serve as an example to others. These believers make up a weak, anemic church that is a blight to what Jesus accomplished on the cross. Did Jesus die for a church full of diseased, depressed people in bondage to the enemy?

There is victory in the cross! The blood wiped out our sin and left Satan powerless. Every blow that drove the nails into His holy hands was also a nail in the coffin of Satan. Every Christian is set free.

Christ's death was a battle in which God achieved an immortal victory. The conflict was furious and mysterious. Our Lord died to win the battle and rose from the dead to enforce the victory.

There is victory in Jesus every day. When Satan comes, we simply remind him of our Savior. If he accuses us, we point to forgiveness. If he desires to tempt us, we let our Lord's words fell him. If he would touch us, we declare that he has no authority over God's property.

chapter 28

FOUNDATIONS FOR VICTORY

S ECOND TIMOTHY 2:3–4 describes every Christian as a soldier at war. If victory is to be enjoyed, then the soldier's battle plan must rest on a solid foundation of sound teaching from the Word of God. The greatest snare of the enemy is in the area of perverting or denying the truth.

God's foundations stand sure, and we must rest our faith, planning, and battle strategy upon three unchanging biblical and spiritual foundations:

1. The finished work of Christ
2. The believer's union with Christ
3. The present work of the Spirit of Christ in the believer

THE FOUNDATION OF THE FINISHED WORK OF CHRIST

All that we have and are able to enjoy in the realm of the Spirit is based upon the glorious fact that the Son of God came in the flesh, invaded this demon-infested world, and wrought the victory though His death and resurrection on the cross.

> How God anointed Jesus of Nazareth with the Holy Spirit and with power, who went about doing good and healing all who were oppressed by the devil, for God was with Him.
>
> —ACTS 10:38

How did God win this victory? Read on in Acts 10:39–40: "Whom they slew and hanged on a tree: Him God raised up the third day" (KJV).

The late Professor James S. Stewart in the Lyman Beecher Lectures at Yale University in the early 1950s mourned the loss of teaching on the demonic and their defeat only through the cross: "I wish to introduce the theme of preaching the cross by suggesting that if for great numbers of our contemporaries the effect of Newton, Darwin, and Freud has been to banish the divine, it has even more emphatically been to banish the demonic."[1]

He further states, "The elimination of the dimension of the demonic has had its effect upon Christian theology…a usurping personal force alive and tyrannical…not simply some phobia of man or divided self."[2]

Jesus Christ's death did at least four things to assure victory.

1. He settled the sin question.

> Therefore, having been justified by faith, we have peace with God through our Lord Jesus Christ, through whom also we have access by faith into this grace in which we stand, and rejoice in hope of the glory of God. And not only that, but we also glory in tribulations, knowing that tribulation produces perseverance; and perseverance, character; and character, hope. Now hope does not disappoint, because the love of God has been poured out in our hearts by the Holy Spirit who was given to us.
>
> —ROMANS 5:1–5

> There is therefore now no condemnation to those who are in Christ Jesus, who do not walk according to the flesh, but according to the Spirit.
>
> —ROMANS 8:1

Jesus Christ died as our sinless substitute to once and for all cancel our sin debt and Satan's right to accuse us.

2. He came to make you acceptable.

> To the praise of the glory of His grace, by which He has made us accepted in the Beloved.
>
> —EPHESIANS 1:6

You now have eternal significance.

3. He came to conquer Satan.

> He has delivered us from the power of darkness and conveyed us into the kingdom of the Son of His love.
>
> —COLOSSIANS 1:13

> Having disarmed principalities and powers, He made a public spectacle of them, triumphing over them in it.
>
> —COLOSSIANS 2:15

> Inasmuch then as the children have partaken of flesh and blood, He Himself likewise shared in the same, that through death He might destroy him who had the power of death, that is, the devil, and release those who through fear of death were all their lifetime subject to bondage.
>
> —HEBREWS 2:14–15

> He who sins is of the devil, for the devil has sinned from the beginning. For this purpose the Son of God was manifested, that He might destroy the works of the devil.
>
> —1 JOHN 3:8

The atonement death of Christ was the battle of the ages. Unseen victories were being won. Theologian Gustav Aulen declares that Jesus is "Christus Victor."[3] His death was triumphant. P. T. Forsyth has said, "The world's awful need is less than Christ's awful victory. And the devils we meet were [already destined to hell] in the Satan He ruined. The wickedness of the world is, after all, 'a bull in a net,' a chained beast kicking himself to death."[4]

John Calvin, in commenting on Colossians 2:8–15, said, "There is no tribunal so magnificent, no throne so stately, no show of triumph so distinguished, no chariot so elevated, as is the gibbet [cross] on which Christ has subdued death and the devil... [and] utterly trodden them under his feet."[5]

The great German theologian Oscar Cullman, in his book *Christ and Time*, said of Christ's finished work, "The principalities and powers between the Resurrection and the Parousia [Second Coming] are tied to a rope, still free enough to evince their demonic character, but nevertheless bound, since Christ has already conquered all demons: the cross and the resurrection being the decisive battle that has turned the tide of the war and settled the issue, even though Victory Day may still lie in a future, out of sight."[6]

We must always understand that we fight on the foundation of a victory already won!

Christ came to cancel everything we inherited from the first Adam.

> Therefore, just as through one man sin entered the world, and death through sin, and thus death spread to all men, because all sinned— (For until the law sin was in the world, but sin is not imputed when there is no law. Nevertheless death reigned from Adam to Moses, even over those who had not sinned according to the likeness of the transgression of Adam, who is a type of Him who was to come. But the free gift is not like the offense. For if by the one man's offense many died, much more the grace of God and the gift by the grace of the one Man, Jesus Christ, abounded to many. And the gift is not like that which came through the one who sinned. For the judgment which came from one offense resulted in condemnation, but the free gift which came from many offenses resulted in justification. For if by the one man's offense death reigned through the one, much more those who receive abundance of grace and of the gift of righteousness will reign in life through the One, Jesus Christ.) Therefore, as through one man's offense judgment came to all men, resulting in condemnation, even so through one Man's righteous act the free gift came to all men, resulting in justification of life. For as by one man's disobedience many were made sinners, so also by one Man's obedience many will be made righteous. Moreover the law entered that the offense might abound. But where sin abounded, grace abounded much more, so that as sin reigned in death, even so grace might reign through righteousness to eternal life through Jesus Christ our Lord.
>
> —ROMANS 5:12–21

In the Garden of Eden, Satan usurped the inheritance of humanity and enthroned death as the king of the earth. A "second Adam"—Jesus Christ—was called forth to break the grip of these principalities and powers and to rescue the race from extinction (Rom. 5:17). You and I must appropriate the finished work of Christ if we are to enjoy His victory. That brings us to the second foundation.

THE FOUNDATION OF OUR UNION WITH CHRIST

> Jesus answered and said to him, "Most assuredly, I say to you, unless one is born again, he cannot see the kingdom of God."
>
> —JOHN 3:3

> And you He made alive, who were dead in trespasses and sins, in which you once walked according to the course of this world, according to the prince of the power of the air, the spirit who now works in the sons of disobedience, among whom also we all once conducted ourselves in the lusts of our flesh, fulfilling the desires of the flesh and of the mind, and were by nature children of wrath, just as the others. But God, who is rich in mercy, because of His great love with which He loved us, even when we were dead in trespasses, made us alive together with Christ (by grace you have been saved), and raised us up together, and made us sit together in the heavenly places in Christ Jesus, that in the ages to come He might show the exceeding riches of His grace in His kindness toward us in Christ Jesus. For by grace you have been saved through faith, and that not of yourselves; it is the gift of God, not of works, lest anyone should boast.
>
> —EPHESIANS 2:1–9

At the new birth (John 3:3), you are made alive by the Holy Spirit (Eph. 2:1–9) and brought into a vital union with Christ. Romans 5:10 says, "Having been reconciled, we shall be saved by His life." Indeed, His death for us secured our salvation. His life in us applies that salvation.

God changes our lives by exchanging our lives for the life of Christ. According to the New Testament, we are now identified with Christ in every aspect of His finished work.

Our death with Christ

> I have been crucified with Christ; it is no longer I who live, but
> Christ lives in me.
>
> —GALATIANS 2:20

Our burial with Christ

Romans 6:4 declares that everything we were in Adam was buried
with Christ; baptism is a picture of that burial.

> Therefore we were buried with Him through baptism into death,
> that just as Christ was raised from the dead by the glory of the
> Father, even so we also should walk in newness of life.

Our resurrection with Christ

> For if we have been united together in the likeness of His death,
> certainly we also shall be in the likeness of His resurrection,
> knowing this, that our old man was crucified with Him, that the
> body of sin might be done away with, that we should no longer be
> slaves of sin.
>
> —ROMANS 6:5–6

> And you He made alive, who were dead in trespasses and sins,
> in which you once walked according to the course of this world,
> according to the prince of the power of the air, the spirit who now
> works in the sons of disobedience, among whom also we all once
> conducted ourselves in the lusts of our flesh, fulfilling the desires of
> the flesh and of the mind, and were by nature children of wrath, just
> as the others. But God, who is rich in mercy, because of His great
> love with which He loved us, even when we were dead in trespasses,
> made us alive together with Christ (by grace you have been saved).
>
> —EPHESIANS 2:1–5

Spiritually the saved person has been raised out of spiritual death.
Though our bodies have not been raised, the resurrection factor lives
by the Holy Spirit in our spirit. In fact, the Holy Spirit is the "earnest"
or guarantee of our bodily resurrection. Eternal life dwells in every
believer.

In Him you also trusted, after you heard the word of truth, the gospel of your salvation; in whom also, having believed, you were sealed with the Holy Spirit of promise, who is the guarantee of our inheritance until the redemption of the purchased possession, to the praise of His glory.

—EPHESIANS 1:13–14

Our enthronement with Christ

Even when we were dead in trespasses, made us alive together with Christ (by grace you have been saved), and raised us up together, and made us sit together in the heavenly places in Christ Jesus.

—EPHESIANS 2:5–6

When you look back at Ephesians 1:20–21, you see that when we take our position in Christ, seated with Him, we are then "far above all principality and power and might and dominion." Now everything that was once over our heads is now under our feet. Our strategic position is identified fully with Christ. First John 4:17 says, "As He is, so are we in this world." This brings us to the final foundation, the fullness of the Holy Spirit.

THE FOUNDATION OF THE FULLNESS AND POWER OF THE HOLY SPIRIT

The Lord on the earth today is the third Person of the Godhead, the blessed Holy Spirit. The Holy Spirit indwells every believer. He may, however, be ignored, insulted, grieved, and quenched. He longs to fill, gift, and bring forth fruit in every believer.

The Holy Spirit alone turns the Word of God into the sword of the Spirit.

And take the helmet of salvation, and the sword of the Spirit, which is the word of God.

—EPHESIANS 6:17

For the word of God is living and powerful, and sharper than any two-edged sword, piercing even to the division of soul and spirit, and of joints and marrow, and is a discerner of the thoughts and intents of the heart.

—Hebrews 4:12

The Holy Spirit alone makes effective praying possible.

Likewise the Spirit also helps in our weaknesses. For we do not know what we should pray for as we ought, but the Spirit Himself makes intercession for us with groanings which cannot be uttered.

—Romans 8:26

But you, beloved, building yourselves up on your most holy faith, praying in the Holy Spirit.

—Jude 20

The Holy Spirit alone gives understanding of the Word of God.

Therefore I also, after I heard of your faith in the Lord Jesus and your love for all the saints, do not cease to give thanks for you, making mention of you in my prayers: that the God of our Lord Jesus Christ, the Father of glory, may give to you the spirit of wisdom and revelation in the knowledge of Him, the eyes of your understanding being enlightened; that you may know what is the hope of His calling, what are the riches of the glory of His inheritance in the saints

—Ephesians 1:15–18

This scripture speaks of the gift of revelation knowledge and understanding by the Holy Spirit. God's Spirit makes it possible to understand and apply spiritual truth.

The Holy Spirit strengthens our inner man.

That He would grant you…to be strengthened with might through His Spirit in the inner man…

—Ephesians 3:16

The Holy Spirit desires to fill every Christian.

Ephesians 5:18 says, "Be filled with the Spirit." This fullness is no less than total control of the individual. This is the lordship of Christ active in the life of a Christian. A Spirit-filled believer cannot be defeated by Satan and his demonic forces. When we are filled with the Spirit, we live in a constant state of triumph.

chapter 29

RESOURCES FOR VICTORY

L ET US SUMMARIZE and organize the truths God has revealed to us. There are five unfailing resources that guarantee spiritual victory.

1. Resource—stand in authority

First, the believer must stand in the authority of his position in Christ. When you were saved, Paul declares in Ephesians 2:6 that you have been raised with Christ and seated with Him in the heavenlies. Back in Ephesians 1:20–21 we discover that the principalities and powers are under our feet when we assume our rightful authority in Christ.

The believer is vested with this authority by virtue of his or her union with Christ. This authority is exercised by the power and authority of the indwelling Holy Spirit. We must stand against the enemy with a firm, unfaltering faith. We must not be afraid to confidently command the enemy to leave our presence and stop interfering with our lives.

2. Resource—Word of God

The second unfailing resource is the Word of God. In the New Testament we discover that two Greek words are translated "word" in reference to Scripture. One is the word *logos*, which means the word in all of its meaning and understanding. *Rhema* is the other expression, and it means "the word spoken and applied." It means "the word unleashed." Ephesians 6:17 calls Scripture "the sword of the Spirit, which is the word of God." *Word* in this verse is *rhema*, which means the word spoken, applied, unleashed, and released. Satan and his demons will flee before the armed believer who speaks forth the Word of God. Our Lord Jesus, when tempted by Satan in the wilderness, used only Scripture to drive him away. (See Matthew 4:1–11.)

3. Resource—prayer and fasting

The third resource is a tag team of prayer and fasting. In Ephesians 6:18 the believer in the full panoply of armor is instructed, "Praying always with all prayer and supplication in the Spirit..."

In extreme cases prayer should be accompanied by fasting. In Mark 9:14–29 Jesus encountered a desperate father with a demonized son. While Jesus was on the Mount of Transfiguration, His remaining disciples had failed in their efforts to bring deliverance to the boy.

The issue with the father was one of faith: "If thou canst believe, all things are possible to him that believeth" (Mark 9:23, kjv). Jesus cast out the demon and then challenged His disciples, saying, "This kind can come out by nothing but prayer and fasting" (v. 29).

Fasting must be added to prayer for Christians who engage in spiritual warfare. Isaiah 58:6–12 defines fasting as giving up one's own possessions in order to help the needy. This kind of fasting is one of God's chosen ways to defeat the enemy.

> Is not this the fast that I have chosen: to loose the bonds of wickedness, to undo heavy burdens, to let the oppressed go free, and that you break every yoke?
>
> —Isaiah 58:6

Prayer and fasting are effective against the enemy.

4. Resource—praise and worship

The fourth resource is praise and worship. In the Old Testament praise was used as a weapon. Second Chronicles 20 records the story of Jehoshaphat and his battle against the Ammonites and Moabites. Look at the strategy for victory:

- The leader offers fervent prayer to God. Second Chronicles 20:6–12 shows us the words of this powerful prayer. Jehoshaphat confesses total reliance on God for the victory. He confesses that his eyes are on the Lord alone.

- Earnest attention is given to the Word of God as proclaimed by a Spirit-filled man of God. In 2 Chronicles 20:13–17, we read that after prayer the prophetic word is declared by Jahaziel. He cries out against fear and encourages faith. The word is released with power!

- Praise and worship go out. In 2 Chronicles 20:18–22, Jehoshaphat dispatched the choirs to sing "with voices loud and high" (v. 19). As they praised "the beauty of holiness" (v. 21), the invisible hosts of God moved into battle formation. "Now when they began to sing and to praise, the LORD set ambushes against the people of Ammon, Moab, and Mount Seir, who had come against Judah; and they were defeated" (v. 22).

Psalm 149:6 says, "Let the high praises to God be in their mouth, and a two-edged sword in their hand." Praise is a strong weapon against the enemy.

5. Resource—presence and virtues of Christ

The fifth resource is the presence and virtues of the Lord Jesus Christ. There are four vital truths about Jesus that guarantee victory in your life.

- You have the blood of Jesus for your sins. First John 1:7 tells us, "The blood of Jesus Christ His Son cleanses us from all sin." Satan and his demons can only penetrate where unconfessed sin gives them a place. The blood is a sure weapon: "And they overcame him [Satan] by the blood of the Lamb..." (Rev. 12:11).

- You have the cross of Jesus to take care of your flesh. "And those who are Christ's have crucified the flesh with its passions and desires" (Gal. 5:24). This identification with Christ's cross puts you out of the sin-enjoying business. Galatians 2:20 says, "I have been crucified with Christ; it is no longer I who live, but Christ lives in me; and the life which I now live in the flesh I live by faith in the Son of God, who loved me and gave Himself for me." The indwelling Christ operates through the believer who lives by faith.

- You have the name of Jesus for defeating the enemy. In Acts 16:18 Paul casts the demon out of a young girl, commanding the spirit "in the name of Jesus Christ to come out of her." In the Bible, names represent the character and authority of a person. The name of Jesus Christ is not a magic word but the recognition of Jesus's awesome presence and power in every situation. Philippians 2:10 says, "That at the name of Jesus every knee should bow, of those in heaven, and of those on earth, and of those under the earth." Obviously demons must bow to the name of Jesus Christ.

• Faith in Jesus is our sure protection. Ephesians 6:16 speaks of "taking the shield of faith, wherewith ye shall be able to quench all the fiery darts of the wicked" (KJV). Christians must believe God in the face of the enemy's accusations, in the crisis of circumstances, and in the storms of difficulty. Faith believes God when something is not so until it is so because God said so!

chapter 30

THE BELIEVER'S POSITION FOR VICTORY

OPERATION DESERT SHIELD is a classic example of battle strategy. No battle was launched until everything and everyone was in the proper position. Then the air attacks began. The Allied planes took the battle to the skies and then to the earth. Then the ground troops moved in to recapture lost territory and set the captives free.

Spiritual warfare uses this same time-tested strategy. Believers must know their enemy, know their strength, and get into battle position. That battle position is described in Ephesians 6:10: "Be strong in the Lord." Salvation is Christ in you. Your exalted position is you in Christ!

UNDERSTANDING THE BELIEVER'S EXALTED POSITION

Paul's favorite description of a Christian is "in Christ." Ephesians uses this expression repeatedly to specify the privileges of being a Christian. Christians are to be "faithful in Jesus Christ." The possibility of faithful living is ours because of our presence in Christ. Also, "every spiritual blessing" (Eph. 1:3) is ours in Christ. Our acceptance in the divine family is secured because "He has made us accepted in the Beloved" (v. 6). In fact, if you read through Ephesians 1, you will discover that all your needs for this life and the life to come are found by understanding what it means to be in Christ. Often the focus is on Christ being in the believer. Yet in Ephesians the believer is viewed as in Christ.

For our purpose in this study it is important to note that the "in Christ" believer has been exalted and enthroned above all principalities and powers "and raised...up together, and made... [to] sit together in the heavenly places in Christ Jesus" (Eph. 2:6). The heavenly places are where Christ is presently enthroned, "which He worked in Christ when He raised Him from the dead and seated Him at His right hand in the heavenly places, far above all principality and power and might and dominion, and every name that is named, not only in this age but also in that which is to come. And He put all things under His feet" (Eph. 1:20–22).

When we understand our position in Christ, then we clearly understand that everything that is under His feet is also under the believer's feet. As ambassadors of heaven believers have the authority of the throne of Jesus Christ! Our battle with Satan and his demons takes place in the heavenly places: "For we do not wrestle against flesh and blood, but against principalities, against powers, against the rulers of the darkness of this age, against spiritual hosts of wickedness in the heavenly places" (Eph. 6:12).

You and I have no authority within ourselves over demons. Yet these wicked spiritual forces are fully aware of the authority that is ours in Jesus Christ. Even though an ambassador of our country lives outside of our own country, he still has citizenship; and when he speaks, he speaks with the authority of Washington DC and all of the might of the United States. Likewise, we are citizens of heaven, and here on the earth we speak with all the authority of heaven.

UNDERSTAND THE BELIEVER'S ETERNAL PURPOSE

God's eternal purpose for every believer is Christlikeness. Our purpose is not to fight for a victory. Our Lord has already won the decisive battle at Calvary. We fight from His victory. We are here to enforce the victory of our Lord. "Be strong in the Lord and the power of His might" (Eph. 6:10).

The verb *be strong in* is a present passive imperative. It is a continuous command. It is passive, indicating that the subject is strengthened by an outside power. It would better be translated, "Go on being strengthened." It is not the believer flexing his spiritual muscles. It is receiving and appropriating God's strength.

God permits Satan to war against believers. Though ultimately this is a mystery, clearly several reasons can be noted.

1. Warfare with Satan sharpens the believer's skill in using Scripture.

2. These earthly battles are freeing us for exalted rule in the next world: "For I consider the sufferings of this present time are not worthy to be compared with the glory which shall be revealed in us" (Rom. 8:18).

3. Spiritual warfare teaches us the tragedy of the human condition because of the fall of mankind. Satan's hatred of the human race and his relentless efforts to control human destiny are clearly exposed in spiritual warfare.

4. Man learns his utter helplessness before evil without Christ. C. S. Lewis has said, "Education without values, as useful as it is, seems rather to make man a more clever devil."[1]

5. Spiritual warfare keeps the believer from becoming too comfortable in this world. Regular struggles with the enemy remind us that we are living in hostile territory. Finally, warfare teaches the believer that the servant is not above his master! Our Lord was a soldier. He battled even to the shedding of His blood. He battled and won the victory.

Now it is the believer's duty to enforce the victory Jesus has won. Our Lord was no stranger to warfare, facing Satan at the beginning of His ministry when He was tempted and at the end of His earthly ministry in the garden and on the cross. It is the purpose of God that every believer know how to do battle following His example.

UNDERSTAND THE BELIEVER'S POWER

Once again let me remind you to "be strong in the Lord and in the power of His might" (Eph. 6:10). When a Christian understands his position, then he can begin to appropriate the power of Jesus. What is "the power of His might"? This same phrase is found in Ephesians 1:19–20. The working of His mighty power is the same power that raised the dead body of Jesus to life. It's the same power that exalted Him above all to the highest position in heaven and on the earth. It is the same power Paul had in mind when he wrote, "I can do all things through Christ who strengthens me" (Phil. 4:13).

When a person accepts Christ as Lord, he is initiated into His victory. It is a fierce and terrible war, but we are in the winning position. How do we appropriate and apply this victory? Prayer, the Word, and faith are the way. We appropriate unlimited power when we are willing to live for the Lord. The Spirit-filled life supplies the strength we need.

Satan has two major goals. First, he desires to keep as many people as possible from salvation through Christ. Second Corinthians 4:4 gives us this terrible strategy: "That they cannot see the light of the gospel of the glory of Christ, who is the image of God" (NIV). Satan believes that his only hope of reprieve is to ensnare so many human beings that God would reverse His plan of redemption and then prove to be unrighteous.

Secondly, Satan desires to neutralize believers by defeating and discouraging them. Wake up to the truth! If you do not take your battle position in Christ, the enemy will destroy you.

Right now you can take your exalted position in Christ. Pray the following prayer:

> *Heavenly Father, I bow in praise and ownership before You. I praise You that the blood of Jesus is my covering. I praise You for the Holy Spirit, who indwells and fills my life. I surrender myself anew to You as a living sacrifice. I repudiate conformity to this world and praise You for the transforming work of Christ. I renounce Satan and all his workers and declare that they have no right to interfere with me in this prayer. I am praying to the true and living God, and I refuse any involvement of the enemy in this prayer.*

I ask You, Lord, to rebuke Satan, and I take now my exalted position in Christ. I recognize that the armor of God is none other than Christ! My sword is the Word of God and praise.

I praise You, Jesus, that in this position on Your throne the enemy is under my feet. I reject, repudiate, and renounce all that Satan has brought against me, and I bring the blood of Jesus against you, Satan, and command you to leave in the name of Jesus Christ. I declare that all principalities and powers take notice that I know who I am in Christ. I will live in Christ and over you in His sure victory. In the strong name of Jesus, amen.

chapter 31

ARMING FOR VICTORY

T HE OLD HYMN "Stand Up for Jesus" has a line in it that goes like this: "Put on the gospel armor / each piece put on with prayer."[1] This thought reflects what Paul is saying to the church. Having declared the believers' position for battle in Ephesians 6:10 and their posture for battle in verses 11–13, Paul moves to their panoply for battle.

Both verses 11 and 13 command the believer to "put on" the whole armor of God. This once-and-for-all command includes the entire outfit. The Greek word for "whole armor," *panoplia*, comes from *pan*, meaning "all," and *hoplon*, meaning "weaponry." The *panoplia* ("whole armor") includes all of the soldier's equipment. One scholar translates it, "Put on the splendid armor."

When Paul wrote the Book of Ephesians, he wrote from personal knowledge about Roman soldiers. He was chained to one guard when he wrote, "I, Paul, the prisoner of Christ Jesus..." (Eph. 3:1); "I, therefore, the prisoner of the Lord, beseech you..." (Eph. 4:1). He described himself as "an ambassador in chains" (Eph. 6:20). Paul saw in the Roman soldier a wonderful illustration of spiritual truth.

Understand that the armor is symbolic. The armor is no less than Christ Himself. Every believer knows Christ as Savior. The problem comes when we do not appropriate all that our Lord brings with Him. You see, it is not Christ available but Christ appropriated that makes the difference. It would be like someone having a million dollars in the bank but living a life of poverty. If you never make a withdrawal and appropriate the funds, what good does it do you? Romans 13:14 says, "Put on the Lord Jesus Christ, and make no provision for the flesh, to fulfill its lusts." The phrase *put on* is translated from the same Greek word *enduo* that is found in Ephesians 6:11. Paul wrote to Timothy, "Be strong in the grace that is in Christ Jesus" (2 Tim. 2:1).

In the battles of life Christ is the answer—but His resources must be appropriated.

In the greater context there are three pieces of armor that should always be in place without question: the belt, the breastplate, and the boots (Eph. 6:14–15). The other pieces are to be taken up decisively and finally. The emphasis here is that it is possible to forget these pieces of armor, such as the shield, helmet, and the sword. We are to take these up regularly into the battle. But in this chapter we will focus on the belt of truth.

THE BELT OF TRUTH DISPLAYS AN ILLUSTRATION OF INTEGRITY

The belt served three primary purposes for the Roman soldier. It held all of his weapons and equipment together. The belt was used to tie his robe so that he would not stumble over it going into battle. Plus, it was ornamental, displaying medals or awards for heroism in battle.

Here it is a spiritual weapon, but the functions are the same. It is called a belt of truth; therefore it pictures the Lord Jesus Christ, who said, "I am…the truth" (John 14:6). It also pictures the written Word of God, which keeps one from tripping over the obstacles in the world. Finally, it pictures the honesty and integrity that ought to characterize the life of all who know Jesus Christ.

THE BELT OF TRUTH EXHIBITS THE INSPIRATION FOR INTEGRITY

As we have already observed, the Lord Jesus Christ is the armor for the believer. Isaiah 11:5 said of Him, "Righteousness shall be the belt of His loins, and faithfulness the belt of His waist."

When Jesus faced Satan, He declared the truth of the Word of God (Matt. 4). He looked at the Pharisees who opposed Him and said, "Which of you convicts Me of sin?" (John 8:46). Pilate looked at Jesus and asked, "What is truth?" And then he declared, "I find no fault in

Him" (John 18:38). Even the thief on the cross cried, "This Man has done nothing wrong" (Luke 23:41).

Our Lord Jesus Christ spoke the truth and lived the truth. He remains the truth today. Revelation 1:12–13 pictures Jesus in His glorified state: He is bound, or girded, by a golden belt. All of our Lord's glory is bound together by His truth.

The belt represents the Lord Jesus Christ and His Word holding everything together in one's life. His truth, His character, and His integrity are to characterize our lives.

A music student walked into his teacher's studio and asked, "What good news do you have today?" The teacher picked up a hammer and hit the tuning fork. He said, "That note is A; it will be A tomorrow; it was A five thousand years ago. It will be A five thousand years from now."

Life can hold together only if it is bound together by unchanging truth. Jesus Christ and His Word are the tuning fork that gives our lives an unchanging reference point to live in harmony in a discordant world.

THE BELT OF TRUTH TEACHES US THE IMPORTANCE OF INTEGRITY

This belt of truth is displayed in the honesty and integrity of the believer. Our lives ought to be lived in such a way that people see the truth. Just as the Roman soldier used the belt to bind his robe to keep from tripping, so the truth of Jesus's Word keeps us from tripping before a watching world.

Also, the believers' medals of victory worn on the belt of integrity are their reputations. Ephesians 4:14–16 warns the believer of false doctrine and deceptive teachers. Verse 15 challenges us to speak "the truth in love" so that we "may grow up in all things."

Let us remember that our enemy can move in to destroy us in the area of honesty and character.

Do you know the truth in a person? Jesus is the truth. You can call on the great philosophers, but Socrates, Plato, and Kant will not answer. You can call on great leaders of the past, and they will not answer. Jesus Christ will answer you today. He proved His truthfulness by rising from the dead. You must admit the truth about yourself and receive the truth of Jesus today. When you do, integrity will characterize your life.

THE HEART OF THE WARRIOR

Stand therefore...having put on the breastplate of righteousness.
—EPHESIANS 6:14

The second piece of armor needed by soldier-saints is the breastplate of righteousness. The Greek word for *breastplate* is *thorax*. This piece of armor was made of metal and leather and fastened around the soldier's body from the neck to the thighs. It protected his vital organs, including the heart and lungs. In the armor of the believer, it is called the breastplate of righteousness. The word *righteousness* literally means "to be made right or to be justified."

The internal organs were considered by first-century people to be the center of the will and emotions. Spiritually, a blow to the mind and emotions is very dangerous. Satan desires to "mess up" your mind. He is an accuser and a slanderer.

What is the righteousness that protects our minds and hearts? First, we will consider what it is not.

Realize there is an impotent righteousness.

We are all like an unclean thing, and all our righteousnesses are like filthy rags.

—ISAIAH 64:6

Romans 3:10 cites several Old Testament passages, declaring, "There is none righteous, no, not one." From these passages we know that this righteousness is not self-righteousness.

This righteousness is not a natural human attribute. This righteousness is not religious activity, charitable activity, or human goodness. Our very best behavior is tainted by sin. Human righteousness is the good that is not good enough. Jesus said, "Unless your righteousness exceeds the righteousness of the scribes and Pharisees, you will by no means enter the kingdom of heaven" (Matt. 5:20). Pharisees lived good lives outwardly. Paul was a Pharisee before his conversion. His testimony in Philippians 3:4–9 was that as a Pharisee he was religious, had zeal, and was blameless.

What does all of this mean? Simply this: you can never be righteous (right with God) on your own merits! How then can a person be righteous?

Receive an imputed righteousness.

Jesus said, "But seek first the kingdom of God and His righteousness, and all these things shall be added to you" (Matt. 6:33). His reign and His righteousness are necessary in our lives, so how can we obtain "the righteousness of God"?

Romans 3:19–26 tells us clearly that Jesus Christ is the righteousness of God: "Being justified freely by His grace through the redemption that is in Christ Jesus, whom God set forth as a propitiation by His blood, through faith, to demonstrate His righteousness" (vv. 24–25).

The only dilemma God ever faced was to be righteous and make sinners righteous at the same time. This dilemma was solved when Christ became the blood sacrifice for the sins of humanity. He died to pay the penalty and bear the curse of the law against all of us.

Romans 3:21–22 declares that the righteousness of God is revealed and received. Then 2 Corinthians 5:21 tells us how this is possible: "For He made Him who knew no sin to be sin for us, that we might become the righteousness of God in Him." Scripture declares that we are righteous because He has imputed His righteousness to us: "And if anyone sins, we have an Advocate with the Father, Jesus Christ the righteous" (1 John 2:1). Scripture also says that we are righteous "just as He is righteous" (1 John 3:7).

Romans 5:17–19 declares that this righteousness of God is a gift of God's grace. Further, this gift enables us to reign in life. The righteousness of Jesus marks us as royalty!

All of these scriptures declare that righteousness is a gift of God and a work of God. Righteousness is the Son of God in our lives. You receive this righteousness by faith.

A breastplate was designed to deflect the blow of the enemy. The righteousness of Christ protects the believer in the same way. When you have accepted Jesus and know that He has accepted you, this deflects the arrows of rejection by others. When you know that God sees you as 100 percent righteous, this deflects the put-downs, the guilt, and the accusations of the enemy.

This righteousness protects from inferiority.

Identity with Christ is the key to a healthy self-image. The world says, "You are nothing," but God says, "You are royalty." (See Romans 5:17.) The enemy says, "You have no future," but God is preparing for you to reign with Him in glory.

The devil will tell you that you are unimportant and what you do is insignificant. Someone said, "All born-again believers, as members of the future bride of Christ, are fully as significant, important, and of great consequence in God's ongoing undertakings, adventures, and creative endeavor as any intelligence in the universe."

We cannot control others. Satan will come against us with all kinds of attacks. The only way he can get through is if we react wrongly. When we respond in the wrong way—whether it be in anger, pouting, self-pity, or self-rejection—we have failed to appropriate the breastplate of righteousness.

Only what touches your spirit can really injure you. If you allow what happens to you or what is said to you affect what God has said about you, then you are not using the breastplate.

What motivated the prodigal son to get out of the hog pen? He realized who he was: he was a son! When he came home, his father said, "This my son was dead and is alive again" (Luke 15:24).

The breastplate of righteousness protects from immorality.

When we know that we are righteous in Jesus and will share in His reign, we do not want to live beneath our position. Why should an heir of God want to live like an animal? Why should a saint want to be a reprobate? Why would a king want to live like a slave?

There was a day when a person would live right to protect the family name. When we realize that we have Jesus and that He is our righteousness, then this motivation enables us to live out what we are in Jesus. You are not a sinner saved by grace; you *were* a sinner. Now you are a saint and a family member. Why would you live less than you are?

By an act of will we can yield our bodies to be controlled by His righteousness (Rom. 6:13). The righteousness of Jesus controls our behavior.

This righteousness protects from insecurity.

> The kingdom of God is not meat and drink; but righteousness, and peace, and joy in the Holy Ghost.
>
> —ROMANS 14:17, KJV

> Seek first the kingdom of God and His righteousness, and all these things shall be added to you.
>
> —MATTHEW 6:33

When Jesus is King in our lives, then we are the beneficiaries of His righteousness. All of the rest of life will fall into place. The things that happen in our lives may be God's way of saying, "Recognize My reign and receive My righteousness."

What do you need to do? Pray the following prayer:

> *Lord, I have no righteousness of my own. I give You my sin for Your righteousness. Lord, I receive Your righteousness as my standing before the Father. I gladly confess that I am now, and forever will be, who You say I am. I confess to being Your child, a saint, an heir of God, a part of Your bride and body. Lord, I yield my body as an instrument of righteousness. I recognize that all I was in Adam is now dead, and that all I am in Jesus makes me Your own. Lord, I accept the Bible as Your very breath of life. I acknowledge 2 Timothy 3:16, which tells us that all Scripture is God-breathed and is profitable for instruction in righteousness. Lord, I thank You that Your death has made me righteous before the Father. In Jesus's name, amen.*

THE WALK OF THE WARRIOR

> And having shod your feet with the preparation of the gospel of peace.
>
> —EPHESIANS 6:15

Jesus Christ Himself is the armor of God: "Put on the Lord Jesus Christ" (Rom. 13:14). Putting on the armor is simply realizing who

Jesus is, recognizing who you are in Him, and appropriating all He has for your life.

The piece of armor we will examine next is the warrior's shoes. Great generals have said that in warfare an army moves on two vital things: its food and its feet. This was especially true of the Roman army, which had to march great distances over rugged terrain. The Roman battle dress for the feet were thick leather soles with hobnails to serve as cleats. They were tied to the feet and leg with leather laces. These boots served three purposes:

1. *To provide firm footing.* The nails dug into the ground to keep the soldiers from slipping.

2. *To furnish protection.* In those days the enemy would drive pegs into the ground and sharpen the tips. A barefoot soldier would receive a painful puncture wound in the foot. Infection would set in and disable the soldier.

3. *To give mobility.* These shoes made it possible for the army to move quickly to the place of battle.

Our spiritual shoes serve essentially the same purpose. They help us see clearly what solid foundation is under us and what keeps us moving.

The identity of the shoes

The believer's spiritual warfare shoes are described as "the gospel of peace." We stand on the sure foundation of the gospel. *Gospel* means "good news." What is "good news"? In 1 Corinthians 15:1–4, Paul described the gospel as the death, burial, and resurrection of Christ. Our firm footing is the unchanging message of Jesus Christ. There are still some unchanging and unalterable truths.

Many people are slipping and sliding in their faith. Many substitutes are offered for the gospel. Paul confronted this problem in Galatians 1:6–10. This false gospel had the following marks: it was different, it was perverted, it was accursed, and it pleased men.

Galatians 5:1 says, "Stand fast therefore in the liberty by which Christ has made us free." We have but one gospel and one way to be saved: "Nor is there salvation in any other, for there is no other name under heaven given among men by which we must be saved" (Acts 4:12, see also verses 10–11). This is where we must stand.

The stability of the shoes

This is the day of spiritual tumbleweeds, blown about by circumstance and false doctrine. Shoes give us stability to keep us from stumbling in the battle. It is possible, even in the battleground of this world, to live a stable life. Ephesians 6:15 speaks of the gospel of peace.

The word *peace* is translated from the Greek word *eirene*. The Hebrew word is *shalom*. Peace is a state of well-being, a sense of contentment. I can have peace with God while I am at war with the devil himself.

> Therefore, having been justified by faith, we have peace with God through our Lord Jesus Christ, through whom also we have access by faith into this grace in which we stand, and rejoice in hope of the glory of God.
>
> —ROMANS 5:1–2

When you know that you stand before God at peace with Him because of the blood of Jesus, then Satan cannot worry you to death. W. D. Cornell must have been experiencing God's peace when he wrote the words to "Wonderful Peace."

> Peace, peace, wonderful peace
> Coming down from the Father above.
> Sweep over my spirit forever, I pray.
> In fathomless billows of love.[2]

If you allow the devil to trouble your mind and cause you anxiety, then all of your life becomes unstable. James 1:8 warns, "A double-minded man [is] unstable in all his ways." Don't allow the enemy to take your shoes off. Remember, in Christ you have what the world longs for—peace (Rom. 5:1–2) and true freedom (Gal. 5:1).

The mobility of the shoes

The word *preparation* is translated from a Greek word that means "readiness." The idea is of one being ready to move into battle at a moment's notice.

Already in Ephesians we have learned that the Christian life is a walk:

- We are not to walk wrongly (Eph. 2:2).
- We are to walk in His works (Eph. 2:10).
- We are to walk worthily (Eph. 4:1).
- We are to walk in love (Eph. 5:1–2).
- We are to walk in the light (Eph. 5:8).

You cannot walk properly without your gospel shoes in place. Too many Christians are sluggish and slow-footed. Others who have walked in the world without their shoes on are wounded and crippled. Today the church is paralyzed and muscle-bound.

Before World War II, General Charles de Gaulle wrote a series of essays warning France that a new kind of warfare was coming. The French had built the Maginot Line on their border. This defensive line consisted of powerful weapons in place facing Germany. De Gaulle warned the nation that new weapons, such as fighter planes and tanks, would make their defenses obsolete. No one listened, and France became a captive nation.[3]

Churches that draw their own lines of defense will stand still. We must be ready to advance with the gospel. Our opportunity for service is today. Now we must use our resources for spreading the gospel of Jesus Christ. We must be ready to move to the front where the battle for souls rages. Let us not flinch in this battle.

We must stand on the secure footing of the truth about Jesus. We must stand with stability of heart, even in the midst of our conflicts. We must be ready to move and stand in the heat of the battles.

Achilles, a hero of Greek mythology, was wounded in his heel. This was the only part of his body exposed, yet the wound killed him. Our feet must not be left unshod if we are to survive and triumph.

THE FAITH OF THE WARRIOR

Above all, taking the shield of faith with which you will be able to quench all the fiery darts of the wicked one.

—EPHESIANS 6:16

In ancient wars, archers would dip their arrows in pitch, set the tips of the arrows on fire, and launch them toward the opponent. The unwary soldier struck by one of these flaming missiles would receive an agonizing wound. His clothing would often be ignited, and he would be severely burned.

To combat these fiery arrows, the Romans invented a large door-shaped shield. The shields would measure four feet by two feet. Leather would be stretched around the frame, and prior to a battle, the shields were soaked in water. This served to repel the fiery arrows of the enemy.

Paul used this weapon to illustrate faith. He changed the verb in the Greek language from *having* to *taking* to describe the believer's use of the last three weapons (Eph. 6:16–17). You can "take" the shield, the helmet, and the sword. This means that you may choose to appropriate faith or not to appropriate faith.

What is faith? New Testament faith is believing to the point of commitment. Faith is trusting and acting on what God has said. Faith is as valid as the object on which it rests. I may believe a chair is sturdy, but I don't exercise biblical faith until I sit down in that chair. Here faith is said to be a shield. A shield like this was used by the Roman soldier to defend against the enemy as well as to advance against the enemy. If I am to put my faith in a shield, I need to know more about that shield.

The shield taken

In order to take the shield, you must understand what—or rather who—the shield is in Scripture. We discover in Genesis 14 and 15 the identity of our shield. In these chapters, Abraham wins a great victory. The king of Sodom offers him a reward that he wisely refuses. Rather, Abraham pays tithes to Melchizedek shortly after Abraham refused the reward of the world. God speaks to him and says, "Do not be afraid, Abram. I am your shield, your exceedingly great reward" (Gen. 15:1).

Abraham put his life in God's hands. God was the shield he needed in order to live in a hostile world.

David also took the shield of faith. He said, "But You, O Lord, are a shield for me" (Ps. 3:3). In Psalm 84:11 we read, "For the Lord God is a sun and shield; the Lord will give grace and glory; no good thing will He withhold from those who walk uprightly."

We take the shield of faith when we trust the Lord. Habakkuk 2:4 says, "The just shall live by his faith." Habakkuk wrote this at a time when the wicked prospered, the enemy threatened, and the people of God needed revival. He asked God hard questions. God's answer was, "Live by faith."

This verse is quoted in Romans 1:17, Galatians 3:11, and Hebrews 10:38. Faith not only gives us life, but it is also the way we live our lives.

We are saved by faith in God's Word about His Son. We also live by faith: "The life which I now live in the flesh I live by faith in the Son of God, who loved me and gave Himself for me" (Gal. 2:20). The songwriter Robert Grant expressed his thoughts this way:

> O worship the King, all glorious above,
> O gratefully sing His power and His love;
> Our Shield and Defender, the Ancient of Days,
> Pavilioned in splendor, and girded with praise.[4]

The shield tested

The test of faith reminds us of the wicked one, whom we meet daily on the battlefield of our lives. This should not surprise us or alarm us. Our Lord was tested by the enemy in the wilderness temptation. When the apostle Paul wrote of this shield of faith, he was in prison.

The shield of faith does not protect us from life. Paul faced difficult circumstances, bodily weaknesses, exhausting labors, and agonizing disappointments, yet he had a shield. You may go through trials of faith, but God won't let anything touch you without His permission. The shield is not meant to make you comfortable in this world. The shield is Christ, and we face everything by His grace.

The devil will hurl his fiery darts. They come sometimes as temptations. They come as distractions. They come as accusations. They come as imaginations. They come as depression. Sometimes they come as persecution! All of these flaming arrows of hellish hate can be answered by Jesus. This shield can take care of all that Satan can hurl at you.

How does faith answer the attacks of the enemy? With the Word of God, always! Faith rests on the character of God, the Word of God, and the promise of God.

When Satan accuses you, let the Word of God answer him. Let the cross of Christ answer the enemy. Refuse the flaming missiles of the enemy.

Someone may ask, "What if I can't remember a scripture?" Just cry out for God. When a child is in trouble and doesn't know what to do, the child cries, "Daddy!" Dear friend, when you don't know how to answer, just cry out for God!

The shield triumphant

All that Satan can hurl at a believer, God can take care of. "This is the victory that has overcome the world—our faith" (1 John 5:4). Faith is always victorious.

Often the Roman army would place their best soldiers on the front line. On occasion that line would stretch a mile. The army would advance behind that formation of brave soldiers who would go forward behind the shield.

The church advances behind the mighty shield of faith. Without faith we are defenseless and useless to God. We cannot please Him without faith. Faith alone is the key to victory. Faith is how we live. Faith is "frontline" Christianity. Faith protects us from Satan. Faith appropriates the promises of God. Faith is always victorious.

THE MIND OF THE WARRIOR

Take the helmet of salvation...

—EPHESIANS 6:17

Every believer is a saint and a soldier, a worshiper and a warrior, in the faith and in the fight! As warriors we fight from a position of strength and victory. We wage war in the right posture, for we are told to stand! We are supplied with a panoply of armor that is adequate to carry us through the battlefields of this life.

We face an intelligent, aggressive enemy who targets the crucial areas of our life for attack. The Greek word for "devil" (*diabolos*) means "a traducer, false accuser, slanderer." He is the "one who hurls through." He is an accuser.

God has provided armor with which to defend our faith and defeat our foes. This armor is comprised of the attributes of our Lord Jesus Christ.

- When you receive the *belt of truth*, it is Jesus who says, "I am...the truth" (John 14:6).

- When you receive the *breastplate of righteousness,* it is Jesus who is the righteousness of God (1 Cor. 1:30).

- When you put on the *shoes of peace,* it is Jesus who says, "My peace I give to you" (John 14:27).

- When you lift the *shield of faith,* it is Jesus alone who can answer every fiery accusation of hell.

Next is the *helmet of salvation.* The Roman helmet, made of metal, covered the head and the cheekbones. It protected against the deathblow of the enemy. The helmet of salvation likewise protects the believer from the deathblow of Satan. Let's look at Satan's attack on the mind.

The attack on the mind

We live in a corrupt world in which people are governed by a "reprobate mind" (Rom. 1:28, KJV). Believers are warned not to walk "in the vanity of their mind" (Eph. 4:17, KJV).

Playwright George Bernard Shaw wrote, "The science I pinned my faith to is bankrupt....For its sake I helped destroy the faith of millions of worshipers....And now look at me and behold the tragedy of an atheist who has lost his faith."[5]

Our world talks about "safe sex" rather than about moral living. Our nation knows a lot about rights and not much about responsibility. Even the church often runs its ministry according to the world. Romans 8:6 says, "To be carnally minded is death." *To be carnally minded* means "to think according to the flesh".

In Luke 12:29 Jesus warned us about the confused mind: "neither be ye of doubtful mind" (KJV). This phrase is translated from the Greek word *meteorizo,* from which our English word *meteor* comes. It means to be "up in the air, suspended, unsettled." There are many who have allowed their lives to be without answer.

Philippians 4:6 says, "Be anxious for nothing." Much discouragement and depression is caused by needless worry. Our minds must not be filled with deception. Second Corinthians 2:11 warns us about a careless mind: "Lest Satan should take advantage of us; for we are not ignorant of his devices." How foolish to live in ignorance of Satan's deceptions. God wants us to think straight.

The assurance of the mind

The helmet is called the helmet of salvation. Salvation is the deliverance of the believers from their lost and condemned position to life in God's kingdom. Salvation has three perspectives:

1. *Salvation is a past event.* In the counsels of eternity, at the cross in history, and in one's personal conversion, salvation is an event that begins in the past.

2. *Salvation is a present experience.* Salvation continues in the life of the Christian. "He who has begun a good work in you will complete it until the day of Jesus Christ" (Phil. 1:6). Salvation goes on happening in the life of the Christian.

3. *Salvation is a promised expectation.* Salvation looks ahead to the believer's future hope. Romans 13:11 speaks of that future perspective: "Now our salvation is nearer than when we first believed."

I am convinced that the helmet of salvation is our assurance of God's protection until the day He comes back. In 1 Thessalonians 5:4–9, the helmet is clearly defined as the "hope of salvation." We can keep our heads straight and our minds from being messed up by remembering that the Lord is in control and that He is coming.

Psychiatrists tell us that for good mental health, a person needs someone to love, something worthwhile to do, and something to hope for. This is true on a practical level. Knowing that Friday is coming gets some of us through the week. The knowledge that present pain will end and health will come gets people through illness and surgery.

The hope of heaven and a better life helps to carry us through this life. Titus 2:13 says, "Looking for the blessed hope and glorious appearing of our great God and Savior Jesus Christ." Hebrews 6:18–19 says, "That...we might have strong consolation, who have fled for refuge to lay hold of the hope set before us. This hope we have as an anchor of the soul." The forerunner, our Lord, has gone before us to glory and anchored our souls to His throne. There is nothing the world can do that our anchor of hope cannot get us through.

I'm reminded again of another great hymn of our faith, "How Firm a Foundation":

> How firm a foundation, ye saints of the Lord
> Is laid for your faith in His excellent Word...
> That soul, though all hell should endeavor to shake
> I'll never, no never, no never forsake.[6]

The answer of the mind

How do we control, then, our thoughts and minds?

First, you must repent in the mind. *Repentance* comes from the Greek word *metanoia*, which means "a change of mind."

Second, you must receive with the mind. "Let this mind be in you which was also in Christ Jesus" (Phil. 2:5). "We have the mind of Christ" (1 Cor. 2:16). "Since Christ suffered for us in the flesh, arm yourselves also with the same mind" (1 Pet. 4:1)

Third, you must renew your mind. "Present your bodies a living sacrifice, holy, acceptable to God, which is your reasonable service. And do not be conformed to this world, but be transformed by the renewing of your mind, that you may prove what is that good and acceptable and perfect will of God" (Rom. 12:1–2). These verses teach us that surrendering our bodies to Him and refusing to be conformed to the world brings the renewal of the mind. This is a daily need.

Steps to a renewed mind

How do you renew the mind? Philippians 4 sets forth the steps to handling troubled thoughts and a messed-up mind.

1. **Rejoice in the Lord.** "Rejoice in the Lord always. Again I will say, rejoice! Let your gentleness be known to all men. The Lord is at hand" (Phil. 4:4–5). Praise is a great antidote to trouble. Rejoicing acknowledges the nearness of the Lord.

2. **Request of God.** "Be anxious for nothing, but in everything by prayer and supplication, with thanksgiving, let your requests be made known to God" (Phil. 4:6). Prayer is an antidote to mental agony. Talk to God about your needs.

3. **Rest in Christ.** "The peace of God, which surpasses all understanding, will guard your hearts and minds through Christ Jesus" (Phil. 4:7). Let God's peace stand guard over your mind.

4. **Reflect on the good things of God.** "Whatever things are true, whatever things are noble, whatever things are just, whatever things are pure, whatever things are lovely, whatever things are of good report, if there is any virtue and if there is anything praiseworthy—meditate on these things. The things which you learned and received and heard and saw in me, these do, and the God of peace will be with you" (Phil. 4:8–9). Think good thoughts. Use the Bible to counter the evil thoughts.

5. **Relax in the Lord.** "But I rejoiced in the Lord greatly that now at last your care for me has flourished again; though you surely did care, but you lacked opportunity. Not that I speak in regard to need, for I have learned in whatever state I am, to be content: I know how to be abased, and I know how to abound. Everywhere and in all things I have learned both to be full and to be hungry, both to abound and to suffer need. I can do all things through Christ who strengthens me" (Phil. 4:10–13). God has promised to supply all our needs. Faith thanks God and receives from His hand all that we need.

Are you wearing the helmet of salvation? Are you living in hope? Is your mind clear? Are you thinking straight? Jesus Christ will give you a new mind. Do you need to repent? Do you need to receive? Do you need to renew your mind? Jesus Christ stands ready to help you today.

THE SWORD OF A WARRIOR

And take…the sword of the Spirit, which is the word of God; praying always with all prayer and supplication in the Spirit, being

watchful to this end with all perseverance and supplication for all
the saints.

—EPHESIANS 6:17–18

This section on warfare calls on every Christian to stand against Satan.
Now Satan comes at us directly—through the world system in which
we live and through our flesh. All of the weapons that we have studied
thus far are defensive in nature. With these weapons we can fend off the
attack of our enemy.

- With our belt and breastplate we have integrity and identity in Christ. Satan cannot attack our character.

- With our shoes and shield we have balance and belief.
  Satan cannot penetrate our commitment.

- With our helmet we have assurance and anticipation of the
  good things of God. Satan cannot destroy our confidence.

James 4:7 tells us, "Resist the devil and he will flee from you." Defensive
weapons can hold off Satan, but only offensive weapons can cause him to
flee! God has supplied just such a weapon in the sword of the Spirit.

The word *sword* is used of the Roman two-edged sword, one used
in hand-to-hand combat. This perfectly balanced weapon was handled
skillfully by the Roman soldiers who practiced several hours daily to
perfect its use. Let's learn about this weapon and its use.

The sword and the soldier

"Take…the sword." The word *take* is an aorist imperative middle verb
in the Greek text. It is a once-and-for-all command for the soldier-saint
to take what God has available. The offensive weapon God offers is His
Word. The Word of God is to be used to attack our enemy, Satan.

This sword is not of human origin. It was forged by the divine decree.
It was not tempered with earthly fire but in the burning flames of the
majestic presence of God. The hammer of heavenly inspiration shaped
the sword that fits in the hand of the believer.

Hebrews 4:12–13 tell us that the Word of God is a living sword. It is
penetrating and powerful. The sharp sword of the Word of God exposes
evil. In this passage the sword is in the hand of our great High Priest, the

Lord Jesus. Using the sword as a surgical tool, He can cut into our lives and discern the thoughts and intentions. With this sword He performed the surgery of salvation. After using the sword on you, the saint, Jesus places the same sword in your hand.

The secret of King Arthur's fighting ability was his sword, Excalibur. This special sword endowed an ordinary warrior with extraordinary power! So it is with the believer. The sword of the Spirit gives the believer a weapon of unlimited power.

The sword of the Spirit

"Take…the sword of the Spirit." Notice carefully that the sword is connected to the Spirit of God. Having the sword of the Spirit is not simply having a Bible! The Holy Spirit inspired the Bible (2 Pet. 1:21). Only the Holy Spirit can teach you the Bible: "The Counselor, the Holy Spirit, whom the Father will send in my name, will teach you all things" (John 14:26, NIV). John 16:13 says of the Spirit, "He will guide you into all truth."

Without the Holy Spirit the truths of the Bible cannot be understood: "But the natural man does not receive the things of the Spirit of God, for they are foolishness to him; nor can he know them, because they are spiritually discerned" (1 Cor. 2:14). The power of the Holy Spirit directs the use of the Word in the life of the believer.

Another way to use the sword is to praise. Psalm 149:6 says, "Let the high praises of God be in their mouth, and a two-edged sword in their hand." Every one of us needs to take the sword of the Spirit. The Word of God must be loved, learned, and lived out in order for it to be a sword. No part of our lives should be lived without prayer and the Word.

In 2 Samuel 23:10 we are told about Eleazar, one of David's mighty men. He fought the Philistines until the sword stuck to his hand. That sword became an extension of his body. May the Word of God, the sword of the Spirit, be that and more to all who would be good soldiers of Jesus Christ.

chapter 32

SLAMMING THE DOOR IN THE ENEMY'S FACE

JESUS CHRIST IS called "the captain of [our] salvation" (Heb. 2:10). One of His stated purposes was to set those free who were captive of Satan.

Jesus came to heal all who were oppressed by the devil. As we read in the Book of Acts, "God anointed Jesus of Nazareth with the Holy Spirit and with power, who went about doing good and healing all who were oppressed by the devil, for God was with Him" (Acts 10:38).

This is the purpose of His church. The first time the church is mentioned in the Scriptures is in Matthew, where we read, "And I also say to you that you are Peter, and on this rock I will build My church, and the gates of Hades shall not prevail against it" (Matt. 16:18). Here is spiritual warfare at the first mention of the church.

The phrase "gates of Hades [or hell] shall not prevail against it" is often misunderstood. We have a picture of us locked behind some gates. Look again at the text. The Greek text indicates that we are attacking the gates of hell! Here is the church on the offensive tearing down the gates of the kingdom of darkness and setting the captives free! You see a militant Christ and a militant church.

We are in an invisible war with a sinister foe. We have weapons of the Spirit that can win. Sadly, many believers live with depression, oppression, fear, habits, family curses, personality changes, addictions, and unexplained illnesses. Where is the victory promised us? What is going on?

Paul speaks of our warfare and satanic attacks on believers in 2 Corinthians 10:3–4. He describes these problems using the term *stronghold*. The Greek word means "fortress." It is derived from a word that means "able, hold, possessed with disease, lack, and need." Strongholds are the way the enemy gains access and control in a Christian's life.

DEFINITION OF A STRONGHOLD

A stronghold is a fortress of wrong thinking that can harbor a demonic entity. This demonic entity can launch attacks from the house our wrong thinking has constructed for him. Yes indeed, we can actually put a gun in the enemy's hand for him to shoot us. Habits and addictions many times are simply demonically infested strongholds. This is not demon possession but demon infestation. Christians can be oppressed, depressed, tempted, harassed, and buffeted—but they cannot be possessed.

Though believers can never be totally overtaken by Satan and his demons, the sad reality is that many are harassed constantly by wicked forces. Whenever the flesh is in control of a Christian's life, demons are given a place in the believer's mind. This place is usually an unconfessed sin, an unbroken bad habit (obsession), or a wrong attitude. Simply stated, the believer has embraced a lie. Second Corinthians 10:5 says, "Casting down arguments and every high thing that exalts itself against the knowledge of God…" The battle rages in the thinking process of a believer; these wrong ideas, bad attitudes, false assumptions, wrong traditions, and lies can become a doorway for demons into our lives. They also can serve as hiding places that harbor demons.

TWELVE ROOT STRONGHOLDS

1. The *spirit of infirmity* affected a believing woman in the New Testament: "And behold, there was a woman who had a spirit of infirmity eighteen years, and was bent over and could in no way raise herself up" (Luke 13:11). This woman was a faithful attendee of the synagogue. She was a daughter of Abraham, yet demons affected her health. Some examples are disorders of the body, attacks on male and female identity, allergies, and strange syndromes.

2. The *spirit of fear.* "For God has not given us a spirit of fear, but of power and of love and of a sound mind" (2 Tim.

1:7). Examples include fright, torment, inferiority, inadequacy, worry, critical spirit, tension, performance, and fear of anything.

3. The *spirit of python*, also called divination. "Now it happened, as we went to prayer, that a certain slave girl possessed with a spirit of divination met us, who brought her masters much profit by fortune-telling. This girl followed Paul and us, and cried out, saying, 'These men are the servants of the Most High God, who proclaim to us the way of salvation.' And this she did for many days. But Paul, greatly annoyed, turned and said to the spirit, 'I command you in the name of Jesus Christ to come out of her.' And he came out that very hour" (Acts 16:16–18). Rebellion, witchcraft, occult practices, and black arts flow from this spirit. Curses follow involvement with these practices.

4. The *spirit of sexual immorality,* called harlotry or whoredoms. "My people ask counsel from their wooden idols, and their staff informs them. For the spirit of harlotry has caused them to stray, and they have played the harlot against their God" (Hosea 4:12). Lust, adultery, pornography, rape, incest, pride, and love of the world are characteristics of this demon. Sexual addiction is also a result of this perverted spirit.

5. An *enslaving spirit* that usually accompanies fear. "For you did not receive the spirit of bondage again to fear, but you received the Spirit of adoption by whom we cry out, 'Abba, Father'" (Rom. 8:15). Addictions, bulimia, anorexia, wrong relationships, codependency, and other obsessive disorders are worsened by this demon.

6. The *spirit of pride* that normally is accompanied by rebellion. "Pride goes before destruction, and a haughty spirit before a fall. Better to be of a humble spirit with the lowly, than to divide the spoil with the proud" (Prov. 16:18–19) Pride, scorn, mockery, lewdness, egotism, prejudice, arro-

gance, gossip, and criticism manifest from this wicked spirit.

7. The *spirit of perversion.* "The LORD has mingled a perverse spirit in her midst; and they have caused Egypt to err in all her work, as a drunken man staggers in his vomit" (Isa. 19:14). Homosexuality, sexual perversion, and abnormal activities are incited by this spirit.

8. The *spirit of Antichrist.* "And every spirit that does not confess that Jesus Christ has come in the flesh is not of God. And this is the spirit of the Antichrist, which you have heard was coming, and is now already in the world" (1 John 4:3). This demon takes glory away from Christ; denies the supernatural gifts, attributing them to Satan; opposes; harasses; persecutes; and divides true ministries.

9. The *spirit of depression* or heaviness. "…to console those who mourn in Zion, to give them beauty for ashes, the oil of joy for mourning, the garment of praise for the spirit of heaviness; that they may be called trees of righteousness, the planting of the LORD, that He may be glorified" (Isa. 61:3). Depression, abnormal grief, despair, hopelessness, and suicidal thoughts flow from this malevolent demon.

10. The *lying spirit,* one of Satan's favorite tools. "We are of God. He who knows God hears us; he who is not of God does not hear us. By this we know the spirit of truth and the spirit of error" (1 John 4:6). Unbelief, deception, compromise, intellectualism, cults, flattery, and legalism flow from this divisive spirit.

11. The *spirit of jealousy,* a relationship-destroying spirit. "If the spirit of jealousy comes upon him and he becomes jealous of his wife, who has defiled herself; or if the spirit of jealousy comes upon him and he becomes jealous of his wife, although she has not defiled herself" (Num. 5:14). Jealousy, anger, rage, cruelty, suspicion, unnatural compe-

tition, insecurity, divorce, and division are the results of allowing this spirit to operate.

12. The *spirit of stupor* or slumber. "Just as it is written: 'God has given them a spirit of stupor, eyes that they should not see and ears that they should not hear, to this very day'" (Rom. 11:8). Constant fatigue, passivity, feeling like a wallflower, and self-pity describe this demon. When allowed to control, this spirit blocks success and brings weariness to life.

TAKING DOWN THE ENEMY'S STRONGHOLDS

In order to take down these strongholds of Satan, you must become an armed believer. Revelation 12:11 declares our threefold weapon to overcome our enemy: "And they overcame him by the blood of the Lamb and by the word of their testimony, and they did not love their lives to the death."

1. The blood cancels Satan's right to oppress you.

2. The word of your testimony. Yes, take the Word of God as a sword, and release it out of your mouth against the enemy. The truth will set you free.

3. A surrendered life to Jesus. You can appropriate all of Jesus's weaponry, and you must capture every thought of the enemy and cast it down.

We see the atoning blood, the witness of the armed believer, and the life abandoned to the will of Jesus. Satan trembles before the believer with God's weapons. Let me share eight steps to the removal of a stronghold.

- Step one—Be sure you have confessed Jesus Christ as your Lord and Savior.

- Step two—Realize only God can remove a stronghold.

- Step three—Identify the stronghold.

- Step four—Confess all sins related to strongholds.

- Step five—Thank God for forgiveness.

- Step six—Visualize the destruction.

- Step seven—Ask God to free you from the negative demonic force associated with strongholds.

- Step eight—Make restitution.

After these steps you must possess the reclaimed territory. Confess that you are no longer affected by that area of stronghold and claim God's fullness. Be finished with the sins that enslaved you, and fill your mind with Scripture in order to reinforce the victory.

In the Old Testament, the Jews were told to drive out the enemy and possess Canaan. The territory of your soul, like Canaan, is full of strongholds that must be torn down. As soldiers we must take what is ours. The abundant life awaits those of us who will drive out the enemy and possess the land of our souls. The fortress of Jericho fell down before the people of God. Satan's fortress will crumble before us if we wield our weapons.

> …and being ready to punish all disobedience when your obedience is fulfilled.
>
> —2 CORINTHIANS 10:6

When you cast away these strongholds, every demon that has lurked behind these lies, habits, sicknesses, and wrong choices is exposed, and God punishes their disobedience. The Greek word for "punish" is *ekdikeo*—or revenge. When we are full of obedience, then God will take revenge on every demon that has dared to threaten you.

SECTION VI

MAINTAINING THE VICTORY OVER YOUR ENEMY

chapter 33

PUTTING THE ENEMY
TO FLIGHT

SATAN HAS BEEN stripped of authority in the life of every believer. Satan and his demonic forces fear the authority of the Word of God through Christ. James 2:19 says, "Even the demons believe—and tremble!" A decisive battle was waged and won at the cross and the empty tomb, and that victory stripped Satan and his hosts of authority. Colossians 2:15 declares that Jesus "disarmed principalities and powers [of their authority]."

When Jesus came to the world, it was an occupied, armed camp of Satan. The forces of evil recognized Him (Mark 1:23–25). In Mark 5, evil forces encamped in a man. Enough demons controlled him to fill two thousand swine. But notice that these forces could not move without the permission of Jesus. Jesus defeated Satan and broke his authority at every point.

Satan could not receive Jesus. He could not get Jesus to yield to temptation. Death could not hold Jesus. Satan used every weapon and found them broken under the feet of Christ. The glorious truth is that you and I can enforce that victory. We can put the enemy to flight. We can see Satan in rapid retreat. Here are the simple steps to victory.

THE REQUIREMENT OF SUBMISSION

God resists the proud, but gives grace to the humble.

—JAMES 4:6

Before a believer can effectively put Satan to flight, he must be under authority himself. God resists the proud. The word *proud* describes a self-sufficient person who runs his own life. The word *resist* means "to arrange an army against." God has placed an army against the self-sufficient.

The key word in James 4:7 is *submit*. It is a military word that means "to place under orders." A believer has authority over Satan by living under the authority of Christ. A rebellious, sinning Christian cannot put Satan to flight. The Christian who lives under God-given authority can put the enemy to flight. Believers must learn to live under authority. The Word of God sets forth God's pattern of authority.

Christians live under the authority of Christ. We also live under the authority of human government (1 Pet. 2:13–15). The wife is to live under the authority of her husband (Eph. 5:22–24). Children are to live under the authority of parents (Eph. 6:1–3). This is for protection and power. All human authority is delegated, but it is invalid if it violates the will of God. "We ought to obey God rather than men" (Acts 5:29).

We are told that if we are to defeat Satan, we must be under orders. Jesus lived under the will of the Father in His earthly sojourn. This was the secret of His power. He lived under authority. "He humbled Himself and became obedient to the point of death" (Phil. 2:8). This was the prelude to victory. This was the path to authority. After His submission came His exaltation. Verse 10 declares that every realm is now under His authority—the spiritual realm, the natural realm, and the demonic realm. Before we can stand in authority, we must submit ourselves to God completely.

THE RESISTANCE OF SATAN

Therefore submit to God. Resist the devil and he will flee from you.

—JAMES 4:7

Once we are under authority, we can stand in Christ's authority. Ephesians 1 and 2 declare these truths. Ephesians 1:19–23 declares the authority of the risen, ascended, and enthroned Christ. We must recognize that we have no authority over Satan in our own flesh and power. We are made lower than the angels. But in Christ we have been given His authority over Satan.

Ephesians 2:1–6 declares that we are now fully identified with Christ in His crucifixion, resurrection, ascension, and in being enthroned. Thus we now share His authority. We are now in Him, elevated above the angelic realm.

We are to *resist* Satan. This word in Ephesians 4:7 is not the same as the word in verse 6. The word in verse 7 implies "to stand alone." It pictures the believer and God against Satan. We stand without human help.

We must learn that we cannot hide from Satan. We cannot run away from Satan. We cannot outrun him, and we cannot get away from him on this planet.

How, then, do we resist Satan?

- Be sure you are living an obedient and clean life under authority.

- Take your stand against Satan in the authority of Christ.

- Stand steadfast in faith, believing God for the victory.

- Verbally attack Satan with the Word of God and the work of Christ.

- Give no place to Satan; give up no ground whatever.

- Demand in the authority of Christ that he leave.

- Give thanks and praise to God and watch the devil run.

chapter 34

TURNING BACK THE ENEMY

THE CHRISTIAN LIFE is always on a collision course with the agenda of Satan. Once a prince, he is now a usurper—a pretender to the throne of the earth.

Satan's rebellion dates back to the pre-Adamic world. Both science and Scripture affirm a great cataclysm that brought ruin and death to this world before Adam. Lucifer became the malicious Satan lurking in the body of a snake in Eden.

Though Satan is defeated, he awaits his final sentence along with those of the human race who will be sent to hell with him. Jesus defeated our ancient enemy and sentenced him to oblivion, preparing a burning hell for him and his angelic cohorts.

Until the final sentence, he remains in our solar system as "the prince of the power of the air." He has permission to operate in the disobedient. He is part and parcel of this fallen world. Therefore we know that the earth for us is not a playground but a battleground.

Psalm 56 is one of those Psalms called a *michtam*, which means "golden song" or "precious song." Its title expresses a longing in David, "The Silent Dove in Distant Lands." This reaches back to Psalm 55:6: "So I said, 'Oh, that I had wings like a dove! I would fly away and be at rest.'"

This psalm was composed when David was being hounded by Saul and fell into the hands of the Philistines. David longed for the days of solitude before the haunting responsibility of leadership fell on him. He had been anointed king, yet instead of a throne, he had war!

This is not unlike our experience: we come to Christ, are anointed by the Spirit, and then the enemy declares war! Yet we know that victory is ours.

FOUR WAYS THE ENEMY OPPRESSES

How does the enemy challenge us? His strategy is to put pressure on you on every side. Here is a clear distinction of satanic oppression and how to identify it.

Satan will surround us with people who distract us. In Psalm 56:2 David feels that he is being hounded by lions. You know there are people in your life whose main goal is to waste your time, distract you, criticize you, or confuse you! When Peter tried to "help" Jesus by denying the need for the cross, Jesus said, "Get behind me, Satan."

Sometimes those close to you will hinder you. At other times people will directly attack you! Remember—the enemy will use anyone! "Be merciful to me, O God, for man would swallow me up; fighting all day he oppresses me" (Ps. 56:1). Notice the word *swallow*; it means "to beat, to curb, and to swallow." Sometimes the enemy just wants to crush your spirit and swallow up your purpose! The phrase "all day" is translated from a Hebrew word that means "all the time; the total of everything." Literally it means that Satan attacks the totality of my life's purpose all the time! He is relentless.

We have already learned of Satan's efforts to intimidate. In the first Gulf War the terms "shock and awe" were introduced, describing an attack that went on from the air for days. The purpose was to crash the will of the ones attacked. Our enemy tries "shock and awe" as the prince of the power of the air.

Satan will use slander to defeat us and turn us away from victory. "All day they twist my words; all their thoughts are against me for evil" (Ps. 56:5). Satan is the accuser! His goal is to slander and to ruin. Remember his vicious attack on Job. The word *twist* is the Hebrew word *atsab*, which means "to fabricate, to carve, to cut up, to inflict pain." Satan will take what you say and do, fashion it into something that causes pain, and misrepresent you and what you believe!

The word *thoughts* means "to weave or fashion." It is used of wrong judgments. Satan will twist and fabricate in order to thwart God's purpose for your life.

Psalm 56:6 declares that Satan stalks believers to hinder their faith: "They gather together, they hide, they mark my steps, when they lie in wait for my life." Here are the final tactics of Satan. Simply notice that more often than not Satan uses people, even believers, to do his dirty work.

SEVEN WINNING RESPONSES TO SATAN'S CHALLENGE

Psalm 56:9 teaches us, "When I cry to You [the Lord], then my enemies will turn back." In tracking through this psalm we discover seven victorious responses to the enemy.

First, we must trust the Lord as the psalmist did. "Whenever I am afraid, I will trust in You" (v. 3). The word *trust* in Hebrew is *batach*, which means "to be confident, secure, safe, and to trust." Its ancient root means "to be stretched out." Here the wrinkles of worry leave as you get spiritual Botox. It also means "to lie safely on the ground."

Psalm 56:4 gives us the second response, which is to trust God's Word. "In God (I will praise His word), in God I have put my trust; I will not fear. What can flesh do to me?" Here the believer takes refuge in God and His Word. He *hallels* the word! He shouts hallelujah in the middle of the attack because he has a word from God! There He trusts in God while the battle rages.

Third, we can take refuge in a God who cares for us and "number[s] my wanderings; put my tears into Your bottle; are they not in Your book?" (Ps. 56:8). Here is trust! While the enemy stalks, God "number[s] my wanderings." The word *number* is "to keep score in order to celebrate later." God will celebrate our victory with us! The word *wandering* is "exile." The enemy has tried to exile us from our land, but God is keeping score. We will get back all that the enemy has taken. God is keeping the book! Our tears are being kept in a wineskin (bottle). That which is bitter God will turn to fine wine. He will take our tears and turn them to joy.

Fourth, prayer brings God's resources on to the scene. "When I cry out to You, then my enemies will turn back; this I know, because God is for me" (Ps. 56:9). Here is passionate prayer that cries out to God in the face of the enemy. This is bold, loud, demanding prayer. God will hear our prayers when they are offered in urgency.

Fifth, I can rest in absolute assurance according to verse 9: "This I know, because God is for me." Wow! Here the believer expresses supreme confidence. Here the mighty shield of faith is lifted up against the enemy. Romans 8:28 affirms this Old Testament promise: "And we know that all things work together for good to those who love God, to those who are the called according to His purpose." God is for you—*believe it!*

Sixth, when we honor our promises, God will protect us. "Vows made to You are binding upon me, O God; I will render praises to You" (Ps. 56:12). A direct interpretation of this would read, "I will fulfill my promises to you, O God, even as I lift my hands in praise." *Towdal* means "to lift the hands while praising God." God views this as a solemn promise to keep our vows. When you do what you promise, victory is guaranteed.

Notice the following warning and promise about vows:

> When you make a vow to God, do not delay to pay it; for He has no pleasure in fools. Pay what you have vowed—better not to vow than to vow and not pay. Do not let your mouth cause your flesh to sin, nor say before the messenger of God that it was an error. Why should God be angry at your excuse and destroy the work of your hands?
> —ECCLESIASTES 5:4–6

The destroyer comes after broken promises to the Lord. "It is a snare for a man to devote rashly something as holy, and afterward to reconsider his vows" (Prov. 20:25).

Seventh, we give witness of God's mighty power as David did in the closing verse of Psalm 56: "For You have delivered my soul from death. Have You not kept my feet from falling, that I may walk before God in the light of the living?" (v. 13). This closing verse declares that God rescues our lives. God keeps us from falling. The word *falling* means "to be pushed." The word *feet* is journey. God will not allow the enemy to push us down or off a cliff on our journey; we will make it home!

God gives us a fresh, new start. The word *living* means "fresh flesh." God renews your life on Earth as you walk before Him in the *light*, or daylight. This speaks of a new beginning. This is how life was meant to be lived!

Here is a proclamation to turn back the enemy:

- I nullify every satanic prayer by the blood of Jesus, in Jesus's name.

- I nullify every satanic challenge by the blood of Jesus, in Jesus's name.

- I nullify every satanic decree against my life, in the name of Jesus.

- I nullify every satanic desire upon my life by the blood of Jesus, in Jesus' name.

- I nullify every satanic expectation concerning my life, in the name of Jesus.

- I nullify every satanic decision taken against my life, in the name of Jesus.

- I nullify every satanic agreement standing against my life, by the blood of Jesus.

- I nullify every satanic conspiracy in the heavenlies against my life in the name of Jesus.

- I nullify every satanic conspiracy on Earth against my life in the name of Jesus.

- I nullify every satanic plan and program for my life in the name of Jesus.

chapter 35

LIVING A LIFE OF WORSHIP

LET'S LOOK BRIEFLY at David's training of his warriors for battle. It is interesting to note that Psalm 18, the "manual of instruction," is framed by praise. Toward the end of the psalm David exclaimed, "The LORD lives! Blessed be my Rock! Let the God of my salvation be exalted" (v. 46). David knew that the worship of God put the enemy to flight.

WORSHIP 101

Yet another psalm seems to be an instruction manual on the art of praise.

> Praise the LORD!
> Sing to the LORD a new song,
> And His praise in the assembly of saints.
> Let Israel rejoice in their Maker;
> Let the children of Zion be joyful in their King.
> Let them praise His name with the dance;
> Let them sing praises to Him with the timbrel and harp.
> For the LORD takes pleasure in His people;
> He will beautify the humble with salvation.
> Let the saints be joyful in glory;
> Let them sing aloud on their beds.
> Let the high praises of God be in their mouth,
> And a two-edged sword in their hand,
> To execute vengeance on the nations,
> And punishments on the peoples;

To bind their kings with chains,
And their nobles with fetters of iron;
To execute on them the written judgment—
This honor have all His saints.
Praise the LORD!

—PSALM 149:1–9

This beautiful psalm tells us that praise isn't just about the music created—it's about the noise of worship. This noise floods the ears of our enemies in battle. It includes laughter, weeping, clapping, and shouting. It even includes the quiet rustle of the breath of the body of Christ when they turn to Him in quiet meditation of His goodness. It is all warfare, the sound of battle in the ear of the enemy.

Worship has even more strength when a whole body of believers does it. This psalm tells us, "Let Israel rejoice." The reference is plural. Something occurs that is powerful during corporate worship where two or three or more are gathered. Jesus promised, "I am there in the midst of them" (Matt. 18:20).

We also know from Hebrews 2:12 that when He shows up in the midst and we are singing, He starts singing. If you think your worship does something to demons, wait until the Lord Jesus starts singing along with you and then the Holy Ghost kicks in and then God the Father starts singing back to you!

Worship should reflect or picture the three parts of the tabernacle or temple. We start at the outer court, where the blood saved us, and we praise the name of Jesus for our salvation. We then proceed into the holy place, where there is the table of shewbread and the candlelight. In that place His Word and His guidance illuminate us a little more, and we enter into those gates with thanksgiving and into those courts with praise.

But then we proceed toward the holy of holies, where there is a veil that has been rent. When the highest praises begin, we go into that place of immunity and intimacy with our Lord where no devil of hell can touch us. The psalmist said, "This honor have all His saints" (Ps. 149:9). At one time, only the priests could enter the holy of holies, but after the cross, Jesus said, "Come on in. You're welcome into this holy place."

Most churches have never entered that place during their corporate worship. They don't know what it is like to get quiet and just lie at His feet and say, "I'm not moving, Lord, until You move. I'm here until You tell me what to do."

Look further at Psalm 149, where the psalmist says that there are many ways to do it. We can play instruments. We can sing. Yes, we can even dance! Verse 3 says, "Let them praise His name with the dance; let them sing praises to Him with the timbrel and harp."

There is more we must learn about worship. Verse 4 continues, "For the LORD takes pleasure in His people." God loves it when you sing. Psalm 22:3 says, "Thou [God] inhabitest the praises…" (KJV). The Hebrew word for "inhabit," *yashab*, means "to dwell with as a husband with the wife he loves." When you begin to sing, He comes not with a whip but with a gift in His hand. When you sing, He comes to kiss you. *Worship* means "to kiss toward." When you sing, God responds as a protector, as a provider, as a lover, as a covering, and as a father.

It doesn't matter if you have a trained voice; God loves to hear you sing! Once in a while my wife, Paulette, will make the request, "Honey, sing to me." My congregation knows that I would never be asked to stand with a microphone and present a special musical offering, but filtered through love, my wife thinks I sound great!

AN EFFECTIVE WEAPON

Our praises of God become a mighty weapon. Psalm 149:6 says, "Let the high praises of God be in [your] mouth, and a [sharp] two-edged sword in [your] hand." Do you long for the power of God's Word to work in your life? Start praising Him!

I often think of David as a youth, running to meet Goliath with stone and sling in hand. The praises of God were on his lips, and the giant couldn't help but laugh, "I'm coming to you as a mighty man, and you send a baby out here." But onward came the singing, praising boy. What Goliath didn't know was that the rock in David's hand was guided by the Rock of Ages, who never misses!

You may feel you have a Goliath arrayed against your life. Pick up the Rock of Ages and begin to praise God. Then take the sword of the Word of God, get that enemy by the hair of its head, and finish it off!

God is restoring the tabernacle of David in these last days. Davidic worship is back. Our churches can incorporate every part of praising

God: instruments, choir, soloists, bands, guitars, clapping, dancing, and shouting.

The praise of God accomplishes so much! God says in Psalm 149:7, "To execute vengeance on the nations, and punishment on the people." When I begin to praise God, the angels of glory go to war for me against every enemy. The next verse states that with this praise, you can bind nobles and kings and put them in chains. You can bind the devil!

Jesus said, "Upon this rock I will build my church; and the gates of hell shall not prevail against the it" (Matt. 16:18, KJV). He then continues in verse 19, "And I will give you the keys of the kingdom of heaven, and whatever you shall bind on earth will be bound in heaven."

What are the keys to the kingdom of heaven? The gospel, of course, is the key. The psalmist said, "Enter into His gates with thanksgiving, and into His courts with praise" (Ps. 100:4). When we do that, we have the keys that will bind the forces of darkness.

At times our praise will bind the spirits that try to harass our lives. The demon of depression will often flee if we just begin to sing. God has promised to give us the garment of praise for the spirit of heaviness (Isa. 61:3). When you feel that darkness start to fall again, just start singing. Victory will come, and He will bind away the devil of depression that has tried to kill you and destroy you.

Music gives you courage. Music has always had a powerful influence on attitudes about warfare. With every war, a theme song seems to arise that becomes the rallying cry. In recent years as America faced crisis in the Persian Gulf and Iraq, you couldn't go a day without hearing Lee Greenwood's powerful song "God Bless the USA." The tired, weary, and sometimes-fearful soul begins to rise and take courage with that music.

Ask Paul and Silas. They were beaten and bloody in the darkness of midnight. "Silas," said Paul, "let's sing!" At the top of their lungs, with pain still coursing through their beaten bodies, they sang, and heaven was torn open. God came down and landed so hard that it burst the doors of the jail open, and the jailer ran in and said, "Sirs, what must I do to be saved?" (See Acts 16.) No sermon…just praise!

Every time David sang, the demons fled out of his life and from those who listened. And Nehemiah—he also knew the power of praising God! He had a ragtag crowd trying to build an incredible wall. Some laughed at the efforts, saying, "Why, if a fox ran up on this wall, the little creature would be able to tear it down!" (See Nehemiah 4:3.) Nehemiah's workers were mocked and made fun of, and they were exhausted beyond imagination. Yet Nehemiah said, "Remember, don't leave your post. If you are weak and tired, the joy of the Lord is your strength." (See Nehemiah 8:10.) Workers began to sing in their own way, and God liked it all. Strength flowed into their spirits.

Praise Births Revival

If you want true revival, you will need to learn true praise and worship. And it may be messy! A time of praise may interrupt your order of service or make that delicious roast burn because the Sunday service runs past noon. But those are insignificant side effects to suffer when you see the altars flooded with crying, repentant, hurting people and then see the power of God flow through His people.

The devil has tried to rob you of your song. It is time to sing again. The psalmist said, "Weeping may endure for a night, but joy comes in the morning" (Ps. 30:5). Well, it is now morning! The night is over. Your Father is singing over you. This is a new day.

chapter 36

LOVING OTHERS UNCONDITIONALLY

I BELIEVE THE GREATEST lesson I've ever learned in spiritual warfare is one I found too late for many opportunities I have had in my life. This powerful weapon is one that has never failed anytime I wielded it. This weapon is agape love, the love of God.

If you take time to read the great love chapter of the Bible, 1 Corinthians 13, you will find that in it the Holy Spirit clearly discusses this powerful gift. Hidden within this priceless treasure that "beareth all things, believeth all things, hopeth all things, and endureth all things" (v. 7, KJV) is an explosive power that can topple many spiritual walls.

In Romans 8:31–39 we read:

> What then shall we say to these things? If God is for us, who can be against us? He who did not spare His own Son, but delivered Him up for us all, how shall He not with Him also freely give us all things? Who shall bring a charge against God's elect? It is God who justifies. Who is he who condemns? It is Christ who died, and furthermore is also risen, who is even at the right hand of God, who also makes intercession for us. Who shall separate us from the love of Christ? Shall tribulation, or distress, or persecution, or famine, or nakedness, or peril, or sword? As it is written: "For Your sake we are killed all day long; we are accounted as sheep for the slaughter." Yet in all these things we are more than conquerors through Him who loved us. For I am persuaded that neither death nor life, nor angels nor principalities nor powers, nor things present nor things to come, nor

height nor depth, nor any other created thing, shall be able to separate us from the love of God which is in Christ Jesus our Lord.

The greatest weapon of spiritual warfare is the love of God. That's why God began with it and promised it from the beginning of time.

For God so loved the world, that he gave his only begotten Son, that whosoever believeth in him should not perish, but have everlasting life.

—John 3:16, kjv

Behold, what manner of love the Father hath bestowed upon us, that we should be called the sons of God.

—1 John 3:1, kjv

The cross of Calvary was a public demonstration of the agape love of God, of the love that knows no limits, of the love that will not hold back, of the love that will go as far as it has to go to bring back its beloved. It is the theme of the Bible. It is the heartbeat of our own song. It is the centerpiece of the gospel that we preach. It is this feature alone that separates Christianity from Islam, Buddhism, and all the "isms" of the world.

We have a God who loves us no matter what we've done. There is no measure to His love. We can't comprehend the height, the depth, the length, or the breadth of His love. This love of Christ surpasses all knowledge. We can't learn it all. We can't study it all. We can't talk about it all. We can't write enough songs. We can't compose enough poems. We can't preach enough sermons. We can't pray enough to express what the love of God is!

One of my favorite old hymns talks of this powerful love, the final verse of which was found written on the walls of an insane asylum:

Could we with ink the ocean fill?
And were the skies of parchment made,
Were every stalk on earth a quill,
And every man a scribe by trade,
To write the love of God above,
Would drain the ocean dry.
Nor could the scroll contain the whole,
Though stretched from sky to sky.

Chorus
O love of God, how rich, how pure,
How measureless and strong.
It shall forevermore endure
The saints' and angels' song.[1]

ELEMENTS OF THE WEAPON

We must clearly understand the many facets of this powerful weapon. It frustrates me to step into churches only to see people going through the motions and playing religious games. I want to just cry out and say, "Do you think God bankrupted heaven to send His beloved Son to hang on a cross for six hours under the noonday sun of Israel and to bleed His life's blood out so you could play some church games? He spent His blood to change you, to heal you inside and out, to transform you forever!" No one who has ever opened his heart and took Christ's embrace has ever been the same. He changes us.

Love undeserved

As His child, no matter what mistakes you may have made, God is for you. Your marriage may have ended in divorce, but God is for you. You may have made some youthful mistakes, failed at your business, or served time in a penitentiary, but God is for you. He cast His vote at Calvary for you. He loved you before you were born. Before the first wave crashed on the shore, He knew your name and knew your heart and loved you! Nothing can separate you from the love of God. You can't do anything to deserve it. That's what agape love is all about.

When you turn that love around and wield it, you discover something of great power. You can love and serve someone without expecting anything back. You will live in victory.

Love undaunted

"Who shall separate us from the love of Christ?" asks Paul. "Shall tribulation or distress?" (See Romans 8:35.) The answer, of course, is no! Your pressures and problems are just ways God can show you He loves you! "Persecution?" Agape love will outlast every controversy. "Famine, or nakedness, or peril, or sword?" None of these influence the power of God's love.

Love undefeated

Romans 8:37 states boldly, "Yet in all these things we are more than conquerors." This phrase "we are more than conquerors" is one word in the Greek—*hupernikao*—and it appears to be a word the apostle Paul just invented, as it appears nowhere else in Greek literature. You see, the word *nikao*, conqueror, was as strong as you could be. It means you have conquered; you have won. You get the spoils. You are in charge. Your enemies are down. Everything you want is in your hands. There was no stronger word than *nikao*. But Paul added *huper* in the Greek, which is like *super* in English. He wanted to communicate something bigger than conquest when he said, "You are *more* than conquerors."

How can I be more than a conqueror? Because of Jesus, there will be certain battles I'm never going to have to fight again. I may have a struggle or two in life, but I don't have to fight for my salvation. He has already won that battle! I don't have to fight for forgiveness. I don't have to fight for my healing. I don't have to fight for the gifts of the Spirit. I am more than a conqueror!

There is a story of a woman whose husband moved to the Philippine Islands for a short-term business opportunity. The couple had raised three children, who were now almost grown. Only a few weeks into his business venture, he sent her a telegram saying, "I don't love you anymore. I have found someone here. I'm not ever coming back. Good-bye. Your husband."

The businessman married a Filipino girl, and they had a child together. But tragically he soon discovered he had a terminal cancer, and he died. The widowed Filipino girl and her baby had nowhere to go, so she wrote the man's first wife: "I was married to your husband. We have a child. I don't know what to do."

Now, this woman was a Christian. "Dearest," she wrote the girl back, "God loves you. Christ died for you. I'm sending you money to come here to the States. We will take care of all the details when you get here. You and the child will live in my house." That is what the power of agape love can do!

Winning and being loved by God does not mean that you won't have pain and be hurt, but it does mean that you will always love. That woman could have simply said, "I'll tell you what, he divorced me. Let his little fling worry about her own self." No, that's how you lose.

Perhaps you are losing your spiritual battle because you cannot forgive. The Bible says, "Love your enemies, bless those who curse you, do good to those who hate you…" (Matt. 5:44). It doesn't matter what the response is to our acts of love. If it is agape love, it doesn't matter. Love is going to love anyway. Love went to the cross, and it kept on loving. It was buried in the ground, and three days later it came alive.

In years past, a counterfeit gospel has been preached. Many have said, "To be a true Christian, it's all about this denomination, belonging to this church, and you have to do this, and you have to be that. You have to dress this way and act that way." But the truth is, the gospel is none of those things. The true gospel is this: Christ loved us, died for us, took our penalty, and loves us anyway in spite of everything. Love wins all the time.

Love undeniable

Paul goes on to write in Romans 8:38, "For I am persuaded…" The word *persuaded* is a passive verb in the Greek. It means "I've been convinced from something beyond myself." It doesn't mean that I've talked myself into it. In the passive voice it means, "I didn't do anything to deserve this. Someone outside of me convinced me." Paul said, "I have enough of it poured on me that I'm absolutely convinced; I am persuaded…"

Paul had been beaten many times. He had been thrown in jail. He had been persecuted. He had been misunderstood. But he said, "I am persuaded." That means in this Greek tense, "I am fully convinced. I will never change my mind. Nothing can rock this in my life. I can't be separated from God's love!" Even death can't separate us from His love.

Until my mother passed away, I called her every Sunday. When I was struggling as a poor freshman college kid, my mama would send me $15 a week. That doesn't sound like a lot now, but in the 1960s, Mama worked for $1.25 an hour. She basically was sending me a day-and-a-half's pay each week!

Looking back, I'm ashamed that I didn't really appreciate it at the time. I watched my mother wear the same dress to church for years. She would clean it up nice so that we could have something new to wear. She gave when it was hard to give. When Daddy was going through all his struggles with alcoholism, I never heard Mama say, "I'm leaving." Long before he came back to God and took the office of a soul-winning deacon the last ten years of his life, my mother was there. She was there when it was tough. Love won!

A DIVINE TRANSFER

You may be reading this and have a need to feel truly loved. Ephesians 1 tells you that you have been accepted in the Beloved. It is time for you to quit blaming yourself for everything and feeling guilty about everything. "There is therefore now no condemnation to those who are in Christ Jesus" (Rom. 8:1). You are loved.

Perhaps you simply need to allow the love that He has given you to be transferred out of your heart and into the lives of those around you. He has poured enough in you that you can let some run out of your life, whether the recipients ever say "I love you" back or not. It is not about getting paid back. Jesus paid it all!

> Oh, the love that drew salvation's plan!
> Oh, the grace that brought it down to man!
> Oh, the mighty gulf that God did span at Calvary![2]

If you will let God's love wash you and flow through you, demons will leave. You will know true victory, for the enemy can't stay where God's love is poured out. Claim your freedom and explode the weapon of His love in your life!

chapter 37

TAKING BACK GROUND

THE OLD TESTAMENT offers beautiful pictures of New Testament truth. These are called types. The greatest picture or type of spiritual warfare is found in the book of Joshua. The very name *Joshua* is the Hebrew *Yeshua*, or Jesus, which means "savior" or "deliverer."

The journey of the children of Israel from Egypt through the wilderness to Canaan is a picture of the Christian life. God used all of these experiences to break His people.

THE RESISTANCE WE FACE

In the Christian life we face a threefold enemy: the world, the flesh, and the devil. Deliverance from Egypt pictures our rescue from the world. The wilderness experience breaks the power of the flesh. We have drawn clear parallels between Canaan and the strongholds in our lives.

Canaan is not a "fair and happy land," nor is it heaven. It represents what is rightfully the believers' now! It is the land flowing with milk and honey. It is the abundant life promised by Jesus in John 10:10.

Most believers have escaped from Egypt, but like the tribe of Gad and the half tribe of Manasseh, they have decided to live in a wilderness, never crossing over into the spiritual territory that flows with milk and honey. Most believers settle for less than the promises of God. God has willed that His sons and daughters be soldiers! He gave them the land of Canaan, and yet it was a veritable armed camp of their enemies. It was filled with fortified cities with great kings who had to be destroyed before they could possess their possessions.

THE RICHES THAT ARE YOURS

Do you see that there are spiritual vistas you have never viewed, mountains you haven't scaled, rivers of life you haven't swum in, fruit you've never tasted, harvests you haven't enjoyed, gifts you've never opened, and abundance you have never experienced?

The towering strongholds have frightened you away. God had given the children of Israel the land, yet they had to claim it, to fight for it (Josh. 1:2). So must you!

In Joshua 3:5 God promises to do wonders, to do the supernatural. In Joshua 4:24 the people praise God for the miracle of the parting of the waters of the Jordan. Immediately the enemy was put on notice that God's people were coming for their land!

After you are saved, you must claim every inch of the territory of your soul. Just as the children of Israel had to march over the land, you must take every inch of what Satan would want to take away from you.

THE REINFORCEMENTS THEN ARE YOURS

The minute the children of Israel stepped out in faith, God showed up with invisible resources—"the Commander of the army of the LORD" (Josh. 5:14). What was going on here?

Here we see the Lord's promise. God had promised never to forsake Joshua. Now the Lord has shown up with His army for the fight. We also see the Lord's presence in that the angel of the Lord has his "sword drawn" (Josh. 5:13). This host of invisible warriors had come to the battle. All Joshua could do was worship and obey. Remember, God never commands His children to fight alone. "I am with you always, even to the end of the age" (Matt. 28:20).

THE REALM THAT IS YOURS

The key passage here is Joshua 6. The children of Israel had to obey the orders to march around Jericho once a day for six days and then seven times on the seventh day. After the seventh time around, they were to blow their trumpets. When this was done, the walls fell and the city was taken. Today if we obey God's commandments, the walls of our strong-holds cannot stand against us.

THE RULE THAT IS YOURS

Give the enemy no place. In Joshua 10:8–25, Joshua was given a clear word from God concerning his enemies. God said no enemy of Israel would be left standing. After hearing from God, Joshua took quick and decisive action. After marching all night, the children of Israel did not rest in the presence of their enemies; instead they attacked them.

In the midst of the battle Joshua needed a miracle if he was going to see the word of God fulfilled in the battle. He prayed. God heard his prayer and stopped the sun from going down on the battle. If God has promised victory, He will not allow darkness to overtake the day.

Five mighty kings, those who would stand against the children of Israel, were delivered into Joshua's hands. With a proclamation of victory, not just for the battle at hand but also for future battles, Joshua destroyed the kings.

God will do for you what he did for Joshua. He will give a clear word. Move quickly in that word, and you will be positioned to see a miracle of God. He will deliver your enemies into your hands.

chapter 38

BREAKING CURSES

Proverbs 18:21 says, "Death and life are in the power of the tongue, and those who love it will eat its fruit." Life and death are powerfully influenced by what we say, what we hear, and what we receive! Just as confessing the Word of God out of our mouth releases blessings and faith to activate the supernatural and defeat the enemy, so negative words bring curses, activate the demonic, and release destructive forces.

OPEN DOORS

Dr. Henry Malone, in his excellent book *Shadow Boxing*, suggests five open doors that allow negative forces to operate in your life.[1]

Disobedience

Willful disobedience brings you into captivity of the enemy.

> Do you not know that to whom you present yourselves slaves to obey, you are that one's slaves whom you obey, whether of sin leading to death, or of obedience leading to righteousness?
> —Romans 6:16

When thoughts of disobedience are spoken, they lead to strongholds.

> Casting down arguments and every high thing that exalts itself against the knowledge of God, bringing every thought into captivity to the obedience of Christ.
> —2 Corinthians 10:5

We must capture our negative and disobedient thoughts rather than confess them.

Unforgiveness

Unforgiveness is the second door that allows the enemy to work in your life. In order to enjoy the benefits of the kingdom of heaven now, you must forgive those who hurt you. Jesus taught unlimited forgiveness.

> Then Peter came to Him and said, "Lord, how often shall my brother sin against me, and I forgive him? Up to seven times?" Jesus said to him, "I do not say to you, up to seven times, but up to seventy times seven."
>
> —MATTHEW 18:21–22

This call to forgive is imperative. Jesus follows it with a parable about debt. A man had a large debt, and his master forgave it. This same forgiven man refused to forgive a smaller debt owed to him. Listen to the verdict of Jesus in Matthew 18:32–35:

> Then his master, after he had called him, said to him, "You wicked servant! I forgave you all that debt because you begged me. Should you not also have had compassion on your fellow servant, just as I had pity on you?" And his master was angry, and delivered him to the torturers until he should pay all that was due to him. So My heavenly Father also will do to you if each of you, from his heart, does not forgive his brother his trespasses.

The tormentors are demons of depression, fear, rage, infirmity, and insomnia. Often, words said or written are the things that people struggle to forgive. Forgiveness is a supernatural act the Holy Spirit does through you.

Emotional trauma

Another tool the enemy uses is emotional trauma, which can result from accidents, abuse, divorce, crime, betrayal, and wrong words. You need healing from things such as fear, unforgiveness, traumas, victimization, and self-pity.

Wrong vows and judgments

Wrong vows and judgments are the fourth avenue used by the enemy. Our wrong words give Satan access.

> But I say to you, do not swear at all: neither by heaven, for it is God's throne; nor by the earth, for it is His footstool; nor by Jerusalem, for it is the city of the great King. Nor shall you swear by your head, because you cannot make one hair white or black. But let your 'Yes' be 'Yes,' and your 'No,' 'No.' For whatever is more than these is from the evil one.
>
> —MATTHEW 5:34–37

People will swear they will never do something. Satan hears it, and then they will repeat the exact act for which they were victims. Most abusers have been abused—and most swore they would never do to others what happened to them. Also, words of judgment against others open the door for the enemy to release the same problem in your life.

> Judge not, that you be not judged. For with what judgment you judge, you will be judged; and with the measure you use, it will be measured back to you.
>
> —MATTHEW 7:1–2

The power of a vow or a judgment will bind you to a fleshly course of action that will control you until the vow is broken. Ecclesiastes 5:5 states, "Better not to vow than to vow and not pay." Be aware of the words "I will never" or "I will always." Until these words are reversed, Satan has ground.

Curses

All of the above can include curses—the fifth open door that allows the work of dark spiritual forces. A curse is an extended evil rope with one end tied to you and one end tied to "who knows what" in the unseen past. You may be living with a curse if it seems that something repeatedly hinders you or creates struggle in a certain area of your life.

Curses, which can also be called habits, affect families, churches, social circles, cities, and nature. They pass down through families if they aren't broken. The invisible realm is where curses operate, and they can be transferred by words or objects.

To determine if you are dealing with a curse, there are several things that may be present in the physical realm if a curse is active in the spiritual realm.

1. **Mental state.** Insanity, personality disorders, and emotional disturbance may be present. "The LORD will make the plague cling to you until He has consumed you from the land which you are going to possess" (Deut. 28:21).

2. **Hereditary afflictions or chronic illness.** "The LORD will strike you with consumption, with fever, with inflammation, with severe burning fever, with the sword, with scorching, and with mildew; they shall pursue you until you perish" (Deut. 28:22).

3. **Female problems and child-bearing difficulties.** While these may have a medical explanation, they can also be the result of a curse. "Cursed shall be the fruit of your body and the produce of your land, the increase of your cattle and the offspring of your flocks" (Deut. 28:18).

4. **Family difficulties or division.** "You shall beget sons and daughters, but they shall not be yours; for they shall go into captivity" (Deut. 28:41).

5. **Financial shortages.** Financial shortages can be a result of unwise choices, but they also can indicate a curse working in your life. "You are cursed with a curse, for you have robbed Me, even this whole nation" (Mal. 3:9).

6. **Accident-prone.** Being accident-prone can also be evidence of a curse working in your life. "The LORD will strike you with madness and blindness and confusion of heart. And you shall grope at noonday, as a blind man gropes in darkness; you shall not prosper in your ways; you shall be only oppressed and plundered continually, and no one shall save you" (Deut. 28:28–29).

Once it has been determined that you may be dealing with a curse, the next step in reversing it is to expose it. "Like a flitting sparrow, like a flying swallow, so a curse without cause shall not alight" (Prov. 26:2).

Causes and Effects of Curses

Curses are always caused by something or someone in the past or present. There are certain sins that curses consistently follow—such as rebellion and disobedience.

> Then Samuel said: "Has the LORD as great delight in burnt offerings and sacrifices, as in obeying the voice of the LORD? Behold, to obey is better than sacrifice, and to heed than the fat of rams. For rebellion is as the sin of witchcraft, and stubbornness is as iniquity and idolatry. Because you have rejected the word of the LORD, He also has rejected you from being king."
>
> —1 SAMUEL 15:22–23

Samuel said that rebellion releases witchcraft. Children's rebellion brings curses.

> Children, obey your parents in the Lord, for this is right. "Honor your father and mother," which is the first commandment with promise: "that it may be well with you and you may live long on the earth."
>
> —EPHESIANS 6:1–3

Curses also come with the occult.

> Now the works of the flesh are evident, which are: adultery, fornication, uncleanness, lewdness, idolatry, sorcery, hatred, contentions, jealousies, outbursts of wrath, selfish ambitions, dissensions, heresies, envy, murders, drunkenness, revelries, and the like; of which I tell you beforehand, just as I also told you in time past, that those who practice such things will not inherit the kingdom of God.
>
> —GALATIANS 5:19–21

Curses follow those who do an injustice to others.

> "Cursed is the one who moves his neighbor's landmark." And all the people shall say, "Amen!" "Cursed is the one who makes the blind to wander off the road." And all the people shall say, "Amen!" "Cursed is the one who perverts the justice due the stranger, the fatherless, and widow." And all the people shall say, "Amen!"
>
> —DEUTERONOMY 27:17–19

Curses follow sexual perversion. All adultery, fornication, homosexuality, bestiality, incest, and pornography bring curses.

> "Cursed is the one who lies with his father's wife, because he has uncovered his father's bed." And all the people shall say, "Amen!" "Cursed is the one who lies with any kind of animal." And all the people shall say, "Amen!" "Cursed is the one who lies with his sister, the daughter of his father or the daughter of his mother." And all the people shall say, "Amen!" "Cursed is the one who lies with his mother-in-law." And all the people shall say, "Amen!"
>
> —DEUTERONOMY 27:20–23

Racism and anti-Semitism will bring a curse on those who feel superior to others.

> I will bless those who bless you, and I will curse him who curses you; and in you all the families of the earth shall be blessed.
>
> —GENESIS 12:3

Trusting human potential, strengths, and influence will cause a curse to fall.

> Thus says the LORD: "Cursed is the man who trusts in man and makes flesh his strength, whose heart departs from the LORD. For he shall be like a shrub in the desert, and shall not see when good comes, but shall inhabit the parched places in the wilderness, in a salt land which is not inhabited."
>
> —JEREMIAH 17:5–6

Curses follow stealing and lying.

> Then he said to me, "This is the curse that goes out over the face of the whole earth: 'Every thief shall be expelled,' according to this side of the scroll; and 'Every perjurer shall be expelled,' according to that side of it. I will send out the curse," says the LORD of hosts; "It shall enter the house of the thief and the house of the one who swears falsely by My name. It shall remain in the midst of his house and consume it, with its timber and stones."
>
> —ZECHARIAH 5:3–4

Stealing and lying include robbing God of the tithe.

> Will a man rob God? Yet you have robbed Me! But you say, "In what way have we robbed You?" In tithes and offerings. You are cursed with a curse, for you have robbed Me, even this whole nation.
>
> —MALACHI 3:8–9

Words spoken by those who are in loving authority can result in curses. When you say something in anger to someone under your authority, you curse that person. Seemingly simple and quickly spoken phrases, such as "You are stupid" or "I hate you," bring lasting effects. Jacob's wife Rachel died young as a result of his words: "'With whomever you find your gods, do not let him live. In the presence of our brethren, identify what I have of yours and take it with you.' For Jacob did not know that Rachel had stolen them" (Gen. 31:32).

Lying, gossiping, and idle religious talk release evil.

> But if you have bitter envy and self-seeking in your heart, do not boast and lie against the truth. This wisdom does not descend from above, but is earthly, sensual, demonic.
>
> —JAMES 3:14–15

> One who turns away his ear from hearing the law, even his prayer is an abomination.
>
> —PROVERBS 28:9

GETTING RID OF THE CURSE

Once a curse has been identified and exposed, the next step is expelling the curse. A critical element in getting rid of curses is to know you are saved! Demons consider your body their home until you are saved.

> When an unclean spirit goes out of a man, he goes through dry places, seeking rest, and finds none. Then he says, "I will return to my house from which I came." And when he comes, he finds it empty, swept, and put in order. Then he goes and takes with him seven other spirits more wicked than himself, and they enter and dwell there; and the last state of that man is worse than the first. So shall it also be with this wicked generation.
>
> —MATTHEW 12:43–45

Confess aloud your willingness to yield to God. Close all doors and take away Satan's access in your life. Repent of rebellion and disobedience. Forgive those who hurt you. Bring all past hurt and trauma to God. Cancel past vows, judgments, and wrong words, whether spoken by you or to you. Confess aloud that Jesus has borne every sin, hurt, and curse for you!

> Christ has redeemed us from the curse of the law, having become a curse for us (for it is written, "Cursed is everyone who hangs on a tree").
>
> —GALATIANS 3:13

In closing, renounce every spirit that has oppressed your life, and receive deliverance and praise God. Confess Psalm 34 as your prayer:

> I will bless the LORD at all times;
> His praise shall continually be in my mouth.
> My soul shall make its boast in the LORD;
> The humble shall hear of it and be glad.
> Oh, magnify the LORD with me,
> And let us exalt His name together.
>
> I sought the Lord, and He heard me,
> And delivered me from all my fears.
> They looked to Him and were radiant,

And their faces were not ashamed.
This poor man cried out, and the LORD heard him,
And saved him out of all his troubles.
The angel of the LORD encamps all around those who fear Him
And delivers them.

Oh, taste and see that the LORD is good;
Blessed is the man who trusts in Him!
Oh, fear the LORD, you His saints!
There is no want to those who fear Him.
The young lions lack and suffer hunger;
But those who seek the LORD shall not lack any good thing.

Come, you children, listen to me;
I will teach you the fear of the LORD.
Who is the man who desires life,
And loves many days, that he may see good?
Keep your tongue from evil,
And your lips from speaking deceit.
Depart from evil and do good;
Seek peace and pursue it.

The eyes of the LORD are on the righteous,
And His ears are open to their cry.
The face of the LORD is against those who do evil,
To cut off the remembrance of them from the earth.

The righteous cry out, and the LORD hears,
And delivers them out of all their troubles.
The LORD is near to those who have a broken heart,
And saves such as have a contrite spirit.

Many are the afflictions of the righteous,
But the LORD delivers him out of them all.
He guards all his bones;
Not one of them is broken.
Evil shall slay the wicked,
And those who hate the righteous shall be condemned.
The LORD redeems the soul of His servants,
And none of those who trust in Him shall be condemned.

chapter 39

BUILDING HEDGES OF SPIRITUAL PROTECTION

THE PROPHET EZEKIEL wrote, "You have not gone up into the gaps to build a wall for the house of Israel to stand in battle on the day of the LORD" (Ezek. 13:5). A hedge in Bible times was a special barrier or fence placed around grape vineyards. Depending on its design, it was placed to keep insects, bugs, rodents, thieves, or birds from coming in and stealing the harvest.

Spiritually, a hedge is God's wall of protection promised for all those who believe on Him, walk with Him, and trust in Him. As Christians believing in His promises, it is time that we declare, "I've come to get back what Satan stole! I want God's protective barrier around my life and that of my family."

God longs for churches and individuals to have the faith to stand in the broken-down gaps so the enemy will have no right to plunder what He has given.

CAN GOD REMOVE A HEDGE?

The Bible indicates at least two times or two reasons why God Himself may allow a hedge to fail. Sometimes He will take down a hedge in judgment. God sang to Isaiah in chapter 5 and basically said, "I gave My Beloved as a vine, and I cleaned out the stones and planted My people into My choice vineyard. I removed everything." Then God says, "I put a hedge around you to protect you. But when I came in there to get

My fruit, instead of a beautiful, sweet cluster of choice grapes, the fruit stunk. It was wild and worthless." God told Isaiah that because of their disobedience, He brought judgment and removed the hedge, allowing destruction to come to the nation.

When God takes down the hedge over a nation, over a church, over a family, or over an individual, deep trouble follows!

God also may take down a hedge to prove Satan is a liar. In the first chapter of Job, the devil shows up. God says to him, "Have you considered My servant Job, that there is none like him on the earth?" (Job 1:8).

The devil replied, "Well, it's no wonder—You have hedged him in. If You will take the hedge down and let me at him, he will curse You to Your face."

God said, "I don't believe he loves Me just because of what I've done for him. I believe he loves Me with all of his heart." So to prove Satan wrong and prove Job's faithfulness, God allowed Satan to afflict Job for a season. When we find Job on the other side of the removal of hedges, his fortune is gone, his family is gone, his health is gone, and his wife is encouraging him to curse God and die. Even so, Job still says, "Though He slay me, yet will I trust Him" (Job 13:15).

Job came through this serious test of faith and lived to see everything returned to him double. That part of his story isn't discussed often enough—we focus so much on his trials that we forget that God rewarded his faithfulness in abundance, above and beyond what had been taken from him.

Job was one of possibly only four men in the Bible whom God could trust with the removal of a hedge. Joseph was another whom God trusted enough to take the hedge down. He allowed him to endure slavery, temptation, imprisonment, and rejection for His glory. Paul also had a hedge down. Thousands were healed under his ministry, but scholars believe his own eyes were his "thorn in the flesh," an infirmity that continued to buffet him unless he be exalted above measure. (See 2 Corinthians 12:7.) God also trusted Jesus enough to take the hedge down and let Him die on the cross, sacrificing Himself for our sins and failures.

IN NEED OF PROTECTION?

Truthfully, most of us with a broken-down or absent protective hedge have not come to it due to our own merit or by being chosen to stand a special test of God. Most gaps in our protective hedges happen because we have made choices that left us open to enemy attack. Because of these choices, we feel miserable. We are hurt. We are bothered. We are struggling. We are failing, and we are walking through difficulty.

The good news is, you can allow God to build a fivefold hedge around you and around your family that the devil cannot touch.

Hedge of prayer

We read in Job, "Now his sons would go and feast in their houses, each on his appointed day, and would send and invite their three sisters to eat and drink with them. So it was, when the days of feasting had run their course, that Job would send and sanctify them, and he would rise early in the morning and offer burnt offerings according to the number of them all. For Job said, 'It may be that my sons have sinned and cursed God in their hearts.' Thus Job did regularly" (Job 1:4–5).

Remember in verse 10 Satan asked God, "Have You not made a hedge around him?" How do you think that hedge got around Job's children? God saw the earnestness of Job's faith. Job wasn't fast asleep, snoring at eight o'clock in the morning—he was up at 4:30 a.m., interceding for his family.

You can imagine those prayers. Perhaps he prayed, "I don't know what my boys and girls have been doing today, but Lord, I'm here with an offering, a memorial to You. God, please put a hedge about my children!"

So many parents feel lost when their children go off to college or move away. It is easy to fall into deep worry and fear about what they are doing at any time of day or night. But here is a practical, tangible way to help them: pray a hedge around them. Lasso them with the Holy Ghost!

Years ago as a young preacher learning lessons from God, I was visiting Natchez, Mississippi. A family put me up for a night, and the mama was a sweet saint of God. This dear woman had a faithful fourteen-year-old girl and an unfaithful twenty-one-year-old son.

About 4:30 a.m. I was returning from getting a drink of water when I heard something that sounded like a wounded animal in an adjacent room. Concerned, I stopped to listen and just caught the broken voice of the saintly mama say, "O God, please save him, Lord. If You have to take my life, Lord, don't let him go to hell. Lord, protect him tonight. I don't know where he is tonight, Lord, but please protect him."

Deeply moved, I went back to bed, but sleep didn't come quickly as I thought of this mother's burden.

The next morning at breakfast, sitting there with her family, I gently said, "I heard you praying last night."

She apologized quickly, "Oh, I'm sorry, Brother Ron. I hope it didn't disturb you."

I said, "No, ma'am, it didn't wake me up, but it sure disturbed me in my own complacent spirit."

She said, "I've been praying for seven years for my son to come out of drugs and alcohol and to come home."

I think back to that story and shake my head to think how many times we pray five minutes about a worry or a need, and when our answer doesn't come, we throw in the towel and give up our intercession. But this saintly mama was like Job. She said, "I didn't give up." And her faithfulness was rewarded—the very next night her boy staggered into a church and gave his heart to Jesus Christ!

You can build a hedge that will draw your family back to God through prayer. You can throw a hedge around your business. If you begin sincerely praying, you will see an amazing difference. If you wonder why the profits are going down or success is not coming, it is because the devil is a thief who loves to steal success from you. Stand in faith and pray God's hedge about you, binding the devil off what you own.

Hedge of spiritual leadership

If you have placed yourself under the authority of a local, Bible-believing church led by a pastor who is sensitive to the Holy Spirit, there is protection in that place. Living under the ministry of a man of God will put a hedge around you. Remember Ezekiel 22:30: "I sought for a man among them, that should make up the hedge, and stand in the gap before me for the land" (KJV).

Too many ministries take up the motto, "We don't want to offend anybody." But God places blessing upon church families who stand for the truth of the Word of God.

Hedge of unity

People in unity can build a hedge. You may recall the story of Abraham pleading with God for Sodom and Gomorrah to be spared. Abraham asked, "Would you spare it for fifty righteous people found there?" God said, "I will spare it for fifty." Abraham bargained all the way down to ten. It is sobering to think that ten righteous, praying people would have spared those evil cities! (See Genesis 19.)

Amazing things could happen if we would begin to seriously pray about the governmental issues that are harming families and churches today. What if we began to pray in unity? If ten righteous people living in purity would have spared Sodom, what could a group of interceding Christians today accomplish in our nation?

Hedge of angelic protection

Holy angels will help you place a hedge around your family. Psalm 34:7 says, "The angel of the LORD encamps around those who fear Him, and delivers them." Imagine the grounds around your home with the angels of the Lord encamped all around! Hebrews 1:14 says, "Are they not all ministering spirits sent forth to minister for those who will inherit salvation?"

This truth became more precious to me when I became the parent of a teenager! When your children hit the age of sixteen and get behind the wheel of the car, it seems your whole prayer life changes! I often teased that I was going to have to buy a timeshare in a junkyard just to park the cars my kids wrecked! But I've learned that God's eye is always on my family; He never sleeps. Even when you fall asleep, thank God that He is watching and that the holy angels can be stationed and arranged around your house, around your possessions, and around your children. No distance is too great, for they travel at the speed of light.

The prophet Daniel once was praying for three weeks over a request. God sent his answer on day one, but Daniel didn't see the evidence of the answer until an angel arrived. The angelic creature identified himself and then said, "I would have gotten here sooner, but I've been wrestling with a demon over Persia. I was on my way with your answer." (See Daniel 10.)

Some of you give up too quickly. You are praying, the angels are at work, demons are fighting them, but God is on His way with the answer.

The angels could be bringing that wayward child of yours home even now, protecting him or her all the way.

Hedge of revival

Revival builds a hedge. Psalm 80:14 says, "Return, we beseech You, O God of hosts; look down from heaven and see, and visit this vine." Again in verse 18 is the plea, "We will not turn back from You; revive us, and we will call upon Your name." When revival comes, it puts a hedge around everything going on in the house.

Recall again the picture of a grape vineyard. Those who raised grapes in Bible times valued their vines and protected them at all costs. The protection around their precious crop was multilayered. Often they would first put a stone wall around it. Then they would follow with a thick hedge of thorns. Then, right before the harvest, they would build a fire to keep the flying insects and birds away.

What a thrilling picture for us! First, that stone wall is a symbol of God the Father, who is eternal, unchanging, and a solid foundation. With our families firmly planted upon the Rock of Ages, we can find peace and security in the Father's strength and guidance.

Next, the hedge of thorns is Jesus, whose blood provides everlasting protection for our souls. I think of the lines from the poem by G. A. Studdert Kennedy:

> When Jesus came to Golgotha they hanged Him on a tree,
> They drave great nails through hands and feet, and made a Calvary;
> They crowned Him with a crown of thorns, red were His wounds and
>   deep,
> For those were crude and cruel days, and human flesh was cheap.[1]

Finally, think of the symbolism of the wall of fire. We arrive at harvest time, when the grapes are ripe, following the long season during which we have waited and waited and waited. The Father has watched over us and the blood has taken care of us, but now the fruit is ripe and the fragrance is wafting. It is when we are at the point of reaping the greatest blessings in our lives that every demon of hell, every insect and fowl bird wants to lodge in the branches! But God says, "I'm sending Holy Ghost fire." And when that fire begins to burn, the smoke of His glory rises, and nothing can come and get our harvest.

When you are saved and He's your Father, you are living under the blood of the crucified Christ; you are baptized, anointed with the Spirit of God and the baptism of fire. No demon of hell is going to touch anything you have! You have immunity! You are walking in His freedom.

Aren't you tired of the enemy coming around and tampering with what is yours? We have a promise from Almighty God to be our protection against the devil's onslaught. Satan has devoured a lot of harvests in the past, but he cannot penetrate the powerful hedge of God. Our children can be safe within that hedge.

It is time for you to have all the protection He's provided. Just pray this prayer:

> *Lord, build a hedge around me, around my church, around my family, and around our nation. Protect my possessions, Lord, because it all really belongs to You. Lord, let me live long enough to see revival, to taste the new wine. Thank You for the harvest that is coming!*

chapter 40

LIVING IN TRIUMPHANT HOPE

How can you maintain a blessed life? Take these eight simple steps and discover how the happy life is the antidote to depression!

1. Do something.

Find something to do. Start serving God! John 13:17 says, "If ye know these things, happy are ye if ye do them" (KJV). Perhaps it could be the simplest task, such as keeping the nursery. In that act of service, you will be happy. Move into action for God, and joy will meet you along the road.

2. Quit complaining about God's correction.

Job 5:17 states, "Behold, happy is the man whom God corrects; therefore do not despise the chastening of the Almighty." Sometimes difficult times don't come from the devil. At times, God is using those circumstances to firmly correct us. Hebrews 12:6 tells us, "Whom the Lord loves He chastens." He is not a sorry parent like some of us who let our kids get away with anything. He is a loving parent who calls His children back into line, not because He doesn't want us to enjoy life but because He sees the whole picture and wants true happiness for us.

3. Learn to abide in God's safety.

Deuteronomy 33:29 says, "Happy are you, O Israel! Who is like you, a people saved by the LORD, the shield of your help and the sword of your majesty! Your enemies shall submit to you, and you shall tread down their high places." Christ is your shield. He is the sword of your majesty.

He will put your enemies under your feet. I'll tell you, you can live a life free of depression if you discover your position in Jesus Christ.

4. Look in the Book!

Become a Bible reader. Proverbs 3:13 states, "Happy is the man who finds wisdom, and the man who gains understanding." God's Word isn't the book of the month; it is the Book of the Ages. This is God's best seller! Within it, there are more than 3,000 promises and all of them are yours. Second Corinthians 1:20 tells us, "All the promises of God in Him are Yes, and in Him Amen." That means they belong to you. Happy are you when you find the treasure. Nearly every depressed person I've ever counseled has lost their devotional life and is not saturating their life with God's promises. If you don't know where to start, begin with the Book of Psalms.

5. Get your priorities in order.

Psalm 128:1–6 tells us, "Blessed is everyone who fears the LORD, who walks in His ways. When you eat the labor of your hands, you shall be happy.... Your wife shall be like a fruitful vine in the very heart of your house, your children like olive plants all around your table. Behold, thus shall the man be blessed who fears the LORD. The LORD bless you out of Zion, and may you see the good of Jerusalem all the days of your life. Yes, may you see your children's children." Take inventory of your priorities, and nail them to the doorpost or place them on the central bulletin board of your home.

6. Stop doing questionable activities.

Too many Christians wonder why they are depressed—after they spend hours watching soap operas, "Hell's Box Office," and other questionable television offerings. If this is an issue for you, unplug the cable if you have to! Get some self-control into your life. Quit reading the wrong things. Saturate yourself with the Bible.

Perhaps you are saying, "I don't really believe that some of these things are wrong for me to do or watch." I must argue—if it is making you miserable, it is wrong! Romans 14:22 says, "Happy is he who does not condemn himself in what he approves." Here is what this verse is saying: "Happy is the man who doesn't walk in condemnation because of the stuff he is allowing in his life." If you feel guilty about it, quit it, regardless of whether others agree or not. If it is something in your life that shouldn't be there, remove it. Get rid of the horoscopes. Throw off any talisman you are wearing around your neck that honors the devil.

Get rid of any kind of music that glorifies the flesh and the enemy. Begin to get your life in order. Begin to sow into your life things that overflow with joy. If you are still not sure if something is right or wrong, ask yourself these questions: "Can I do this activity without hurting a fellow Christian? Can I maintain my witness to the lost? Can I do it and not live under condemnation?"

7. Learn to roll with the punches.

James 5:11 says, "Behold, we count them happy which endure" (KJV). I may have battle wounds now and then, but I'm here to tell you that the blood of Jesus is on your side! It is time for Christians to find some backbone, to be those who will not run every time the devil raises his ugly head and hisses. "Happy are you," James said, "when you can endure the trials that are coming your way."

8. Finally, remember who is in charge.

Print out Psalm 144:15 and hang it somewhere where you will see it every morning when you get up. It says, "Happy are those people who are in such a state; happy are the people whose God is the LORD!" Your God is in charge! He is Lord over all. Not one thing could happen to topple Him from His throne. We have been given the last chapters of the book, and Revelation 22 reveals that when the whole thing is over, He is still proclaimed to be King of kings and Lord of lords! There has never been a kingdom He is not King over. Your circumstances may be too big for you, but they are not too big for Him.

Introduction

1. Ted Rowlands and Michael Cary, "Army Honors Dead, Searches for Motive in Fort Hood Shootings," CNN.com, November 7, 2009, http://www.cnn .com/2009/CRIME/11/06/texas.fort.hood.shootings/index.html (accessed April 28, 2010).

2. Aaron Cooper, Ted Rowlands, Barbara Star, and Brian Todd, "Fort Hood Suspect Charged With Murder," CNN.com, November 12, 2009, http://www.cnn .com/2009/CRIME/11/12/fort.hood.investigation/index.html (accessed April 28, 2010).

Chapter 2
Gaining a Victory Perspective

1. Oscar Cullman, *Christ and Time* (n.p.: n.p., 1964), 84.

2. James S. Stewart, *A Faith to Proclaim* (London: Hodder and Stoughton, 1962), 102–103.

Chapter 3
End Time Misconceptions About Spiritual Warfare

1. NotableBiographies.com, "Joy Adamson," http://www.notablebiographies .com/A-An/Adamson-Joy.html (accessed June 1, 2010).

Chapter 4
Training for Reigning

1. I heard Senator Denton make this statement at a meeting I attended.

2. As quoted in "Top Ten Armies of the World," StrategyPage.com, http:// www.strategypage.com/militaryforums/30-2212/page23.aspx (accessed April 29, 2010).

Chapter 5
Battle Beyond the Stars

1. Sun Tzu, *The Art of War*, trans. Lionel Giles, Project Gutenberg, http://www .gutenberg.org/files/17405/17405-h/17405-h.htm (accessed April 29, 2010).

2. Joseph DelGrippo, "Cowboys-49ers: Breaking Down the Best 12 Games in NFL's Best Rivalry," BleacherReport.com, http://bleacherreport.com/

articles/243827-the-dozen-best-games-in-the-nfls-best-rivalry-dallas-and-san -francisco (accessed April 29, 2010).

Chapter 6
The Continuous War in Eden

1. Book of Jasher 16:11, http://www.ccel.org/a/anonymous/jasher/16.htm; 24:17, http://www.ccel.org/a/anonymous/jasher/24.htm; 28:18, http://www.ccel.org/a/ anonymous/jasher/28.htm (accessed April 29, 2010).

Chapter 10
Seven Demons That Attack the Church

1. Publius Cornelius Tacitus, *Annals* 14.27, trans. Alfred John Church and William Jackson Brodribb, http://mcadams.posc.mu.edu/txt/ah/tacitus/ TacitusAnnals14.html (accessed May 3, 2010).

2. As quoted in sermon "Revival Recovers All" by Dr. Harold L. White, http:// www.angelfire.com/az3/hlw1932/1sam3011revrecovers.html (accessed May 3, 2010).

3. *Lambeth and the Vatican: or, Anecdotes of the Church of Rome, of the Reformed Churches, and of Sects and Sectaries*, vol. 3 (London: Oxford University, 1825), 149.

Chapter 13
Unmasking the Enemy

1. William F. Arndt and F. Wilber Gingrich, *A Greek-English Lexicon of the New Testament* (Chicago: University of Chicago Press, 1979).

2. C. Fred Dickason, *Demon Possession and the Christian: A New Perspective* (Wheaton, IL: Crossway Books, 1989).

3. Kurt E. Koch, *Occult Bondage and Deliverance* (Grand Rapids, MI: Kregel Publications, 1972).

Chapter 17
Strategy of Depression

1. Bruce Levine, *Commonsense Rebellion: Debunking Psychiatry, Confronting Society* (n.p.: Continuum International Publishing Group, 2001), referenced in Christopher Kemp, "Respectable Drugs and the Mental Health Craze," CityBeat .com, August 9, 2001, http://www.citybeat.com/cincinnati/article-6075 -respectable-drugs-and-the-mental-health-craze.html (accessed May 4, 2010).

Chapter 19
The Strategy of Error

1. Neil T. Anderson, *The Bondage Breaker* (Eugene, OR: Harvest House, 2000), 23.

2. As quoted in Percy Williams, "The Christian Family Series: The Role of the Church in Creating and Maintaining Strong Families," *The Vision Speaks*, vol. 48, issue 1, Spring 2004, http://www.thechurchofgodntj.org/strongfamilies.html (accessed May 4, 2010).

Chapter 20
The Strategy of Perversion

1. Associated Press, "Amanda Knox Judges: Murder Was Impulsive," CBSNews.com, March 4, 2010, http://www.cbsnews.com/stories/2010/03/04/world/main6266494.shtml?source=related_story&tag=related (accessed May 4, 2010).

2. CBS/Associated Press, "Amanda Knox Found Guilty of Murder," CBSNews .com, December 4, 2009, http://www.cbsnews.com/stories/2009/12/04/world/main5893278.shtml (accessed May 4, 2010).

3. Child Welfare Information Gateway, "What Is Child Abuse and Neglect?" ChildWelfare.gov, http://www.childwelfare.gov/pubs/factsheets/whatiscan.cfm (accessed April 21, 2010).

4. Lord Byron, "On My Thirty-sixth Year," Bartleby.com, http://www.bartleby .com/100/368.187.html (accessed June 1, 2010).

5. NOH8 Campaign, Photos: Cindy McCain, http://www.noh8campaign.com/photo-gallery/familiar-faces/photo/5722 (accessed May 4, 2010).

Chapter 21
The Strategy of Confusion

1. Matthew George Easton, *Easton's Illustrated Bible Dictionary* (New York: T. Nelson and Sons, 1894), s.v. "Leviathan," 420.

2. PCStudy Bible, online Bible, *Brown-Driver-Briggs Hebrew Lexicon*, copyright © 1993, Woodside Bible Fellowship, Ontario, Canada; licensed from the Institute of Creation Research; used by permission; s.v. "Leviathan."

Chapter 22
The Strategy of Bitterness

1. Fullerton.edu, "The French Revolution," http://faculty.fullerton.edu/nfitch/history110b/rev.html (accessed May 4, 2010).

Chapter 23
The Strategy of Death

1. ProjectAvalon.net, "Soviet Policy and the Ukranian Genocide of 1932–33," http://projectavalon.net/forum/showthread.php?t=8690 (accessed May 5, 2010).

Chapter 27
The Victory at Calvary

1. John Bunyan, *The Pilgrim's Progress* (New York: Oxford University Press, Inc., 1996), 45.

2. Stewart, *A Faith to Proclaim*, 95–97.

Chapter 28
Foundations for Victory

1. Stewart, *A Faith to Proclaim*.

2. Ibid.

3. Gustav Aulen, *Christus Victor: An Historical Study of the Three Main Types of the Idea of the Atonement* (n.p.: Society for Promoting Christian Knowledge, 1945).

4. P. T. Forsyth, "The Fatherhood of Death," in *Missions in State—and Church* (New York: A. C. Armstrong and Son, 1908), http://www.archive.org/stream/missionsinstatec00fors/missionsinstatec00fors_djvu.txt (accessed May 5, 2010).

5. John Calvin, *Calvin's Bible Commentaries: Philippians, Colossians, and Thessalonians*, first published 1847 (n.p.: Forgotten Books, 2007), 161.

6. Cullman, *Christ and Time*, 198.

Chapter 30
The Believer's Position for Victory

1. C. S. Lewis Society of California, "Quotes by C. S. Lewis," http://www.lewissociety.org/quotes.php (accessed May 5, 2010).

Chapter 31
Arming for Victory

1. "Stand Up for Jesus" by George Duffield Jr. Public domain.

2. "Wonderful Peace" by Warren D. Cornell. Public domain.

3. NotableBiographies.com, "Charles de Gaulle," http://www.notablebiographies.com/De-Du/de-Gaulle-Charles.html (accessed May 6, 2010).

4. "O Worship the King" by Robert Grant. Public domain.

5. George Bernard Shaw, *Too Good to Be True: A Political Extravaganza* (n.p.: Samuel French, Inc., 1933, 1934, 1960, 1961), 99.

6. "How Firm a Foundation" by John Rippon. Public domain.

Chapter 36
Loving Others Unconditionally

1. "The Love of God" by Frederick M. Lehman. Public domain.
2. "At Calvary" by William R. Newell. Public domain.

Chapter 38
Breaking Curses

1. Henry Malone, *Shadow Boxing* (n.p.: Vision Life Publications, 2004).

Chapter 39
Building Hedges of Spiritual Protection

1. G. A. Studdert Kennedy, "Indifference," in *The Unutterable Beauty* (London: Hodder and Stoughton, 1927), 24; http://www.mun.ca/rels/restmov/texts/dasc/TUB.HTM (accessed May 7, 2010).

"An incredible overview of the special messengers God uses."
—MARCUS D. LAMB, *President and CEO,*
Daystar Television Network

Ron Phillips brings
you a definitive guide to
angels, describing where
they originated, how they
operate, and how you
can engage their help
in your own life.

Open your
eyes to a
whole new
world!

Our INVISIBLE
ALLIES

The story of
ANGELS
and how they work
behind the scenes

RON PHILLIPS

978-1-59979-523-2 | $14.99

Charisma
HOUSE
A STRANG COMPANY
9410B

VISIT YOUR LOCAL BOOKSTORE.

FREE NEWSLETTERS
TO HELP EMPOWER YOUR LIFE

Why subscribe today?

☐ **DELIVERED DIRECTLY TO YOU.** All you have to do is open your inbox and read.

☐ **EXCLUSIVE CONTENT.** We cover the news overlooked by the mainstream press.

☐ **STAY CURRENT.** Find the latest court rulings, revivals, and cultural trends.

☐ **UPDATE OTHERS.** Easy to forward to friends and family with the click of your mouse.

CHOOSE THE E-NEWSLETTER THAT INTERESTS YOU MOST:

- Christian news
- Daily devotionals
- Spiritual empowerment
- And much, much more

SIGN UP AT: **http://freenewsletters.charismamag.com**

8178